RAPHAEL'S ASTRONOMICAL

Ephemeris of the Planets' Places

for 2000

A Complete Aspectarian

Mean Obliquity of the Ecliptic, 2000, 23° 26′ 21″

INTRODUCTION

Greenwich Mean Time (G.M.T.) has been used as the basis for all tabulations and times. The tabular data are for Greenwich Mean Noon (12h. G.M.T.), except for the Moon tabulations headed "MIDNIGHT". All phenomena and aspect times are now in G.M.T. To obtain Local Mean Time of aspect, add the time equivalent of the longitude if East and subtract if West.

In the aspectarian am denotes morning; pm denotes afternoon.

☽ ☌ ● *Eclipse of* ☉. ☽ ☍ ☉ *Eclipse of* ☽.

☌ *Occultation by* ☽.

BRITISH SUMMER TIME

British Summer Time begins on March 26 and ends on October 29. When *British Summer Time* (one hour in advance of G.M.T.) is used, subtract one hour from B.S.T. before entering this Ephemeris.

These dates are believed to be correct at the time of printing.

Printed in Great Britain

ISBN 0-572-02384-7

Published by

. FOULSHAM & CO. LTD.

SE, SLOUGH, BERKS. ENGLAND

ꞔONTO CAPE TOWN SYDNEY

NEW MOON-Jan. 6, 6h.14m. pm. (15°♑44′)

D M	D W	Sidereal Time	☉ Long.	☉ Dec.	☽ Long.	☽ Lat.	☽ Dec.	☽ Node	Midnight ☽ Long.	Midnight ☽ Dec.
		H. M. S.	° ′ ″	° ′	° ′ ″	° ′	° ′	° ′	° ′ ″	° ′
1	S	18 41 50	10 ♑ 22 8	23 S 2	13 ♏ 19 26	5 N10	10 S 54	5 ♌ 3	19 ♏ 19 2	12 S 41
2	Su	18 45 47	11 23 18	22 57	25 16 52	4 53	14 20	4 59	1 ♐ 13 19	15 50
3	M	18 49 44	12 24 29	22 52	7 ♐ 8 48	4 23	17 10	4 56	13 3 38	18 20
4	T	18 53 40	13 25 39	22 46	18 58 10	3 42	19 17	4 53	24 52 40	20 2
5	W	18 57 37	14 26 50	22 39	0 ♑ 47 27	2 52	20 34	4 50	6 ♑ 42 44	20 53
6	Th	19 1 33	15 28 1	22 32	12 38 46	1 54	20 57	4 47	18 35 47	20 47
7	F	19 5 30	16 29 11	22 25	24 34 0	0 N50	20 23	4 44	0 ♒ 33 41	19 45
8	S	19 9 26	17 30 22	22 18	6 ♒ 35 2	0 S16	18 53	4 40	12 38 19	17 48
9	Su	19 13 23	18 31 32	22 9	18 43 47	1 23	16 31	4 37	24 51 44	15 2
10	M	19 17 19	19 32 42	22 1	1 ♓ 2 27	2 26	13 23	4 34	7 ♓ 16 16	11 34
11	T	19 21 16	20 33 51	21 52	13 33 30	3 24	9 36	4 31	19 54 30	7 31
12	W	19 25 13	21 35 0	21 42	26 19 37	4 12	5 19	4 28	2 ♈ 49 12	3 S 3
13	Th	19 29 9	22 36 8	21 33	9 ♈ 23 35	4 49	0 S 43	4 25	16 3 4	1 N39
14	F	19 33 6	23 37 15	21 22	22 47 54	5 12	4 N 2	4 21	29 38 17	6 24
15	S	19 37 2	24 38 22	21 12	6 ♉ 34 20	5 17	8 43	4 18	13 ♉ 36 4	10 56
16	Su	19 40 59	25 39 28	21 1	20 43 21	5 4	13 3	4 15	27 55 58	14 59
17	M	19 44 55	26 40 34	20 49	5 ♊ 13 30	4 31	16 44	4 12	12 ♊ 35 25	18 13
18	T	19 48 52	27 41 38	20 37	20 1 2	3 40	19 25	4 9	27 29 29	20 17
19	W	19 52 48	28 42 42	20 25	4 ♋ 59 50	2 33	20 48	4 5	12 ♋ 31 3	20 56
20	Th	19 56 45	29 ♑ 43 46	20 12	20 2 1	1 S15	20 42	4 2	27 31 39	20 6
21	F	20 0 42	0 ♒ 44 48	19 59	4 ♌ 58 51	0 N 7	19 8	3 59	12 ♌ 22 38	17 51
22	S	20 4 38	1 45 50	19 46	19 42 3	1 28	16 18	3 56	26 56 22	14 30
23	Su	20 8 35	2 46 51	19 32	4 ♍ 4 57	2 41	12 31	3 53	11 ♍ 7 18	10 23
24	M	20 12 31	3 47 52	19 18	18 3 10	3 43	8 8	3 50	24 52 23	5 50
25	T	20 16 28	4 48 52	19 4	1 ♎ 34 57	4 29	3 N29	3 46	8 ♎ 11 1	1 N 9
26	W	20 20 24	5 49 52	18 49	14 40 50	5 1	1 S10	3 43	21 4 46	3 S26
27	Th	20 24 21	6 50 50	18 34	27 23 14	5 16	5 37	3 40	3 ♏ 36 43	7 44
28	F	20 28 17	7 51 49	18 18	9 ♏ 45 47	5 16	9 44	3 37	15 50 59	11 37
29	S	20 32 14	8 52 47	18 2	21 52 53	5 2	13 22	3 34	27 52 6	14 58
30	Su	20 36 11	9 53 44	17 46	3 ♐ 49 12	4 35	16 24	3 31	9 ♐ 44 45	17 40
31	M	20 40 7	10 ♒ 54 40	17 S 30	15 ♐ 39 19	3 N57	18 S 45	3 ♌ 27	21 ♐ 33 24	19 S 37

D M	Mercury Lat.	Mercury Dec.		Venus Lat.	Venus Dec.		Mars Lat.	Mars Dec.		Jupiter Lat.	Jupiter Dec.
	° ′	° ′	° ′	° ′	° ′	° ′	° ′	° ′	° ′	° ′	° ′
1	1 S 0	24 S 25	24 S 29	2 N 4	18 S 27	18 S 43	1 S 4	13 S 11	12 S 54	1 S 16	8 N36
3	1 11	24 32	24 33	2 0	18 58	19 13	1 3	12 37	12 20	1 15	8 38
5	1 21	24 33	24 31	1 57	19 28	19 42	1 1	12 3	11 45	1 14	8 41
7	1 31	24 28	24 24	1 53	19 55	20 8	1 0	11 28	11 10	1 14	8 44
9	1 40	24 18	24 11	1 48	20 21	20 32	0 58	10 53	10 35	1 13	8 47
11	1 47	24 2	23 52	1 44	20 44	20 54	0 56	10 17	9 59	1 13	8 51
13	1 54	23 40	23 27	1 39	21 5	21 14	0 55	9 41	9 23	1 12	8 55
15	1 59	23 12	22 56	1 34	21 23	21 32	0 53	9 5	8 47	1 11	8 59
17	2 3	22 38	22 19	1 29	21 40	21 47	0 52	8 29	8 11	1 11	9 3
19	2 5	21 58	21 36	1 23	21 53	21 59	0 50	7 52	7 34	1 10	9 8
21	2 6	21 12	20 47	1 18	22 5	22 9	0 49	7 15	6 57	1 10	9 13
23	2 5	20 20	19 51	1 12	22 13	22 17	0 47	6 38	6 19	1 9	9 18
25	2 2	19 21	18 50	1 7	22 20	22 22	0 46	6 1	5 42	1 9	9 23
27	1 57	18 17	17 43	1 1	22 23	22 24	0 44	5 23	5 4	1 8	9 29
29	1 49	17 7	16 S 29	0 55	22 24	22 S 24	0 42	4 46	4 S 27	1 8	9 35
31	1 S 39	15 S 51		0 N 49	22 S 22		0 S 41	4 S 8		1 S 7	9 N41

FIRST QUARTER-Jan.14, 1h.34m. pm. (23°♈41′)

FULL MOON-Jan.21, 4h.40m. am. (0°♌26′)

EPHEMERIS] JANUARY 2000

D M	☿ Long.	♀ Long.	♂ Long.	♃ Long.	♄ Long.	♅ Long.	♆ Long.	♇ Long.	☉	☿	♀	♂	♃	♄	♅	♆	♇
	Lunar Aspects																
	° ′	° ′	° ′	° ′	° ′	° ′	° ′	° ′									
1	1♑53	1♐34	27♒58	25♈15	10♉24	14♒49	3♒12	11♐27	⚹	∠				☍	□		⚺
2	3 27	2 47	28 44	25 18	10R 23	14 52	3 14	11 29	∠			□					
3	5 1	3 59	29♒31	25 20	10 22	14 55	3 16	11 31	⚺	⚺	☌		⚼			⚹	☌
4	6 35	5 12	0♓17	25 23	10 21	14 58	3 18	11 33							⚹	∠	
5	8 10	6 25	1 4	25 27	10 20	15 1	3 20	11 36				⚹	△	⚼	∠	⚺	
6	9 44	7 37	1 51	25 30	10 19	15 4	3 22	11 38	☌	☌	⚺	∠		△	⚺		⚺
7	11 20	8 50	2 37	25 33	10 19	15 7	3 25	11 40			∠		□				∠
8	12 55	10 3	3 24	25 37	10 18	15 10	3 27	11 42			⚹	⚺		□		☌	⚹
9	14 31	11 16	4 10	25 41	10 18	15 14	3 29	11 44	⚺	⚺					☌		
10	16 8	12 29	4 57	25 45	10 17	15 17	3 31	11 46	∠	∠		☌	⚹			⚺	
11	17 45	13 42	5 43	25 50	10 17	15 20	3 33	11 47		⚹	□		∠	⚹	⚺	∠	□
12	19 22	14 55	6 30	25 54	10D 17	15 23	3 36	11 49	⚹				⚺	∠	∠		
13	21 0	16 9	7 16	25 59	10 17	15 26	3 38	11 51				⚺		⚺	⚹	⚹	△
14	22 38	17 22	8 3	26 4	10 18	15 30	3 40	11 53	□	□	△	∠	☌				⚼
15	24 17	18 35	8 49	26 9	10 18	15 33	3 42	11 55			⚼	⚹		☌		□	
16	25 57	19 48	9 35	26 14	10 18	15 36	3 45	11 57	△	△			⚺		□		
17	27 36	21 2	10 22	26 19	10 19	15 40	3 47	11 59	⚼			□	∠	⚺		△	☍
18	29♑17	22 15	11 8	26 25	10 20	15 43	3 49	12 0		⚼	☍		⚹	∠	△	⚼	
19	0♒57	23 28	11 55	26 31	10 20	15 46	3 52	12 2				△		⚹	⚼		
20	2 39	24 42	12 41	26 37	10 21	15 50	3 54	12 4					□				⚼
21	4 21	25 55	13 27	26 43	10 22	15 53	3 56	12 6	☍	☍	⚼	⚼		□		☍	△
22	6 3	27 9	14 14	26 49	10 23	15 57	3 58	12 7					△		☍		
23	7 46	28 22	15 0	26 56	10 25	16 0	4 1	12 9			△			△			
24	9 29	29♐36	15 46	27 2	10 26	16 3	4 3	12 11	⚼			☍	⚼			⚼	□
25	11 13	0♑49	16 32	27 9	10 27	16 7	4 5	12 12	△	⚼	□			⚼	⚼	△	
26	12 57	2 3	17 19	27 16	10 29	16 10	4 7	12 14		△					△		⚹
27	14 41	3 17	18 5	27 23	10 30	16 14	4 10	12 15					⚼	☍			∠
28	16 26	4 30	18 51	27 30	10 32	16 17	4 12	12 17	□		⚹				☍	□	⚺
29	18 11	5 44	19 37	27 38	10 34	16 21	4 14	12 18		□	∠	△			□		
30	19 56	6 58	20 23	27 45	10 36	16 24	4 17	12 20			⚺					⚹	
31	21♒41	8♑12	21♓9	27♈53	10♉38	16♒28	4♒19	12♐21	⚹			□	⚼		⚹	∠	☌

D M	Saturn Lat.	Saturn Dec.	Uranus Lat.	Uranus Dec.	Neptune Lat.	Neptune Dec.	Pluto Lat.	Pluto Dec.
	° ′	° ′	° ′	° ′	° ′	° ′	° ′	° ′
1	2S27	12N37	0S39	17S 1	0N14	19S13	10N51	11S24
3	2 26	12 37	0 39	16 59	0 14	19 12	10 52	11 24
5	2 26	12 37	0 39	16 58	0 14	19 11	10 52	11 24
7	2 25	12 37	0 39	16 56	0 14	19 10	10 52	11 25
9	2 24	12 37	0 39	16 54	0 14	19 9	10 52	11 25
11	2 24	12 38	0 39	16 52	0 14	19 8	10 52	11 25
13	2 23	12 38	0 39	16 50	0 14	19 7	10 53	11 25
15	2 23	12 39	0 39	16 48	0 14	19 6	10 53	11 25
17	2 22	12 40	0 39	16 46	0 14	19 5	10 53	11 26
19	2 21	12 41	0 39	16 44	0 14	19 4	10 54	11 26
21	2 21	12 42	0 39	16 42	0 14	19 3	10 54	11 26
23	2 20	12 43	0 39	16 40	0 14	19 2	10 54	11 26
25	2 20	12 45	0 39	16 38	0 14	19 1	10 55	11 26
27	2 19	12 46	0 39	16 36	0 14	19 0	10 55	11 26
29	2 18	12 48	0 39	16 34	0 14	18 58	10 56	11 26
31	2S18	12N50	0S39	16S32	0N14	18S57	10N56	11S26

Mutual Aspects

1 ☉△♄. ♀±♃.
2 ☉⚺♇. ☿⚺♆. ♀Q♅. ♀⚹♆. ♂Q♄.
3 ♂P♄. 4 ♀P♆.
6 ☉⚺♅. ☿△♄. ☿⊥♅.
7 ☿⚺♇. ♂P♇.
8 ☉⊥♇. ♀⚼♃. ♀∇♄. ♂⚺♆.
9 ☿⚺♅. ♀☌♇.
11 ☿⊥♇.
12 ☉∠♂. ♀⚹♅. ♄ Stat.
13 ♀±♄.
14 ☿∠♂. ☉P♀.
15 ☉⊥♀. ♀∠♆. ♂P♃.
16 ☉☌☿. ☿⊥♀. ☿□♃. ♂⊥♆.
17 ☉□♃. ☉∠♇. ☿∠♇. ♂⚹♄.
18 ♂∠♃.
19 ♂□♇. ☿P♀.
21 ☿☌♆. ♀⚼♄.
22 ♀△♃. 23 ♀⊥♆.
24 ☉☌♆. ☿⊥♂. ♂⚺♅.
25 ☿□♄. ♀∠♅. ☉P♆.
26 ☿⚹♇. ♃⚼♇. ☉P☿. ☿P♆.
27 ☿Q♃.
28 ☿☌♅. ♀⚺♆. ♂∠♆.
30 ☿⚺♂. ☿P♅.
31 ☉□♄.

LAST QUARTER-Jan.28, 7h.57m. am. (7°♏42′)

NEW MOON-Feb. 5, 1h. 3m. pm. (16°♒ 2′)

D M	D W	Sidereal Time	☉ Long.	☉ Dec.	☽ Long.	☽ Lat.	☽ Dec.	☽ Node	Midnight ☽ Long.	Midnight ☽ Dec.
		H. M. S.	° ′ ″	° ′	° ′ ″	° ′	° ′	° ′	° ′ ″	° ′
1	T	20 44 4	11 ♒ 55 36	17 S 13	27 ♐ 27 32	3 N 8	20 S 17	3 ☊ 24	3 ♑ 22 9	20 S 43
2	W	20 48 0	12 56 31	16 56	9 ♑ 17 41	2 12	20 55	3 21	15 14 32	20 54
3	Th	20 51 57	13 57 25	16 38	21 13 3	1 9	20 38	3 18	27 13 32	20 7
4	F	20 55 53	14 58 18	16 21	3 ♒ 16 16	0 N 3	19 23	3 15	9 ♒ 21 29	18 25
5	S	20 59 50	15 59 9	16 3	15 29 23	1 S 5	17 13	3 11	21 40 7	15 49
6	Su	21 3 46	17 0 0	15 44	27 53 52	2 10	14 14	3 8	4 ♓ 10 42	12 28
7	M	21 7 43	18 0 49	15 26	10 ♓ 30 43	3 10	10 33	3 5	16 54 0	8 30
8	T	21 11 40	19 1 37	15 7	23 20 37	4 1	6 20	3 2	29 50 35	4 S 5
9	W	21 15 36	20 2 24	14 48	6 ♈ 23 59	4 41	1 S 46	2 59	13 ♈ 0 51	0 N 36
10	Th	21 19 33	21 3 9	14 29	19 41 11	5 7	2 N 58	2 56	26 25 3	5 19
11	F	21 23 29	22 3 52	14 9	3 ♉ 12 26	5 16	7 38	2 52	10 ♉ 3 23	9 52
12	S	21 27 26	23 4 34	13 49	16 57 50	5 7	11 59	2 49	23 55 47	13 58
13	Su	21 31 22	24 5 15	13 30	0 ♊ 57 8	4 41	15 46	2 46	8 ♊ 1 44	17 21
14	M	21 35 19	25 5 53	13 9	15 9 26	3 56	18 42	2 43	22 19 56	19 45
15	T	21 39 15	26 6 30	12 49	29 32 56	2 57	20 29	2 40	6 ♋ 47 59	20 53
16	W	21 43 12	27 7 6	12 28	14 ♋ 4 37	1 46	20 57	2 37	21 22 14	20 38
17	Th	21 47 9	28 7 39	12 7	28 40 12	0 S 27	19 59	2 33	5 ♌ 57 47	18 59
18	F	21 51 5	29 ♒ 8 11	11 46	13 ♌ 14 14	0 N 53	17 41	2 30	20 28 49	16 6
19	S	21 55 2	0 ♓ 8 41	11 25	27 40 44	2 9	14 17	2 27	4 ♍ 49 17	12 16
20	Su	21 58 58	1 9 10	11 4	11 ♍ 53 48	3 15	10 6	2 24	18 53 41	7 49
21	M	22 2 55	2 9 37	10 42	25 48 27	4 8	5 28	2 21	2 ♎ 37 46	3 N 4
22	T	22 6 51	3 10 2	10 21	9 ♎ 21 21	4 46	0 N 41	2 17	15 59 7	1 S 41
23	W	22 10 48	4 10 26	9 59	22 31 4	5 7	4 S 0	2 14	28 57 21	6 14
24	Th	22 14 44	5 10 49	9 37	5 ♏ 18 11	5 13	8 22	2 11	11 ♏ 33 55	10 23
25	F	22 18 41	6 11 10	9 14	17 44 58	5 3	12 16	2 8	23 51 50	14 0
26	S	22 22 38	7 11 30	8 52	29 55 3	4 40	15 35	2 5	5 ♐ 55 12	16 58
27	Su	22 26 34	8 11 48	8 30	11 ♐ 52 55	4 4	18 10	2 2	17 48 50	19 11
28	M	22 30 31	9 12 5	8 7	23 43 35	3 19	19 58	1 58	29 37 49	20 33
29	T	22 34 27	10 ♓ 12 21	7 S 44	5 ♑ 32 11	2 N 25	20 S 54	1 ☊ 55	11 ♑ 27 16	21 S 1

D M	Mercury Lat.	Mercury Dec.		Venus Lat.	Venus Dec.		Mars Lat.	Mars Dec.		Jupiter Lat.	Jupiter Dec.
	° ′	° ′	° ′	° ′	° ′	° ′	° ′	° ′	° ′	° ′	° ′
1	1 S 34	15 S 11	14 S 30	0 N 46	22 S 21	22 S 18	0 S 40	3 S 49	3 S 30	1 S 7	9 N 44
3	1 20	13 48	13 5	0 40	22 15	22 11	0 38	3 11	2 52	1 6	9 50
5	1 3	12 22	11 37	0 34	22 6	22 1	0 37	2 33	2 14	1 6	9 56
7	0 43	10 52	10 8	0 28	21 55	21 49	0 35	1 55	1 36	1 5	10 3
9	0 S 20	9 23	8 38	0 22	21 42	21 34	0 34	1 17	0 58	1 5	10 10
11	0 N 5	7 55	7 12	0 15	21 26	21 17	0 32	0 39	0 S 21	1 4	10 17
13	0 34	6 31	5 51	0 10	21 7	20 57	0 31	0 S 2	0 N 17	1 4	10 24
15	1 4	5 14	4 39	0 N 4	20 46	20 34	0 29	0 N 36	0 55	1 3	10 31
17	1 35	4 8	3 40	0 S 2	20 22	20 9	0 28	1 14	1 33	1 3	10 38
19	2 7	3 15	2 55	0 8	19 56	19 42	0 26	1 51	2 10	1 2	10 46
21	2 36	2 40	2 29	0 14	19 27	19 12	0 24	2 29	2 47	1 2	10 54
23	3 2	2 23	2 22	0 19	18 57	18 41	0 23	3 6	3 24	1 2	11 1
25	3 23	2 26	2 35	0 25	18 24	18 7	0 21	3 43	4 1	1 1	11 9
27	3 37	2 48	3 5	0 30	17 49	17 30	0 20	4 20	4 38	1 1	11 17
29	3 43	3 26	3 S 50	0 35	17 12	16 S 52	0 18	4 56	5 N 15	1 0	11 25
31	3 N 39	4 S 16		0 S 40	16 S 33		0 S 17	5 N 33		1 S 0	11 N 33

FIRST QUARTER-Feb.12,11h.21m. pm. (23° ♉ 33′)

FULL MOON-Feb.19, 4h.27m. pm. (0°♍20′)

D M	☿ Long.	♀ Long.	♂ Long.	♃ Long.	♄ Long.	♅ Long.	♆ Long.	♇ Long.	Lunar Aspects ☉	☿	♀	♂	♃	♄	♅	♆	♇
	° ′	° ′	° ′	° ′	° ′	° ′	° ′	° ′									
1	23♒25	9♑25	21♓56	28♈ 1	10♉40	16♒31	4♒21	12♐23	∠	⚹			△	⚼	∠		
2	25 9	10 39	22 42	28 9	10 43	16 35	4 23	12 24	⚺	∠	☌			△		⚺	⚺
3	26 53	11 53	23 28	28 17	10 45	16 38	4 26	12 26				⚹			⚺		
4	28♒35	13 7	24 14	28 25	10 48	16 42	4 28	12 27		⚺			□			☌	∠
5	0♓16	14 21	25 0	28 34	10 50	16 45	4 30	12 28	●		⚺	∠		□	☌		⚹
6	1 56	15 35	25 46	28 42	10 53	16 49	4 32	12 30		☌	∠	⚺	⚹				
7	3 33	16 49	26 32	28 51	10 56	16 52	4 35	12 31					∠	⚹		⚺	□
8	5 8	18 3	27 18	29 0	10 59	16 56	4 37	12 32	⚺		⚹	☌	⚺	∠	⚺	∠	
9	6 40	19 17	28 3	29 9	11 2	16 59	4 39	12 33	∠	⚺				⚺	∠	⚹	△
10	8 9	20 31	28 49	29 18	11 5	17 3	4 41	12 34	⚹	∠	□				⚹		
11	9 33	21 44	29♓35	29 27	11 8	17 6	4 43	12 35				⚺	☌			□	⚼
12	10 52	22 58	0♈21	29 37	11 11	17 10	4 46	12 37	□	⚹	△	∠		☌	□		
13	12 5	24 12	1 7	29 46	11 15	17 13	4 48	12 38				⚹	⚺			△	
14	13 13	25 26	1 52	29♈56	11 18	17 16	4 50	12 39		□	⚼		∠	⚺	△	⚼	☍
15	14 13	26 40	2 38	0♉ 6	11 22	17 20	4 52	12 40	△			□	⚹	∠	⚼		
16	15 5	27 54	3 24	0 16	11 26	17 23	4 54	12 41	⚼	△				⚹			
17	15 49	29♑ 8	4 9	0 26	11 29	17 27	4 56	12 42		⚼	☍	△	□			☍	⚼
18	16 24	0♒22	4 55	0 36	11 33	17 30	4 59	12 42				⚼		□	☍		△
19	16 50	1 36	5 40	0 46	11 37	17 34	5 1	12 43	☍				△				
20	17 5	2 51	6 26	0 57	11 41	17 37	5 3	12 44		☍	⚼		⚼	△			□
21	17 11	4 5	7 11	1 7	11 46	17 41	5 5	12 45						⚼		⚼	
22	17R 6	5 19	7 57	1 18	11 50	17 44	5 7	12 46			△	☍			⚼	△	⚹
23	16 51	6 33	8 42	1 28	11 54	17 47	5 9	12 47	⚼						△		∠
24	16 27	7 47	9 27	1 39	11 59	17 51	5 11	12 47	△	⚼	□		☍			□	
25	15 53	9 1	10 13	1 50	12 3	17 54	5 13	12 48		△				☍	□		⚺
26	15 12	10 15	10 58	2 1	12 8	17 57	5 15	12 49				⚼				⚹	
27	14 23	11 29	11 43	2 12	12 12	18 1	5 17	12 49	□	□	⚹	△	⚼				☌
28	13 29	12 43	12 28	2 23	12 17	18 4	5 19	12 50			∠			⚼	⚹	∠	
29	12♓30	13♒57	13♈13	2♉35	12♉22	18♒ 7	5♒21	12♐50	⚹				△		∠	⚺	

D M	Saturn Lat.	Saturn Dec.	Uranus Lat.	Uranus Dec.	Neptune Lat.	Neptune Dec.	Pluto Lat.	Pluto Dec.
	° ′	° ′	° ′	° ′	° ′	° ′	° ′	° ′
1	2S18	12N51	0S39	16S31	0N14	18S57	10N56	11S26
3	2 17	12 53	0 39	16 28	0 14	18 56	10 57	11 25
5	2 16	12 55	0 39	16 26	0 14	18 55	10 57	11 25
7	2 16	12 57	0 39	16 24	0 14	18 54	10 58	11 25
9	2 15	12 59	0 39	16 22	0 14	18 53	10 58	11 25
11	2 15	13 2	0 39	16 20	0 14	18 52	10 59	11 25
13	2 14	13 5	0 39	16 18	0 14	18 51	10 59	11 24
15	2 14	13 7	0 39	16 16	0 14	18 50	11 0	11 24
17	2 13	13 10	0 39	16 14	0 14	18 49	11 0	11 24
19	2 13	13 13	0 39	16 12	0 14	18 48	11 1	11 23
21	2 12	13 16	0 39	16 10	0 14	18 47	11 1	11 23
23	2 12	13 19	0 39	16 8	0 14	18 46	11 2	11 23
25	2 11	13 22	0 39	16 5	0 14	18 45	11 3	11 22
27	2 11	13 26	0 39	16 3	0 14	18 44	11 3	11 22
29	2 10	13 29	0 40	16 1	0 14	18 43	11 4	11 21
31	2S10	13N32	0S40	15S59	0N13	18S42	11N 4	11S21

Mutual Aspects

1 ☉⚹♇. ♂⊥♃.
2 ☿Q♇. ♀Q♂. ♀△♄. ♀⊥♅. ♂⊥♅.
3 ☿∠♀. ♀⚺♇.
4 ☿⚹♃. ☿Q♄. ☉P♅. ☿P♄.
6 ☉Q♃. ☉☌♅. ♂∠♄. ☿P♇.
7 ♀⚺♅. ♃Q♅.
8 ☿⚺♆. ♀⊥♇. ☿P♃.
11 ♂⚺♃.
12 ☉⚺♀. ☿⚹♄. ☿⊥♆.
13 ☿□♇.
14 ☉Q♇. ☉P♄.
15 ♂∠♅.
16 ☿∠♃. ♀∠♇.
17 ☉⊥♂.
18 ☉Q♄. ♀□♃. ♂⚹♆.
19 ☿∠♀. ♂⊥♄. ☉P♇.
20 ☉⚹♃.
21 ☉P♃. ☿P♂. ☿Stat.
22 ♀☌♆.
24 ☉⚺♆. ☿∠♃. ♀P♆.
25 ☿⊥♀. 27 ♀⚹♂.
28 ☿⚺♀. ♀□♄. ♀⚹♇. ♂⚺♄. ♂△♇.
♃P♇.
29 ☿⚺♂. ☿⚹♄. ☿□♇.

LAST QUARTER-Feb.27, 3h.53m. am. (7°♐51′)

NEW MOON-Mar. 6, 5h.17m. am. (15° ♓ 57′)

D M	D W	Sidereal Time	☉ Long.	☉ Dec.	☽ Long.	☽ Lat.	☽ Dec.	☽ Node	Midnight ☽ Long.	Midnight ☽ Dec.
		H. M. S.	° ′ ″	° ′	° ′ ″	° ′	° ′	° ′	° ′ ″	° ′
1	W	22 38 24	11 ♓ 12 35	7 S 22	17 ♑ 23 41	1 N25	20 S 54	1 ☊ 52	23 ♑ 21 59	20 S 32
2	Th	22 42 20	12 12 48	6 59	29 22 39	0 N21	19 56	1 49	5 ♒ 26 11	19 6
3	F	22 46 17	13 12 58	6 36	11 ♒ 32 57	0 S 45	18 2	1 46	17 43 19	16 45
4	S	22 50 13	14 13 8	6 13	23 57 34	1 50	15 16	1 43	0 ♓ 15 52	13 35
5	Su	22 54 10	15 13 15	5 49	6 ♓ 38 22	2 51	11 43	1 39	13 5 5	9 43
6	M	22 58 7	16 13 20	5 26	19 36 0	3 45	7 34	1 36	26 11 1	5 18
7	T	23 2 3	17 13 24	5 3	2 ♈ 49 56	4 27	2 S 57	1 33	9 ♈ 32 33	0 S 34
8	W	23 6 0	18 13 26	4 39	16 18 34	4 56	1 N52	1 30	23 7 41	4 N17
9	Th	23 9 56	19 13 25	4 16	29 59 33	5 8	6 40	1 27	6 ♉ 53 52	8 58
10	F	23 13 53	20 13 23	3 52	13 ♉ 50 17	5 2	11 11	1 23	20 48 30	13 15
11	S	23 17 49	21 13 18	3 29	27 48 14	4 39	15 8	1 20	4 ♊ 49 14	16 50
12	Su	23 21 46	22 13 12	3 5	11 ♊ 51 18	3 58	18 16	1 17	18 54 12	19 27
13	M	23 25 42	23 13 3	2 42	25 57 49	3 4	20 19	1 14	3 ♋ 1 58	20 53
14	T	23 29 39	24 12 52	2 18	10 ♋ 6 30	1 57	21 6	1 11	17 11 17	20 59
15	W	23 33 36	25 12 38	1 54	24 16 6	0 S 44	20 32	1 8	1 ♌ 20 44	19 46
16	Th	23 37 32	26 12 22	1 30	8 ♌ 24 58	0 N32	18 40	1 4	15 28 27	17 18
17	F	23 41 29	27 12 4	1 7	22 30 51	1 46	15 40	1 1	29 31 46	13 49
18	S	23 45 25	28 11 44	0 43	6 ♍ 30 47	2 52	11 47	0 58	13 ♍ 27 25	9 36
19	Su	23 49 22	29 ♓ 11 22	0 S 19	20 21 15	3 48	7 18	0 55	27 11 48	4 56
20	M	23 53 18	0 ♈ 10 57	0 N 4	3 ♎ 58 39	4 29	2 N32	0 52	10 ♎ 41 27	0 N 7
21	T	23 57 15	1 10 31	0 28	17 19 54	4 55	2 S 16	0 48	23 53 45	4 S 36
22	W	0 1 11	2 10 2	0 52	0 ♏ 22 54	5 4	6 51	0 45	6 ♏ 47 17	9 0
23	Th	0 5 8	3 9 32	1 15	13 7 0	4 58	11 2	0 42	19 22 12	12 55
24	F	0 9 5	4 9 0	1 39	25 33 8	4 38	14 39	0 39	1 ♐ 40 8	16 12
25	S	0 13 1	5 8 26	2 3	7 ♐ 43 39	4 6	17 33	0 36	13 44 8	18 43
26	Su	0 16 58	6 7 51	2 26	19 42 10	3 23	19 40	0 33	25 38 20	20 24
27	M	0 20 54	7 7 13	2 50	1 ♑ 33 15	2 32	20 54	0 29	7 ♑ 27 36	21 10
28	T	0 24 51	8 6 34	3 13	13 22 3	1 34	21 12	0 26	19 17 17	21 0
29	W	0 28 47	9 5 53	3 36	25 14 0	0 N32	20 34	0 23	1 ♒ 12 51	19 53
30	Th	0 32 44	10 5 11	4 0	7 ♒ 14 29	0 S 32	18 58	0 20	13 19 30	17 50
31	F	0 36 40	11 ♈ 4 26	4 N23	19 ♒ 28 29	1 S 35	16 S 29	0 ☊ 17	25 ♒ 41 55	14 S 56

D M	Mercury Lat.	Mercury Dec.		Venus Lat.	Venus Dec.		Mars Lat.	Mars Dec.		Jupiter Lat.	Jupiter Dec.
	° ′	° ′	° ′	° ′	° ′	° ′	° ′	° ′	° ′	° ′	° ′
1	3 N42	3 S 50	4 S 16	0 S 37	16 S 52	16 S 33	0 S 18	5 N15	5 N 33	1 S 0	11 N29
3	3 34	4 44	5 13	0 42	16 13	15 52	0 16	5 51	6 9	1 0	11 38
5	3 19	5 42	6 12	0 47	15 31	15 9	0 15	6 27	6 44	0 59	11 46
7	2 58	6 40	7 8	0 51	14 47	14 25	0 13	7 2	7 20	0 59	11 54
9	2 33	7 34	7 58	0 56	14 2	13 39	0 12	7 38	7 55	0 59	12 3
11	2 5	8 20	8 40	1 0	13 15	12 51	0 10	8 12	8 30	0 58	12 11
13	1 35	8 58	9 13	1 3	12 27	12 3	0 9	8 47	9 4	0 58	12 20
15	1 6	9 27	9 37	1 7	11 38	11 13	0 7	9 21	9 38	0 58	12 28
17	0 38	9 46	9 52	1 10	10 47	10 21	0 6	9 55	10 12	0 57	12 37
19	0 N12	9 56	9 58	1 14	9 55	9 29	0 4	10 28	10 45	0 57	12 46
21	0 S 14	9 58	9 55	1 16	9 2	8 35	0 3	11 1	11 18	0 57	12 55
23	0 37	9 51	9 45	1 19	8 8	7 41	0 S 1	11 34	11 50	0 56	13 3
25	0 58	9 36	9 26	1 21	7 13	6 45	0 0	12 6	12 21	0 56	13 12
27	1 17	9 15	9 1	1 23	6 17	5 49	0 N 1	12 37	12 53	0 56	13 21
29	1 34	8 46	8 S 29	1 25	5 21	4 S 53	0 3	13 8	13 N 23	0 56	13 30
31	1 S 49	8 S 10		1 S 27	4 S 24		0 N 4	13 N39		0 S 55	13 N39

FIRST QUARTER-Mar.13, 6h.59m. am. (23° ♊ 1′)

FULL MOON-Mar.20, 4h.44m. am. (7°♉43′)

EPHEMERIS] MARCH 2000

D M	☿ Long.	♀ Long.	♂ Long.	♃ Long.	♄ Long.	♅ Long.	♆ Long.	♇ Long.	☉	☿	♀	♂	♃	♄	♅	♆	♇
	° ′	° ′	° ′	° ′	° ′	° ′	° ′	° ′									
1	11♓29	15♒12	13♈58	2♉46	12♉27	18♒11	5♒23	12♐51		⚹	⚺	□		△	⚺		⚺
2	10R 26	16 26	14 43	2 58	12 32	18 14	5 25	12 51	∠	∠			□			☌	∠
3	9 23	17 40	15 28	3 9	12 37	18 17	5 27	12 52	⚺	⚺		⚹		□			⚹
4	8 22	18 54	16 13	3 21	12 42	18 20	5 29	12 52			●				☌		
5	7 24	20 8	16 58	3 33	12 47	18 24	5 31	12 52		☌		∠	⚹	⚹		⚺	□
6	6 30	21 22	17 43	3 44	12 53	18 27	5 32	12 53	☌		⚺	⚺	∠		⚺	∠	
7	5 40	22 36	18 28	3 56	12 58	18 30	5 34	12 53		⚺	∠		⚺	∠	∠	⚹	
8	4 56	23 51	19 13	4 8	13 4	18 33	5 36	12 53	⚺	∠		☌		⚺	⚹		△
9	4 19	25 5	19 58	4 20	13 9	18 36	5 38	12 53	∠	⚹	⚹		☌			□	⚼
10	3 47	26 19	20 42	4 33	13 15	18 39	5 40	12 54	⚹					☌	□		
11	3 22	27 33	21 27	4 45	13 20	18 42	5 41	12 54		□	□	⚺					
12	3 4	28♒47	22 12	4 57	13 26	18 46	5 43	12 54				∠	⚺	⚺	△	△	☍
13	2 52	0♓ 1	22 56	5 10	13 32	18 49	5 45	12 54	□	△	△	⚹	∠	∠		⚼	
14	2 47	1 15	23 41	5 22	13 38	18 52	5 46	12 54			⚼		⚹	⚹	⚼		
15	2D 48	2 29	24 25	5 35	13 44	18 55	5 48	12R 54	△	⚼		□					⚼
16	2 55	3 44	25 10	5 47	13 50	18 58	5 50	12 54	⚼				□	□		☍	△
17	3 7	4 58	25 54	6 0	13 56	19 0	5 51	12 54				△			☍		
18	3 25	6 12	26 38	6 13	14 2	19 3	5 53	12 54		☍	☍	⚼	△				□
19	3 48	7 26	27 23	6 26	14 8	19 6	5 54	12 54					⚼	△		⚼	
20	4 16	8 40	28 7	6 38	14 14	19 9	5 56	12 54	☍					⚼	⚼	△	
21	4 48	9 54	28 51	6 51	14 21	19 12	5 57	12 53		⚼					△		⚹
22	5 24	11 8	29♈35	7 4	14 27	19 15	5 59	12 53		△	⚼	☍				□	∠
23	6 5	12 22	0♉19	7 17	14 33	19 17	6 0	12 53	⚼		△		☍	☍	□		⚺
24	6 49	13 36	1 3	7 30	14 40	19 20	6 2	12 53									
25	7 37	14 51	1 48	7 44	14 46	19 23	6 3	12 52	△	□						⚹	☌
26	8 28	16 5	2 31	7 57	14 53	19 25	6 5	12 52			□	⚼	⚼		⚹	∠	
27	9 22	17 19	3 15	8 10	15 0	19 28	6 6	12 52				△		⚼	∠	⚺	
28	10 19	18 33	3 59	8 23	15 6	19 31	6 7	12 51	□	⚹	⚹		△	△			⚺
29	11 19	19 47	4 43	8 37	15 13	19 33	6 8	12 51		∠					⚺		∠
30	12 22	21 1	5 27	8 50	15 20	19 36	6 10	12 50	⚹	⚺	∠	□	□			☌	⚹
31	13♓27	22♓15	6♉11	9♉ 4	15♉27	19♒38	6♒11	12♐50			⚺			□	☌		

D M	Saturn Lat.	Saturn Dec.	Uranus Lat.	Uranus Dec.	Neptune Lat.	Neptune Dec.	Pluto Lat.	Pluto Dec.
	° ′	° ′	° ′	° ′	° ′	° ′	° ′	° ′
1	2S10	13N31	0S40	16S 0	0N14	18S42	11N 4	11S21
3	2 9	13 34	0 40	15 58	0 13	18 41	11 5	11 21
5	2 9	13 38	0 40	15 57	0 13	18 40	11 5	11 20
7	2 8	13 41	0 40	15 55	0 13	18 40	11 6	11 20
9	2 8	13 45	0 40	15 53	0 13	18 39	11 6	11 19
11	2 8	13 49	0 40	15 51	0 13	18 38	11 7	11 19
13	2 7	13 53	0 40	15 49	0 13	18 37	11 7	11 18
15	2 7	13 57	0 40	15 47	0 13	18 36	11 8	11 18
17	2 6	14 0	0 40	15 45	0 13	18 35	11 9	11 17
19	2 6	14 4	0 40	15 44	0 13	18 35	11 9	11 17
21	2 6	14 9	0 40	15 42	0 13	18 34	11 10	11 16
23	2 5	14 13	0 40	15 40	0 13	18 33	11 10	11 15
25	2 5	14 17	0 40	15 39	0 13	18 33	11 11	11 15
27	2 5	14 21	0 40	15 37	0 13	18 32	11 11	11 14
29	2 4	14 25	0 40	15 35	0 13	18 31	11 12	11 14
31	2S 4	14N29	0S40	15S34	0N13	18S31	11N12	11S13

Mutual Aspects

1 ☉☌☿. ☉⊥♆. ☿⊥♆.
2 ☉⚹♄.
3 ☉□♇. ☿⊥♂.
4 ♀☌♅. ☉P♂. ♀P♅.
5 ☉P☿.
6 ♀Q♃. ♂Q♆. ♄∇♇.
7 ☿⚺♆. ♂⚹♅.
8 ☉⚺♅.
9 ☉∠♃. ☿∠♂. ☿⚹♃. ♀Q♇.
10 ☉∠♆. ☿P♂. ♀P♄.
12 ☉⚺♂. 13 ♀P♃.
14 ♀Q♄. ☿Stat.
15 ☉⊥♅. ☿☌♀. ♇Stat.
16 ♃□♆. ☿P♂. ♀P♇.
18 ♀⚹♃. ♀⚺♆. ♀P♂.
19 ☉∠♄. ☿P♀.
20 ♂⚼♇.
21 ☉⊥♃. ♃±♇.
22 ♂P♇.
23 ☿⚺♆. ♀⊥♆. ♀□♇.
24 ☉∠♅. ♂Q♅.
25 ☿⚹♃. ♀⚹♄.
26 ☉⚹♆. 28 ☉⚺♃.
29 ☉⊥♄. ♀∠♂. ♀⚺♅.
30 ☿⊥♆. ☿□♇. ♀∠♆.
31 ♂□♆. ☉P♀. ♂P♃.

LAST QUARTER-Mar.28, 0h.21m. am. (7°♑38′)

NEW MOON-Apr. 4, 6h.12m. pm. (15°♈16′)

D M	D W	Sidereal Time	☉ Long.	☉ Dec.	☽ Long.	☽ Lat.	☽ Dec.	☽ Node	Midnight ☽ Long.	Midnight ☽ Dec.
		H. M. S.	° ′ ″	° ′	° ′ ″	° ′	° ′	° ′	° ′ ″	° ′
1	S	0 40 37	12 ♈ 3 40	4 N46	2 ♓ 0 12	2 S 36	13 S 11	0 ☊ 14	8 ♓ 23 41	11 S 16
2	Su	0 44 34	13 2 52	5 9	14 52 35	3 30	9 11	0 10	21 27 0	6 58
3	M	0 48 30	14 2 1	5 32	28 6 56	4 14	4 S 38	0 7	4 ♈ 52 12	2 S 13
4	T	0 52 27	15 1 9	5 55	11 ♈ 42 33	4 45	0 N 15	0 4	18 37 35	2 N 45
5	W	0 56 23	16 0 15	6 18	25 36 47	5 0	5 14	0 ☊ 1	2 ♉ 39 34	7 41
6	Th	1 0 20	16 59 19	6 40	9 ♉ 45 15	4 57	10 2	29 ♋ 58	16 53 9	12 16
7	F	1 4 16	17 58 20	7 3	24 2 34	4 36	14 19	29 54	1 ♊ 12 48	16 11
8	S	1 8 13	18 57 20	7 25	8 ♊ 23 15	3 57	17 48	29 51	15 33 20	19 9
9	Su	1 12 9	19 56 17	7 48	22 42 36	3 3	20 11	29 48	29 50 38	20 54
10	M	1 16 6	20 55 12	8 10	6 ♋ 57 9	1 58	21 17	29 45	14 ♋ 1 56	21 19
11	T	1 20 3	21 54 5	8 32	21 4 51	0 S 47	21 1	29 42	28 5 49	20 23
12	W	1 23 59	22 52 55	8 54	5 ♌ 4 47	0 N 27	19 26	29 39	12 ♌ 1 44	18 12
13	Th	1 27 56	23 51 43	9 16	18 56 39	1 39	16 43	29 35	25 49 30	14 59
14	F	1 31 52	24 50 29	9 37	2 ♍ 40 15	2 44	13 4	29 32	9 ♍ 28 49	10 59
15	S	1 35 49	25 49 12	9 59	16 15 6	3 39	8 47	29 29	22 58 57	6 29
16	Su	1 39 45	26 47 54	10 20	29 40 14	4 21	4 N 7	29 26	6 ♎ 18 45	1 N 43
17	M	1 43 42	27 46 33	10 41	12 ♎ 54 17	4 48	0 S 40	29 23	19 26 41	3 S 3
18	T	1 47 38	28 45 10	11 2	25 55 44	5 0	5 22	29 20	2 ♏ 21 19	7 36
19	W	1 51 35	29 ♈ 43 45	11 23	8 ♏ 43 19	4 56	9 44	29 16	15 1 41	11 44
20	Th	1 55 32	0 ♉ 42 19	11 43	21 16 26	4 38	13 36	29 13	27 27 37	15 18
21	F	1 59 28	1 40 50	12 3	3 ♐ 35 25	4 7	16 50	29 10	9 ♐ 40 2	18 9
22	S	2 3 25	2 39 20	12 24	15 41 45	3 25	19 16	29 7	21 40 58	20 10
23	Su	2 7 21	3 37 48	12 44	27 38 5	2 35	20 50	29 4	3 ♑ 33 36	21 16
24	M	2 11 18	4 36 15	13 3	9 ♑ 28 2	1 38	21 28	29 0	15 22 0	21 26
25	T	2 15 14	5 34 40	13 23	21 16 7	0 N 37	21 9	28 57	27 11 3	20 37
26	W	2 19 11	6 33 3	13 42	3 ♒ 7 27	0 S 26	19 52	28 54	9 ♒ 6 2	18 54
27	Th	2 23 7	7 31 25	14 1	15 7 30	1 28	17 42	28 51	21 12 30	16 18
28	F	2 27 4	8 29 45	14 20	27 21 42	2 28	14 42	28 48	3 ♓ 35 42	12 55
29	S	2 31 1	9 28 3	14 39	9 ♓ 55 5	3 22	10 58	28 45	16 20 18	8 51
30	Su	2 34 57	10 ♉ 26 20	14 N57	22 ♓ 51 43	4 S 7	6 S 37	28 ♋ 41	29 ♓ 29 37	4 S 16

D M	Mercury Lat.	Mercury Dec.	Mercury Dec.	Venus Lat.	Venus Dec.	Venus Dec.	Mars Lat.	Mars Dec.	Mars Dec.	Jupiter Lat.	Jupiter Dec.
	° ′	° ′	° ′	° ′	° ′	° ′	° ′	° ′	° ′	° ′	° ′
1	1 S 55	7 S 50	7 S 29	1 S 27	3 S 55	3 S 27	0 N 5	13 N54	14 N 8	0 S 55	13 N43
3	2 7	7 6	6 42	1 29	2 58	2 29	0 6	14 23	14 38	0 55	13 52
5	2 17	6 16	5 49	1 29	2 0	1 31	0 7	14 52	15 7	0 55	14 1
7	2 24	5 20	4 51	1 30	1 1	0 S 32	0 9	15 21	15 35	0 54	14 9
9	2 30	4 20	3 47	1 30	0 S 3	0 N27	0 10	15 49	16 2	0 54	14 18
11	2 33	3 14	2 40	1 30	0 N56	1 25	0 11	16 16	16 29	0 54	14 27
13	2 34	2 4	1 27	1 30	1 54	2 24	0 13	16 42	16 55	0 54	14 36
15	2 34	0 S 49	0 S 10	1 30	2 53	3 22	0 14	17 8	17 21	0 54	14 44
17	2 31	0 N30	1 N 11	1 29	3 51	4 20	0 15	17 34	17 46	0 53	14 53
19	2 26	1 53	2 35	1 28	4 49	5 18	0 16	17 58	18 10	0 53	15 2
21	2 19	3 19	4 4	1 27	5 47	6 16	0 18	18 22	18 34	0 53	15 10
23	2 10	4 49	5 35	1 25	6 44	7 12	0 19	18 45	18 57	0 53	15 19
25	1 59	6 22	7 10	1 24	7 41	8 9	0 20	19 8	19 19	0 53	15 27
27	1 46	7 58	8 46	1 22	8 37	9 4	0 21	19 29	19 40	0 53	15 36
29	1 31	9 35	10 N 24	1 19	9 32	9 N59	0 22	19 51	20 N 1	0 52	15 44
31	1 S 15	11 N14		1 S 17	10 N26		0 N 23	20 N11		0 S 52	15 N53

FIRST QUARTER-Apr.11, 1h.30m. pm. (21°♋58′)

FULL MOON-Apr.18, 5h.41m. pm. (28°♎59′)

EPHEMERIS]			APRIL 2000														9
D	☿	♀	♂	♃	♄	♅	♆	♇	Lunar Aspects								
M	Long.	Long.	Long.	Long.	Long.	Long.	Long.	Long.	☉	☿	♀	♂	♃	♄	♅	♆	♇
	° ′	° ′	° ′	° ′	° ′	° ′	° ′	° ′									
1	14♓35	23♓29	6♉54	9♉17	15♉33	19♒41	6♒12	12♐49	∠			✱				⊻	
2	15 45	24 43	7 38	9 31	15 40	19 43	6 13	12R 49	⊻	☌			✱	✱	⊻	∠	□
3	16 57	25 57	8 22	9 44	15 47	19 46	6 14	12 48			☌	∠	∠	∠	∠		
4	18 11	27 11	9 5	9 58	15 54	19 48	6 16	12 47	☌			⊻	⊻	⊻		✱	△
5	19 28	28 26	9 49	10 12	16 1	19 50	6 17	12 47		⊻	⊻				✱		⚻
6	20 46	29♓40	10 32	10 26	16 8	19 52	6 18	12 46		∠	∠	☌	☌	☌		□	
7	22 6	0♈54	11 16	10 39	16 15	19 55	6 19	12 45	⊻	✱					□		
8	23 28	2 8	11 59	10 53	16 23	19 57	6 20	12 45	∠		✱	⊻	⊻			△	☍
9	24 52	3 22	12 42	11 7	16 30	19 59	6 21	12 44	✱	□		∠	∠	⊻	△	⚻	
10	26 17	4 36	13 25	11 21	16 37	20 1	6 22	12 43			□	✱	✱	∠	⚻		
11	27 45	5 50	14 9	11 35	16 44	20 3	6 22	12 42	□					✱			⚻
12	29♓14	7 4	14 52	11 49	16 52	20 5	6 23	12 41		△	△		□			☍	
13	0♈44	8 18	15 35	12 3	16 59	20 7	6 24	12 40	△	⚻	⚻	□		□	☍		△
14	2 17	9 32	16 18	12 17	17 6	20 9	6 25	12 39									
15	3 51	10 46	17 1	12 31	17 14	20 11	6 26	12 38	⚻			△	△	△		⚻	□
16	5 27	12 0	17 44	12 45	17 21	20 13	6 26	12 38		☍		⚻	⚻	⚻	⚻		
17	7 4	13 14	18 27	12 59	17 28	20 15	6 27	12 37			☍					△	✱
18	8 43	14 27	19 10	13 13	17 36	20 17	6 28	12 35	☍						△		∠
19	10 24	15 41	19 53	13 27	17 43	20 18	6 28	12 34					☍			□	⊻
20	12 6	16 55	20 35	13 41	17 51	20 20	6 29	12 33				☍		☍	□		
21	13 50	18 9	21 18	13 55	17 58	20 22	6 30	12 32		⚻	⚻					✱	
22	15 35	19 23	22 1	14 9	18 6	20 23	6 30	12 31	⚻	△	△				✱	∠	☌
23	17 23	20 37	22 43	14 23	18 13	20 25	6 31	12 30					⚻	⚻			
24	19 11	21 51	23 26	14 38	18 21	20 26	6 31	12 29	△			⚻	△		∠	⊻	⊻
25	21 2	23 5	24 9	14 52	18 29	20 28	6 32	12 28		□	□	△		△	⊻		
26	22 54	24 19	24 51	15 6	18 36	20 29	6 32	12 26	□							☌	∠
27	24 48	25 33	25 33	15 20	18 44	20 31	6 32	12 25					□	□	☌		✱
28	26 44	26 47	26 16	15 35	18 51	20 32	6 33	12 24		✱	✱	□					
29	28♈41	28 1	26 58	15 49	18 59	20 33	6 33	12 23	✱	∠	∠		✱			⊻	□
30	0♉40	29♈14	27♉41	16♉3	19♉7	20♒34	6♒33	12♐21	∠			✱		✱	⊻	∠	

D	Saturn		Uranus		Neptune		Pluto	
M	Lat.	Dec.	Lat.	Dec.	Lat.	Dec.	Lat.	Dec.
	° ′	° ′	° ′	° ′	° ′	° ′	° ′	° ′
1	2S 4	14N31	0S40	15S33	0N13	18S30	11N13	11S13
3	2 3	14 36	0 40	15 32	0 13	18 30	11 13	11 12
5	2 3	14 40	0 40	15 30	0 13	18 29	11 14	11 11
7	2 3	14 44	0 40	15 29	0 13	18 29	11 14	11 11
9	2 3	14 49	0 41	15 28	0 13	18 28	11 14	11 10
11	2 2	14 53	0 41	15 26	0 13	18 28	11 15	11 9
13	2 2	14 57	0 41	15 25	0 13	18 27	11 15	11 9
15	2 2	15 2	0 41	15 24	0 13	18 27	11 16	11 8
17	2 2	15 6	0 41	15 23	0 13	18 27	11 16	11 8
19	2 1	15 10	0 41	15 22	0 13	18 26	11 16	11 7
21	2 1	15 15	0 41	15 21	0 13	18 26	11 17	11 6
23	2 1	15 19	0 41	15 20	0 13	18 26	11 17	11 6
25	2 1	15 23	0 41	15 19	0 13	18 26	11 17	11 5
27	2 1	15 28	0 41	15 18	0 13	18 25	11 18	11 5
29	2 1	15 32	0 41	15 17	0 13	18 25	11 18	11 4
31	2S 0	15N36	0S41	15S17	0N13	18S25	11N18	11S 4

Mutual Aspects

1 ♂±♇.
2 ☉△♇. ☿✱♄. ♀∠♃.
3 ♀⊥♅. 4 ♂P♄.
5 ☉⊻♄. ☿⊻♅. ☉P☿.
6 ☿∠♆. ♂☌♃.
7 ☉Q♆. ♀∠♄.
8 ♂P♅.
9 ☉✱♅. ♂▽♇.
10 ☿∠♃. ☿⊥♅. ♀∠♅.
11 ♀⊥♃. ♀✱♆.
13 ☿∠♂. ☿P♀.
14 ☿∠♄.
15 ♀⊥♂. ♀⊥♄. ♂☌♄.
16 ☿∠♅. ♃▽♇.
17 ☉⚻♇. ☿⊥♃. ☿✱♆. ♀⊻♃. ♀△♇.
18 ☉P♇.
20 ☿⊥♄. ☿△♇. ♂□♅.
21 ☿⊻♃. ♀⊻♄. ♀Q♆. ♂P♆.
22 ☉Q♅. ☿⊥♂.
23 ♀✱♅. ♃P♄. ♃P♅. ♄P♅.
24 ☿⊻♄. ☿Q♆.
25 ☿✱♅.
26 ☉□♆. ☉±♇.
27 ♀⊻♂.
28 ☿☌♀. ☿⊻♂. ☿⚻♇. ♀⚻♇.
29 ☿P♀.

LAST QUARTER-Apr.26, 7h.30m. pm. (6°♒51′)

NEW MOON-May 4, 4h.12m. am. (14° ♉ 0′)

D M	D W	Sidereal Time	☉ Long.	☉ Dec.	☽ Long.	☽ Lat.	☽ Dec.	☽ Node	Midnight ☽ Long.	Midnight ☽ Dec.
		H. M. S.	° ′ ″	° ′	° ′ ″	° ′	° ′	° ′	° ′ ″	° ′
1	M	2 38 54	11 ♉ 24 36	15 N15	6 ♈ 14 4	4 S41	1 S49	28 ♋ 38	13 ♈ 5 4	0 N41
2	T	2 42 50	12 22 49	15 33	20 2 24	4 59	3 N13	28 35	27 5 40	5 45
3	W	2 46 47	13 21 2	15 51	4 ♉ 14 19	5 0	8 13	28 32	11 ♉ 27 39	10 37
4	Th	2 50 43	14 19 12	16 8	18 44 50	4 41	12 53	28 29	26 4 56	14 58
5	F	2 54 40	15 17 21	16 25	3 ♊ 26 57	4 4	16 51	28 26	10 ♊ 49 53	18 27
6	S	2 58 36	16 15 29	16 42	18 12 45	3 11	19 45	28 22	25 34 39	20 43
7	Su	3 2 33	17 13 34	16 59	2 ♋ 54 47	2 5	21 20	28 19	10 ♋ 12 27	21 35
8	M	3 6 30	18 11 38	17 15	17 27 6	0 S51	21 27	28 16	24 38 20	20 59
9	T	3 10 26	19 9 39	17 31	1 ♌ 45 51	0 N25	20 10	28 13	8 ♌ 49 28	19 3
10	W	3 14 23	20 7 39	17 46	15 49 8	1 38	17 39	28 10	22 44 51	16 1
11	Th	3 18 19	21 5 37	18 2	29 36 41	2 44	14 10	28 6	6 ♍ 24 44	12 9
12	F	3 22 16	22 3 33	18 17	13 ♍ 9 8	3 40	10 0	28 3	19 50 2	7 45
13	S	3 26 12	23 1 27	18 32	26 27 33	4 22	5 25	28 0	3 ♎ 1 48	3 N 3
14	Su	3 30 9	23 59 19	18 46	9 ♎ 32 53	4 50	0 N40	27 57	16 0 55	1 S42
15	M	3 34 5	24 57 9	19 0	22 25 55	5 3	4 S 2	27 54	28 47 58	6 19
16	T	3 38 2	25 54 58	19 14	5 ♏ 7 5	5 1	8 30	27 51	11 ♏ 23 20	10 35
17	W	3 41 59	26 52 46	19 28	17 36 44	4 44	12 33	27 47	23 47 22	14 21
18	Th	3 45 55	27 50 32	19 41	29 55 17	4 14	16 0	27 44	6 ♐ 0 37	17 28
19	F	3 49 52	28 48 16	19 54	12 ♐ 3 30	3 32	18 44	27 41	18 4 7	19 47
20	S	3 53 48	29 ♉ 46 0	20 6	24 2 41	2 42	20 36	27 38	29 59 30	21 12
21	Su	3 57 45	0 ♊ 43 42	20 18	5 ♑ 54 54	1 45	21 34	27 35	11 ♑ 49 13	21 40
22	M	4 1 41	1 41 23	20 30	17 42 55	0 N43	21 33	27 32	23 36 28	21 11
23	T	4 5 38	2 39 3	20 41	29 30 21	0 S20	20 35	27 28	5 ♒ 25 10	19 45
24	W	4 9 34	3 36 42	20 52	11 ♒ 21 28	1 23	18 42	27 25	17 19 54	17 26
25	Th	4 13 31	4 34 19	21 3	23 21 5	2 23	15 59	27 22	29 25 40	14 21
26	F	4 17 28	5 31 56	21 14	5 ♓ 34 19	3 18	12 32	27 19	11 ♓ 47 38	10 34
27	S	4 21 24	6 29 32	21 24	18 6 13	4 5	8 27	27 16	24 30 39	6 13
28	Su	4 25 21	7 27 7	21 33	1 ♈ 1 22	4 41	3 S53	27 12	7 ♈ 38 47	1 S28
29	M	4 29 17	8 24 41	21 42	14 23 9	5 3	1 N 1	27 9	21 14 36	3 N32
30	T	4 33 14	9 22 14	21 51	28 13 5	5 8	6 2	27 6	5 ♉ 18 24	8 30
31	W	4 37 10	10 ♊ 19 46	22 N 0	12 ♉ 30 7	4 S55	10 N54	27 ♋ 3	19 ♉ 47 40	13 N10

D M	Mercury Lat.	Mercury Dec.	Mercury Dec. (even days)	Venus Lat.	Venus Dec.	Venus Dec. (even days)	Mars Lat.	Mars Dec.	Mars Dec. (even days)	Jupiter Lat.	Jupiter Dec.
	° ′	° ′	° ′	° ′	° ′	° ′	° ′	° ′	° ′	° ′	° ′
1	1 S15	11 N14	12 N 4	1 S 17	10 N26	10 N53	0 N 23	20 N11	20 N 21	0 S 52	15 N53
3	0 57	12 53	13 43	1 14	11 20	11 46	0 25	20 30	20 40	0 52	16 1
5	0 37	14 32	15 21	1 11	12 12	12 38	0 26	20 49	20 58	0 52	16 9
7	0 S17	16 9	16 56	1 8	13 3	13 28	0 27	21 7	21 16	0 52	16 17
9	0 N 4	17 42	18 27	1 5	13 53	14 17	0 28	21 24	21 32	0 52	16 25
11	0 26	19 10	19 52	1 2	14 42	15 5	0 29	21 41	21 48	0 52	16 33
13	0 46	20 31	21 9	0 58	15 29	15 52	0 30	21 56	22 4	0 51	16 41
15	1 5	21 45	22 18	0 54	16 14	16 37	0 31	22 11	22 18	0 51	16 49
17	1 23	22 49	23 17	0 50	16 58	17 20	0 32	22 25	22 31	0 51	16 57
19	1 39	23 42	24 5	0 46	17 41	18 1	0 33	22 38	22 44	0 51	17 4
21	1 52	24 26	24 43	0 42	18 21	18 41	0 34	22 50	22 56	0 51	17 12
23	2 2	24 58	25 11	0 38	19 0	19 18	0 35	23 2	23 7	0 51	17 19
25	2 8	25 21	25 29	0 33	19 36	19 54	0 36	23 12	23 17	0 51	17 27
27	2 12	25 34	25 38	0 29	20 10	20 27	0 37	23 22	23 26	0 51	17 34
29	2 13	25 39	25 N 38	0 24	20 43	20 N58	0 38	23 31	23 N 35	0 51	17 41
31	2 N10	25 N36		0 S 20	21 N13		0 N 39	23 N39		0 S 51	17 N48

FIRST QUARTER-May 10, 8h. 0m. pm. (20° ♌ 27′)

FULL MOON-May 18, 7h.34m. am. (27°♏40′)

D M	☿ Long.	♀ Long.	♂ Long.	♃ Long.	♄ Long.	♅ Long.	♆ Long.	♇ Long.	☉	☿	♀	♂	♃	♄	♅	♆	♇
	° ′	° ′	° ′	° ′	° ′	° ′	° ′	° ′									
1	2♉41	0♉28	28♉23	16♉17	19♉14	20♒36	6♒34	12♐20	⚺	⚺	⚺		∠	∠	∠	⚹	△
2	4 43	1 42	29 5	16 32	19 22	20 37	6 34	12R 19				∠	⚺	⚺	⚹		
3	6 47	2 56	29♉47	16 46	19 30	20 38	6 34	12 17		☌	☌	⚺				□	⚼
4	8 52	4 10	0♊29	17 0	19 38	20 39	6 34	12 16	☌				☌	☌	□		
5	10 58	5 24	1 11	17 14	19 45	20 40	6 34	12 15			⚺	☌				△	
6	13 6	6 38	1 53	17 29	19 53	20 41	6 34	12 13	⚺	⚺	∠		⚺	⚺	△	⚼	☍
7	15 15	7 51	2 35	17 43	20 1	20 42	6 34	12 12	∠	∠	⚹	⚺	∠	∠	⚼		
8	17 24	9 5	3 17	17 57	20 8	20 43	6 34	12 10	⚹	⚹		∠	⚹	⚹			
9	19 34	10 19	3 59	18 12	20 16	20 43	6R 34	12 9				⚹				☍	⚼
10	21 45	11 33	4 41	18 26	20 24	20 44	6 34	12 7	□		□		□	□	☍		△
11	23 56	12 47	5 23	18 40	20 32	20 45	6 34	12 6		□		□					
12	26 6	14 0	6 5	18 54	20 39	20 45	6 34	12 4			△		△				□
13	28♉16	15 14	6 46	19 9	20 47	20 46	6 34	12 3	△	△	⚼			△		⚼	
14	0♊26	16 28	7 28	19 23	20 55	20 47	6 34	12 1	⚼			△	⚼	⚼	⚼	△	⚹
15	2 35	17 42	8 10	19 37	21 2	20 47	6 34	12 0		⚼		⚼			△		∠
16	4 42	18 56	8 51	19 51	21 10	20 48	6 33	11 58								□	
17	6 48	20 9	9 33	20 6	21 18	20 48	6 33	11 57			☍		☍	☍	□		⚺
18	8 52	21 23	10 14	20 20	21 26	20 48	6 33	11 55	☍								
19	10 54	22 37	10 56	20 34	21 33	20 49	6 32	11 54		☍		☍				⚹	☌
20	12 54	23 51	11 37	20 48	21 41	20 49	6 32	11 52							⚹	∠	
21	14 52	25 4	12 18	21 2	21 49	20 49	6 32	11 51			⚼		⚼	⚼	∠	⚺	
22	16 47	26 18	13 0	21 16	21 56	20 49	6 31	11 49	⚼				△	△	⚺		⚺
23	18 40	27 32	13 41	21 31	22 4	20 49	6 31	11 47	△	⚼	△	⚼					∠
24	20 30	28 45	14 22	21 45	22 12	20 49	6 30	11 46				△				☌	⚹
25	22 17	29♉59	15 3	21 59	22 19	20R 49	6 30	11 44		△			□	□	☌		
26	24 1	1♊13	15 45	22 13	22 27	20 49	6 29	11 43	□		□					⚺	□
27	25 42	2 27	16 26	22 27	22 34	20 49	6 29	11 41				□	⚹	⚹	⚺	∠	
28	27 21	3 40	17 7	22 41	22 42	20 49	6 28	11 39		□	⚹				∠	⚹	
29	28♊56	4 54	17 48	22 55	22 50	20 49	6 27	11 38	⚹		∠	⚹	∠	∠	⚹		△
30	0♋29	6 8	18 29	23 9	22 57	20 49	6 27	11 36	∠	⚹		∠	⚺	⚺			⚼
31	1♋58	7♊22	19♊10	23♉23	23♉5	20♒49	6♒26	11♐34	⚺	∠	⚺	⚺				□	

(Columns ☉ to ♇ on the right: Lunar Aspects)

D M	Saturn Lat.	Saturn Dec.	Uranus Lat.	Uranus Dec.	Neptune Lat.	Neptune Dec.	Pluto Lat.	Pluto Dec.
	° ′	° ′	° ′	° ′	° ′	° ′	° ′	° ′
1	2S 0	15N36	0S41	15S17	0N13	18S25	11N18	11S 4
3	2 0	15 40	0 41	15 16	0 13	18 25	11 18	11 3
5	2 0	15 45	0 41	15 15	0 13	18 25	11 19	11 2
7	2 0	15 49	0 42	15 15	0 13	18 25	11 19	11 2
9	2 0	15 53	0 42	15 15	0 13	18 25	11 19	11 1
11	2 0	15 57	0 42	15 14	0 13	18 25	11 19	11 1
13	2 0	16 1	0 42	15 14	0 13	18 25	11 19	11 1
15	2 0	16 5	0 42	15 14	0 13	18 25	11 19	11 0
17	2 0	16 10	0 42	15 13	0 13	18 25	11 19	11 0
19	2 0	16 14	0 42	15 13	0 13	18 25	11 19	10 59
21	2 0	16 17	0 42	15 13	0 13	18 26	11 19	10 59
23	2 0	16 21	0 42	15 13	0 13	18 26	11 19	10 59
25	2 0	16 25	0 42	15 13	0 13	18 26	11 19	10 58
27	2 0	16 29	0 42	15 13	0 13	18 26	11 19	10 58
29	2 0	16 33	0 42	15 13	0 13	18 27	11 19	10 58
31	2S 0	16N37	0S42	15S14	0N13	18S27	11N19	10S57

Mutual Aspects

1 ☿ Q ♅. ☉ P ♅. ☿ P ♇.
2 ☉ ⚻ ♇. ☉ P ♄. ♀ P ♇.
3 ☿ □ ♆. ☿ ± ♇. ♀ Q ♅.
4 ☉ P ♃.
6 ☿ ⚻ ♇. ♀ □ ♆. ♀ ± ♇. ☿ P ♅.
7 ☿ P ♃. ☿ P ♄.
8 ☉ ☌ ♃. ☿ ☌ ♃. ♆ Stat.
9 ☉ ☌ ☿. ☿ ☌ ♄. ☉ P ☿.
10 ☉ ☌ ♄. ☿ □ ♅. ♀ ⚻ ♇. ☿ P ♆.
11 ☉ □ ♅. 12 ♀ P ♅.
13 ♂ △ ♆. ♄ □ ♅. ☉ P ♆.
15 ♀ P ♄. 16 ☿ P ♂.
17 ☿ △ ♆. ♀ ☌ ♃. ♀ P ♃.
18 ♀ ☌ ♄. ♀ □ ♅.
19 ☿ ☌ ♂. ☿ ☍ ♇.
20 ♂ ☍ ♇. ♃ □ ♅.
21 ♀ P ♆. 24 ☿ △ ♅.
25 ☿ ⚺ ♃. ☿ ⚺ ♄. ☿ ⚼ ♆. ♅ Stat.
27 ☉ △ ♆. 28 ♃ ☌ ♄.
29 ☿ ⊥ ♃. ☿ ⊥ ♄.
30 ☿ ± ♆. ♀ △ ♆.

LAST QUARTER-May 26,11h.55m. am. (5°♓32′)

NEW MOON-June 2, 0h.14m. pm. (12°♊15′)

D M	D W	Sidereal Time	☉ Long.	☉ Dec.	☽ Long.	☽ Lat.	☽ Dec.	☽ Node	Midnight ☽ Long.	Midnight ☽ Dec.
		H. M. S.	° ′ ″	° ′	° ′ ″	° ′	° ′	° ′	° ′ ″	° ′
1	Th	4 41 7	11 ♊ 17 18	22 N 8	27 ♉ 10 14	4 S 23	15 N 15	27 ♋ 0	4 ♊ 36 55	17 N 8
2	F	4 45 3	12 14 49	22 16	12 ♊ 6 38	3 32	18 44	26 57	19 38 16	20 2
3	S	4 49 0	13 12 18	22 23	27 10 36	2 26	20 58	26 53	4 ♋ 42 29	21 32
4	Su	4 52 57	14 9 47	22 30	12 ♋ 12 49	1 S 10	21 43	26 50	19 40 37	21 30
5	M	4 56 53	15 7 14	22 36	27 4 59	0 N 10	20 55	26 47	4 ♌ 25 13	19 58
6	T	5 0 50	16 4 41	22 43	11 ♌ 40 45	1 29	18 42	26 44	18 51 10	17 9
7	W	5 4 46	17 2 6	22 48	25 56 15	2 40	15 23	26 41	2 ♍ 55 52	13 24
8	Th	5 8 43	17 59 30	22 54	9 ♍ 50 0	3 39	11 16	26 37	16 38 45	9 1
9	F	5 12 39	18 56 52	22 59	23 22 17	4 25	6 41	26 34	0 ♎ 0 49	4 N 19
10	S	5 16 36	19 54 14	23 3	6 ♎ 34 37	4 56	1 N 55	26 31	13 3 58	0 S 28
11	Su	5 20 32	20 51 35	23 7	19 29 10	5 10	2 S 50	26 28	25 50 29	5 8
12	M	5 24 29	21 48 54	23 11	2 ♏ 8 13	5 10	7 22	26 25	8 ♏ 22 40	9 30
13	T	5 28 26	22 46 13	23 14	14 34 5	4 54	11 31	26 22	20 42 42	13 24
14	W	5 32 22	23 43 31	23 17	26 48 48	4 25	15 8	26 18	2 ♐ 52 34	16 42
15	Th	5 36 19	24 40 48	23 20	8 ♐ 54 15	3 45	18 5	26 15	14 54 5	19 15
16	F	5 40 15	25 38 5	23 22	20 52 15	2 55	20 13	26 12	26 49 1	20 57
17	S	5 44 12	26 35 21	23 24	2 ♑ 44 36	1 58	21 27	26 9	8 ♑ 39 17	21 43
18	Su	5 48 8	27 32 36	23 25	14 33 19	0 N 55	21 43	26 6	20 27 2	21 30
19	M	5 52 5	28 29 51	23 26	26 20 45	0 S 9	21 2	26 3	2 ♒ 14 49	20 20
20	T	5 56 1	29 ♊ 27 6	23 26	8 ♒ 9 38	1 14	19 25	25 59	14 5 38	18 16
21	W	5 59 58	0 ♋ 24 20	23 26	20 3 16	2 15	16 56	25 56	26 2 59	15 25
22	Th	6 3 55	1 21 34	23 26	2 ♓ 5 20	3 12	13 43	25 53	8 ♓ 10 48	11 52
23	F	6 7 51	2 18 48	23 25	14 19 57	4 1	9 52	25 50	20 33 19	7 45
24	S	6 11 48	3 16 2	23 24	26 51 26	4 39	5 31	25 47	3 ♈ 14 48	3 S 12
25	Su	6 15 44	4 13 16	23 22	9 ♈ 43 55	5 5	0 S 49	25 43	16 19 10	1 N 36
26	M	6 19 41	5 10 29	23 20	23 0 54	5 16	4 N 3	25 40	29 49 22	6 30
27	T	6 23 37	6 7 43	23 18	6 ♉ 44 41	5 9	8 54	25 37	13 ♉ 46 50	11 13
28	W	6 27 34	7 4 57	23 15	20 55 38	4 44	13 25	25 34	28 10 42	15 28
29	Th	6 31 30	8 2 11	23 12	5 ♊ 31 32	3 59	17 18	25 31	12 ♊ 57 22	18 52
30	F	6 35 27	8 ♋ 59 25	23 N 8	20 ♊ 27 22	2 S 58	20 N 8	25 ♋ 28	28 ♊ 0 29	21 N 3

D M	Mercury Lat.	Mercury Dec.		Venus Lat.	Venus Dec.		Mars Lat.	Mars Dec.		Jupiter Lat.	Jupiter Dec.
	° ′	° ′	° ′	° ′	° ′	° ′	° ′	° ′	° ′	° ′	° ′
1	2 N 8	25 N 31	25 N 25	0 S 17	21 N 27	21 N 40	0 N 40	23 N 42	23 N 46	0 S 51	17 N 51
3	2 0	25 18	25 9	0 13	21 53	22 6	0 41	23 49	23 52	0 51	17 58
5	1 49	24 59	24 47	0 8	22 17	22 28	0 42	23 55	23 58	0 51	18 5
7	1 36	24 35	24 21	0 S 3	22 39	22 48	0 42	24 0	24 2	0 50	18 12
9	1 19	24 7	23 52	0 N 1	22 57	23 6	0 43	24 4	24 6	0 50	18 18
11	0 59	23 36	23 20	0 6	23 14	23 21	0 44	24 8	24 9	0 50	18 25
13	0 37	23 3	22 46	0 11	23 27	23 33	0 45	24 10	24 11	0 50	18 31
15	0 N 12	22 28	22 10	0 16	23 38	23 42	0 46	24 12	24 13	0 50	18 37
17	0 S 16	21 53	21 35	0 20	23 46	23 49	0 47	24 13	24 13	0 50	18 43
19	0 45	21 17	21 0	0 25	23 51	23 53	0 48	24 13	24 13	0 50	18 49
21	1 17	20 43	20 26	0 29	23 53	23 54	0 48	24 12	24 11	0 50	18 55
23	1 49	20 10	19 54	0 34	23 53	23 52	0 49	24 10	24 9	0 50	19 1
25	2 21	19 39	19 25	0 38	23 50	23 47	0 50	24 8	24 6	0 50	19 7
27	2 53	19 11	18 59	0 43	23 44	23 39	0 51	24 5	24 3	0 50	19 12
29	3 24	18 47	18 N 37	0 47	23 35	23 N 29	0 52	24 1	23 N 58	0 50	19 18
31	3 S 51	18 N 27		0 N 51	23 N 23		0 N 52	23 N 56		0 S 50	19 N 23

FIRST QUARTER-June 9, 3h.29m. am. (18°♍37′)

FULL MOON-June16,10h.27m. pm. (26°♐ 3′)

D M	☿ Long.	♀ Long.	♂ Long.	♃ Long.	♄ Long.	♅ Long.	♆ Long.	♇ Long.	☉	☿	♀	♂	♃	♄	♅	♆	♇
	° ′	° ′	° ′	° ′	° ′	° ′	° ′	° ′	Lunar Aspects								
1	3♋24	8♊35	19♊51	23♉37	23♉12	20♒48	6♒25	11♐33		⚺			☌	☌	□		
2	4 47	9 49	20 31	23 51	23 20	20R 48	6R 25	11R 31	☌		☌					△	☍
3	6 7	11 3	21 12	24 4	23 27	20 47	6 24	11 30				☌	⚺	⚺	△	⚼	
4	7 24	12 17	21 53	24 18	23 34	20 47	6 23	11 28	⚺	☌	⚺		∠	∠	⚼		
5	8 38	13 30	22 34	24 32	23 42	20 46	6 22	11 26	∠		∠	⚺	⚹	⚹			⚼
6	9 48	14 44	23 14	24 46	23 49	20 46	6 21	11 25	⚹	⚺	⚹	∠				☍	△
7	10 55	15 58	23 55	25 0	23 57	20 45	6 20	11 23		∠		⚹	□	□	☍		
8	11 58	17 11	24 36	25 13	24 4	20 45	6 19	11 21		⚹							□
9	12 58	18 25	25 16	25 27	24 11	20 44	6 18	11 20	□		□	□	△	△		⚼	
10	13 54	19 39	25 57	25 40	24 18	20 43	6 17	11 18					⚼	⚼	⚼	△	⚹
11	14 47	20 53	26 37	25 54	24 26	20 42	6 16	11 17	△	□	△				△		
12	15 35	22 6	27 18	26 8	24 33	20 42	6 15	11 15	⚼		⚼	△				□	∠
13	16 20	23 20	27 58	26 21	24 40	20 41	6 14	11 13		△		⚼			□		⚺
14	17 1	24 34	28 39	26 34	24 47	20 40	6 13	11 12		⚼			☍	☍			
15	17 38	25 47	29 19	26 48	24 54	20 39	6 12	11 10								⚹	☌
16	18 11	27 1	29♊59	27 1	25 1	20 38	6 11	11 9	☍						⚹	∠	
17	18 40	28 15	0♋39	27 14	25 8	20 37	6 10	11 7			☍	☍			∠	⚺	
18	19 4	29♊29	1 20	27 28	25 15	20 36	6 9	11 6		☍			⚼	⚼			⚺
19	19 24	0♋42	2 0	27 41	25 22	20 34	6 8	11 4					△	△	⚺		∠
20	19 39	1 56	2 40	27 54	25 29	20 33	6 6	11 3								☌	⚹
21	19 50	3 10	3 20	28 7	25 36	20 32	6 5	11 1	⚼		⚼	⚼		□	☌		
22	19 56	4 23	4 0	28 20	25 43	20 31	6 4	11 0	△	⚼	△	△	□			⚺	
23	19R 58	5 37	4 40	28 33	25 49	20 29	6 3	10 58		△					⚺		□
24	19 55	6 51	5 20	28 46	25 56	20 28	6 1	10 57					⚹	⚹		∠	
25	19 47	8 5	6 0	28 59	26 3	20 27	6 0	10 55	□		□	□	∠	∠	∠	⚹	△
26	19 36	9 18	6 40	29 12	26 9	20 25	5 59	10 54		□			⚺	⚺	⚹		⚼
27	19 20	10 32	7 20	29 24	26 16	20 24	5 57	10 52	⚹		⚹	⚹				□	
28	19 0	11 46	8 0	29 37	26 22	20 22	5 56	10 51	∠	⚹	∠	∠		☌	□		
29	18 36	13 0	8 40	29♉50	26 29	20 21	5 55	10 49	⚺	∠		⚺	☌			△	☍
30	18♋ 9	14♋13	9♋20	0♊ 2	26♉35	20♒19	5♒53	10♐48		⚺	⚺			⚺	△	⚼	

D M	Saturn Lat.	Saturn Dec.	Uranus Lat.	Uranus Dec.	Neptune Lat.	Neptune Dec.	Pluto Lat.	Pluto Dec.
	° ′	° ′	° ′	° ′	° ′	° ′	° ′	° ′
1	2S 0	16N39	0S42	15S14	0N13	18S27	11N19	10S57
3	2 0	16 42	0 43	15 14	0 13	18 28	11 18	10 57
5	2 0	16 46	0 43	15 15	0 13	18 28	11 18	10 57
7	2 0	16 49	0 43	15 15	0 13	18 29	11 18	10 57
9	2 0	16 53	0 43	15 15	0 13	18 29	11 18	10 57
11	2 0	16 56	0 43	15 16	0 13	18 30	11 17	10 56
13	2 0	17 0	0 43	15 17	0 13	18 30	11 17	10 56
15	2 0	17 3	0 43	15 17	0 13	18 31	11 17	10 56
17	2 0	17 6	0 43	15 18	0 13	18 31	11 16	10 56
19	2 0	17 9	0 43	15 19	0 13	18 32	11 16	10 56
21	2 1	17 12	0 43	15 20	0 13	18 32	11 16	10 56
23	2 1	17 15	0 43	15 21	0 13	18 33	11 15	10 56
25	2 1	17 18	0 43	15 21	0 13	18 34	11 15	10 56
27	2 1	17 21	0 43	15 22	0 13	18 34	11 14	10 57
29	2 1	17 24	0 43	15 23	0 13	18 35	11 14	10 57
31	2S 1	17N27	0S44	15S25	0N13	18S36	11N13	10S57

Mutual Aspects

1 ☉☍♇. 2 ♂△♅.
3 ☿⚼♅. ☿▽♆. ♀☍♇. ♂⚼♆.
5 ☿∠♄. 6 ☿∠♃.
7 ☿▽♇. ♂⚺♄.
9 ♂⚺♃. ☉P♀. ☿P♂.
11 ☉☌♀. ☉△♅. ☉⚼♆. ☿±♅. ♀△♅.
♀⚼♆.
12 ☉P☿. ☿P♀.
13 ♃P♆.
14 ☿±♇. ♀⚺♄.
15 ☉⚺♄.
16 ♀⚺♃. ♂±♆.
18 ☉⚺♃. ♂⊥♄.
19 ♀±♆. 20 ♀⊥♄.
21 ☉±♆. ♀☌♂.
22 ☉⊥♄. ♀⊥♃.
23 ♀⚼♅. ♀▽♆. ♂⊥♃. ☿Stat.
24 ♂⚼♅. 25 ♂▽♆.
26 ☉⊥♃. ☉⚼♅.
27 ☉▽♆. ♀▽♇. ☿P♃.
28 ♀∠♄.
30 ♀±♅. ☿P♆.

LAST QUARTER-June25, 1h. 0m. am. (3°♈47′)

NEW MOON-July 1, 7h.20m. pm. (10°♋14′) & July31, 2h.25m. am. (8°♌12′)

D M	D W	Sidereal Time	☉ Long.	☉ Dec.	☽ Long.	☽ Lat.	☽ Dec.	☽ Node	Midnight ☽ Long.	Midnight ☽ Dec.
		H. M. S.	° ′ ″	° ′	° ′ ″	° ′	° ′	° ′	° ′ ″	° ′
1	S	6 39 24	9 ♋ 56 38	23 N 4	5 ♋ 35 36	1 S 43	21 N36	25 ♋ 24	13 ♋ 11 30	21 N44
2	Su	6 43 20	10 53 52	22 59	20 47 0	0 S 21	21 29	25 21	28 20 54	20 50
3	M	6 47 17	11 51 6	22 55	5 ♌ 52 6	1 N 2	19 48	25 18	13 ♌ 19 35	18 27
4	T	6 51 13	12 48 19	22 49	20 42 29	2 20	16 48	25 15	28 0 7	14 54
5	W	6 55 10	13 45 33	22 44	5 ♍ 11 57	3 27	12 48	25 12	12 ♍ 17 36	10 34
6	Th	6 59 6	14 42 46	22 38	19 16 51	4 19	8 13	25 9	26 9 40	5 48
7	F	7 3 3	15 39 58	22 31	2 ♎ 56 5	4 55	3 N21	25 5	9 ♎ 36 19	0 N54
8	S	7 6 59	16 37 11	22 24	16 10 36	5 14	1 S 32	25 2	22 39 17	3 S 54
9	Su	7 10 56	17 34 23	22 17	29 2 46	5 17	6 12	24 59	5 ♏ 21 26	8 24
10	M	7 14 53	18 31 35	22 9	11 ♏ 35 46	5 4	10 29	24 56	17 46 12	12 27
11	T	7 18 49	19 28 47	22 1	23 53 10	4 37	14 16	24 53	29 57 9	15 55
12	W	7 22 46	20 26 0	21 53	5 ♐ 58 34	3 59	17 23	24 49	11 ♐ 57 49	18 40
13	Th	7 26 42	21 23 12	21 44	17 55 18	3 10	19 44	24 46	23 51 23	20 35
14	F	7 30 39	22 20 25	21 35	29 46 27	2 14	21 12	24 43	5 ♑ 40 48	21 36
15	S	7 34 35	23 17 37	21 26	11 ♑ 34 45	1 12	21 44	24 40	17 28 38	21 38
16	Su	7 38 32	24 14 50	21 16	23 22 43	0 N 7	21 18	24 37	29 17 18	20 43
17	M	7 42 28	25 12 4	21 6	5 ♒ 12 40	0 S 59	19 55	24 34	11 ♒ 9 5	18 53
18	T	7 46 25	26 9 17	20 55	17 6 51	2 2	17 38	24 30	23 6 16	16 12
19	W	7 50 22	27 6 32	20 44	29 7 37	3 0	14 35	24 27	5 ♓ 11 14	12 49
20	Th	7 54 18	28 3 46	20 33	11 ♓ 17 27	3 51	10 54	24 24	17 26 36	8 51
21	F	7 58 15	29 1 2	20 21	23 39 2	4 33	6 41	24 21	29 55 7	4 S 27
22	S	8 2 11	29 ♋ 58 18	20 9	6 ♈ 15 14	5 2	2 S 8	24 18	12 ♈ 39 44	0 N14
23	Su	8 6 8	0 ♌ 55 35	19 57	19 8 58	5 16	2 N37	24 15	25 43 17	5 0
24	M	8 10 4	1 52 53	19 44	2 ♉ 22 58	5 15	7 22	24 11	9 ♉ 8 15	9 41
25	T	8 14 1	2 50 12	19 31	15 59 20	4 56	11 54	24 8	22 56 18	14 0
26	W	8 17 57	3 47 32	19 18	29 59 8	4 19	15 55	24 5	7 ♊ 7 43	17 39
27	Th	8 21 54	4 44 53	19 5	14 ♊ 21 46	3 25	19 7	24 2	21 40 52	20 18
28	F	8 25 51	5 42 15	18 51	29 4 27	2 17	21 9	23 59	6 ♋ 31 50	21 38
29	S	8 29 47	6 39 38	18 36	14 ♋ 2 7	0 S 58	21 44	23 55	21 34 21	21 26
30	Su	8 33 44	7 37 2	18 22	29 7 28	0 N25	20 44	23 52	6 ♌ 40 22	19 40
31	M	8 37 40	8 ♌ 34 26	18 N 7	14 ♌ 11 53	1 N46	18 N16	23 ♋ 49	21 ♌ 40 55	16 N33

D M	Mercury Lat.	Mercury Dec.		Venus Lat.	Venus Dec.		Mars Lat.	Mars Dec.		Jupiter Lat.	Jupiter Dec.
	° ′	° ′	° ′	° ′	° ′	° ′	° ′	° ′	° ′	° ′	° ′
1	3 S 51	18 N27	18 N 19	0 N 51	23 N23	23 N16	0 N 52	23 N56	23 N 53	0 S 50	19 N23
3	4 14	18 12	18 7	0 54	23 8	23 0	0 53	23 50	23 47	0 50	19 28
5	4 33	18 2	17 59	0 58	22 51	22 42	0 54	23 44	23 40	0 51	19 33
7	4 46	17 58	17 57	1 2	22 31	22 20	0 54	23 37	23 33	0 51	19 38
9	4 52	17 58	18 1	1 5	22 9	21 56	0 55	23 29	23 24	0 51	19 43
11	4 52	18 4	18 9	1 8	21 44	21 30	0 56	23 20	23 15	0 51	19 47
13	4 45	18 14	18 21	1 11	21 16	21 1	0 57	23 10	23 5	0 51	19 52
15	4 33	18 29	18 38	1 14	20 46	20 30	0 57	23 0	22 55	0 51	19 56
17	4 16	18 47	18 57	1 17	20 13	19 56	0 58	22 49	22 44	0 51	20 0
19	3 54	19 8	19 19	1 19	19 39	19 20	0 58	22 38	22 32	0 51	20 4
21	3 29	19 30	19 41	1 21	19 2	18 42	0 59	22 26	22 19	0 51	20 8
23	3 2	19 52	20 3	1 23	18 23	18 2	1 0	22 13	22 6	0 51	20 12
25	2 33	20 14	20 24	1 24	17 42	17 20	1 0	21 59	21 52	0 51	20 16
27	2 3	20 33	20 41	1 26	16 59	16 36	1 1	21 45	21 37	0 51	20 20
29	1 33	20 48	20 N 54	1 27	16 14	15 N50	1 2	21 30	21 N 22	0 51	20 23
31	1 S 3	20 N58		1 N 28	15 N27		1 N 2	21 N14		0 S 51	20 N26

FIRST QUARTER-July 8, 0h.53m. pm. (16°♎39′)

FULL MOON-July16, 1h.55m. pm. (24°♑19′)

D M	☿ Long.	♀ Long.	♂ Long.	♃ Long.	♄ Long.	♅ Long.	♆ Long.	♇ Long.	⊙	☿	♀	♂	♃	♄	♅	♆	♇
	° ′	° ′	° ′	° ′	° ′	° ′	° ′	° ′	Lunar Aspects								
1	17♋39	15♋27	9♋59	0♊15	26♉42	20♒18	5♒52	10♐47	☌			☌	⚺	∠	⚻		
2	17R 6	16 41	10 39	0 27	26 48	20R 16	5R 50	10R 45		☌	☌		∠	⚹			⚻
3	16 32	17 55	11 19	0 40	26 54	20 14	5 49	10 44	⚺			⚺	⚹			☍	△
4	15 55	19 8	11 59	0 52	27 0	20 13	5 48	10 43		⚺	⚺	∠		□	☍		
5	15 18	20 22	12 38	1 4	27 7	20 11	5 46	10 41	∠	∠	∠		□				□
6	14 41	21 36	13 18	1 16	27 13	20 9	5 45	10 40	⚹	⚹	⚹	⚹				⚻	
7	14 4	22 50	13 57	1 28	27 19	20 7	5 43	10 39					△	△	⚻	△	
8	13 28	24 3	14 37	1 40	27 25	20 5	5 42	10 38	□	□		□	⚻	⚻	△		⚹
9	12 54	25 17	15 16	1 52	27 31	20 3	5 40	10 36			□						∠
10	12 22	26 31	15 56	2 4	27 36	20 2	5 39	10 35		△		△				□	⚺
11	11 53	27 45	16 35	2 16	27 42	20 0	5 37	10 34	△	⚻	△			☍	□		
12	11 27	28♋58	17 15	2 27	27 48	19 58	5 36	10 33	⚻			⚻	☍			⚹	☌
13	11 5	0♌12	17 54	2 39	27 54	19 56	5 34	10 32			⚻				⚹	∠	
14	10 47	1 26	18 34	2 51	27 59	19 54	5 32	10 31							∠	⚺	
15	10 34	2 40	19 13	3 2	28 5	19 52	5 31	10 30		☍				⚻			⚺
16	10 26	3 53	19 52	3 13	28 10	19 50	5 29	10 28	☍			☍	⚻	△	⚺		∠
17	10 23	5 7	20 31	3 25	28 15	19 48	5 28	10 27			☍		△			☌	⚹
18	10D 26	6 21	21 11	3 36	28 21	19 45	5 26	10 26							☌		
19	10 34	7 35	21 50	3 47	28 26	19 43	5 24	10 25		⚻			□	□			
20	10 47	8 49	22 29	3 58	28 31	19 41	5 23	10 25	⚻	△		⚻				⚺	□
21	11 7	10 2	23 8	4 9	28 36	19 39	5 21	10 24	△		⚻	△		⚹	⚺	∠	
22	11 32	11 16	23 47	4 19	28 41	19 37	5 20	10 23		□	△		⚹		∠	⚹	△
23	12 2	12 30	24 26	4 30	28 46	19 35	5 18	10 22				□	∠	∠	⚹		⚻
24	12 39	13 44	25 6	4 41	28 51	19 32	5 16	10 21	□				⚺	⚺		□	
25	13 21	14 57	25 45	4 51	28 56	19 30	5 15	10 20		⚹	□				□		
26	14 10	16 11	26 24	5 1	29 1	19 28	5 13	10 19	⚹	∠		⚹	☌	☌		△	
27	15 3	17 25	27 3	5 12	29 5	19 26	5 11	10 19	∠	⚺	⚹	∠			△	⚻	☍
28	16 2	18 39	27 42	5 22	29 10	19 23	5 10	10 18	⚺		∠	⚺	⚺	⚺	⚻		
29	17 7	19 53	28 21	5 32	29 14	19 21	5 8	10 17		☌	⚺		∠	∠			
30	18 17	21 6	28 59	5 42	29 19	19 19	5 7	10 16				☌	⚹	⚹		☍	⚻
31	19♋32	22♌20	29♋38	5♊52	29♉23	19♒16	5♒5	10♐16	☌	⚺					☍		△

D M	Saturn Lat.	Saturn Dec.	Uranus Lat.	Uranus Dec.	Neptune Lat.	Neptune Dec.	Pluto Lat.	Pluto Dec.
	° ′	° ′	° ′	° ′	° ′	° ′	° ′	° ′
1	2S 1	17N27	0S44	15S25	0N13	18S36	11N13	10S57
3	2 2	17 30	0 44	15 26	0 13	18 36	11 13	10 57
5	2 2	17 32	0 44	15 27	0 13	18 37	11 12	10 57
7	2 2	17 35	0 44	15 28	0 13	18 38	11 11	10 58
9	2 2	17 37	0 44	15 29	0 13	18 39	11 11	10 58
11	2 2	17 40	0 44	15 30	0 13	18 39	11 10	10 58
13	2 3	17 42	0 44	15 32	0 13	18 40	11 9	10 59
15	2 3	17 44	0 44	15 33	0 13	18 41	11 9	10 59
17	2 3	17 46	0 44	15 34	0 13	18 42	11 8	10 59
19	2 3	17 48	0 44	15 36	0 13	18 43	11 7	11 0
21	2 4	17 50	0 44	15 37	0 13	18 43	11 6	11 0
23	2 4	17 52	0 44	15 39	0 13	18 44	11 6	11 1
25	2 4	17 54	0 44	15 40	0 13	18 45	11 5	11 1
27	2 5	17 56	0 44	15 42	0 13	18 46	11 4	11 2
29	2 5	17 57	0 44	15 43	0 13	18 47	11 3	11 3
31	2S 5	17N59	0S44	15S44	0N13	18S47	11N 3	11S 3

Mutual Aspects

1 ⊙☌♂. ♀∠♃.
2 ⊙▽♇. ☿☌♀. ♀±♇. ♂▽♇.
3 ⊙∠♄. ☿±♇.
4 ☿∠♃. ♂∠♄.
5 ⊙±♅. ♀▽♅.
6 ⊙☌☿.
7 ☿☌♂. ☿±♅. ♂±♅. ⊙P♀.
8 ⊙∠♃. ⊙±♇.
9 ♀⚻♇. 10 ☿∠♄.
11 ♀⚹♄. ♂±♇.
12 ⊙▽♅. ♂∠♃.
15 ♀⚹♃.
16 ☿▽♇. ♂▽♅. ☿P♆.
17 ⊙⚻♇. ♀☍♆. ☿Stat.
18 ☿▽♇. ♀P♃.
20 ☿P♀.
21 ⊙⚹♄. ♀Q♄. ♀△♇.
22 ☿⚺♀. ⊙P♃. ♀P♆.
23 ⊙P☿.
24 ♂⚻♇. ♀P♄.
25 ☿±♅. ☿P♃.
26 ☿∠♄.
27 ⊙☍♆. ♀Q♃. ♃△♆.
28 ⊙⚹♃. ☿±♇. ⊙P♆.
29 ♀☍♅. 30 ♀P♅.
31 ☿▽♅. ♂⚹♄.

LAST QUARTER-July24,11h. 2m. am. (1°♉51′)

NEW MOON-Aug.29,10h.19m. am. (6°♍23′)

D M	D W	Sidereal Time	☉ Long.	☉ Dec.	☽ Long.	☽ Lat.	☽ Dec.	☽ Node	Midnight ☽ Long.	Midnight ☽ Dec.
		H. M. S.	° ′ ″	° ′	° ′ ″	° ′	° ′	° ′	° ′ ″	° ′
1	T	8 41 37	9 ♌ 31 52	17 N52	29 ♌ 6 27	3 N 0	14 N35	23 ♋ 46	6 ♍ 27 33	12 N25
2	W	8 45 33	10 29 18	17 37	13 ♍ 43 24	4 0	10 5	23 43	20 53 22	7 39
3	Th	8 49 30	11 26 45	17 21	27 56 59	4 43	5 8	23 40	4 ♎ 53 57	2 N37
4	F	8 53 26	12 24 12	17 5	11 ♎ 44 7	5 8	0 N 6	23 36	18 27 32	2 S23
5	S	8 57 23	13 21 40	16 49	25 4 19	5 16	4 S48	23 33	1 ♏ 34 46	7 7
6	Su	9 1 20	14 19 9	16 32	7 ♏ 59 14	5 7	9 19	23 30	14 18 10	11 23
7	M	9 5 16	15 16 39	16 15	20 32 4	4 44	13 19	23 27	26 41 29	15 4
8	T	9 9 13	16 14 10	15 58	2 ♐ 46 58	4 8	16 39	23 24	8 ♐ 49 7	18 3
9	W	9 13 9	17 11 41	15 41	14 48 29	3 22	19 14	23 21	20 45 40	20 12
10	Th	9 17 6	18 9 13	15 23	26 41 12	2 28	20 56	23 17	2 ♑ 35 36	21 27
11	F	9 21 2	19 6 46	15 5	8 ♑ 29 23	1 27	21 43	23 14	14 23 2	21 44
12	S	9 24 59	20 4 21	14 47	20 16 57	0 N24	21 31	23 11	26 11 34	21 3
13	Su	9 28 55	21 1 56	14 29	2 ♒ 7 13	0 S41	20 22	23 8	8 ♒ 4 15	19 26
14	M	9 32 52	21 59 32	14 11	14 2 58	1 45	18 17	23 5	20 3 36	16 56
15	T	9 36 49	22 57 10	13 52	26 6 24	2 45	15 24	23 1	2 ♓ 11 35	13 41
16	W	9 40 45	23 54 48	13 33	8 ♓ 19 17	3 37	11 48	22 58	14 29 43	9 48
17	Th	9 44 42	24 52 28	13 14	20 42 59	4 20	7 40	22 55	26 59 16	5 27
18	F	9 48 38	25 50 10	12 54	3 ♈ 18 39	4 52	3 S 9	22 52	9 ♈ 41 18	0 S48
19	S	9 52 35	26 47 53	12 35	16 7 21	5 9	1 N35	22 49	22 36 54	3 N58
20	Su	9 56 31	27 45 37	12 15	29 10 8	5 11	6 20	22 46	5 ♉ 47 10	8 38
21	M	10 0 28	28 43 23	11 55	12 ♉ 28 8	4 56	10 52	22 42	19 13 10	13 0
22	T	10 4 24	29 ♌ 41 11	11 35	26 2 23	4 25	14 58	22 39	2 ♊ 55 51	16 46
23	W	10 8 21	0 ♍ 39 1	11 15	9 ♊ 53 38	3 38	18 21	22 36	16 55 42	19 40
24	Th	10 12 18	1 36 53	10 54	24 1 58	2 37	20 42	22 33	1 ♋ 12 16	21 24
25	F	10 16 14	2 34 46	10 33	8 ♋ 26 20	1 24	21 46	22 30	15 43 46	21 46
26	S	10 20 11	3 32 41	10 12	23 4 4	0 S 6	21 22	22 26	0 ♌ 26 36	20 37
27	Su	10 24 7	4 30 38	9 51	7 ♌ 50 38	1 N14	19 30	22 23	15 15 21	18 3
28	M	10 28 4	5 28 36	9 30	22 39 48	2 29	16 18	22 20	0 ♍ 3 2	14 18
29	T	10 32 0	6 26 36	9 9	7 ♍ 24 5	3 33	12 5	22 17	14 42 0	9 43
30	W	10 35 57	7 24 38	8 47	21 55 55	4 23	7 13	22 14	29 5 2	4 N39
31	Th	10 39 53	8 ♍ 22 41	8 N26	6 ♎ 8 42	4 N54	2 N 4	22 ♋ 11	13 ♎ 6 25	0 S31

D M	Mercury Lat.	Mercury Dec.		Venus Lat.	Venus Dec.		Mars Lat.	Mars Dec.		Jupiter Lat.	Jupiter Dec.
	° ′	° ′	° ′	° ′	° ′	° ′	° ′	° ′	° ′	° ′	° ′
1	0 S49	21 N 1	21 N 2	1 N28	15 N 3	14 N39	1 N 2	21 N 6	20 N58	0 S51	20 N28
3	0 S20	21 1	20 57	1 29	14 14	13 49	1 3	20 50	20 41	0 52	20 31
5	0 N 6	20 51	20 43	1 29	13 23	12 57	1 4	20 33	20 24	0 52	20 34
7	0 30	20 32	20 18	1 29	12 31	12 5	1 4	20 15	20 6	0 52	20 37
9	0 51	20 2	19 43	1 28	11 38	11 11	1 5	19 57	19 48	0 52	20 40
11	1 8	19 22	18 58	1 28	10 43	10 15	1 5	19 38	19 29	0 52	20 43
13	1 22	18 31	18 2	1 27	9 47	9 19	1 6	19 19	19 9	0 52	20 45
15	1 33	17 31	16 58	1 26	8 51	8 22	1 6	18 59	18 49	0 52	20 48
17	1 41	16 22	15 46	1 24	7 53	7 24	1 7	18 39	18 29	0 52	20 50
19	1 45	15 7	14 27	1 22	6 54	6 25	1 7	18 18	18 7	0 53	20 52
21	1 46	13 46	13 4	1 20	5 55	5 25	1 8	17 57	17 46	0 53	20 54
23	1 44	12 20	11 36	1 18	4 55	4 25	1 8	17 35	17 24	0 53	20 56
25	1 40	10 52	10 6	1 16	3 55	3 24	1 8	17 13	17 2	0 53	20 58
27	1 34	9 20	8 34	1 13	2 54	2 23	1 9	16 50	16 39	0 53	21 0
29	1 26	7 48	7 N 1	1 10	1 52	1 N22	1 9	16 27	16 N16	0 53	21 1
31	1 N17	6 N14		1 N 7	0 N51		1 N10	16 N 4		0 S53	21 N 3

FIRST QUARTER-Aug. 7, 1h. 2m. am. (14°♏50′)

FULL MOON-Aug.15, 5h.13m. am. (22°♒41′)

D M	☿ Long.	♀ Long.	♂ Long.	♃ Long.	♄ Long.	♅ Long.	♆ Long.	♇ Long.	Lunar Aspects ☉	☿	♀	♂	♃	♄	♅	♆	♇
	° ′	° ′	° ′	° ′	° ′	° ′	° ′	° ′									
1	20♋52	23♌34	0♌17	6♊ 2	29♉27	19♒14	5♒ 3	10♐15			●	⚺	□	□			
2	22 18	24 48	0 56	6 11	29 31	19R 12	5R 2	10R 15	⚺	∠		∠				⚼	□
3	23 47	26 2	1 35	6 21	29 35	19 9	5 0	10 14	∠	⚹	⚺	⚹		△	⚼		
4	25 22	27 15	2 14	6 30	29 39	19 7	4 58	10 13	⚹		∠		△	⚼		△	⚹
5	27 0	28 29	2 52	6 39	29 43	19 4	4 57	10 13		□	⚹		⚼		△		∠
6	28♋42	29♌43	3 31	6 48	29 47	19 2	4 55	10 12				□				□	⚺
7	0♌28	0♍57	4 10	6 57	29 51	19 0	4 54	10 12	□						□		
8	2 17	2 11	4 49	7 6	29 54	18 57	4 52	10 12		△	□	△	☍	☍		⚹	
9	4 9	3 24	5 27	7 15	29♉58	18 55	4 50	10 11	△	⚼					⚹	∠	☌
10	6 4	4 38	6 6	7 24	0♊ 1	18 53	4 49	10 11				⚼					
11	8 1	5 52	6 45	7 32	0 5	18 50	4 47	10 11	⚼		△				∠	⚺	⚺
12	9 59	7 6	7 23	7 41	0 8	18 48	4 46	10 10			⚼		⚼	⚼	⚺		∠
13	11 59	8 19	8 2	7 49	0 11	18 45	4 44	10 10					△	△		☌	
14	14 0	9 33	8 40	7 57	0 14	18 43	4 43	10 10		☍		☍			☌		⚹
15	16 1	10 47	9 19	8 5	0 17	18 41	4 41	10 10	☍					□			
16	18 3	12 0	9 57	8 13	0 20	18 38	4 40	10 9			☍		□			⚺	□
17	20 5	13 14	10 36	8 20	0 23	18 36	4 38	10 9				⚼			⚺	∠	
18	22 7	14 28	11 14	8 28	0 25	18 33	4 37	10 9		⚼			⚹	⚹	∠	⚹	
19	24 9	15 42	11 53	8 35	0 28	18 31	4 35	10 9	⚼			△		∠	⚹		△
20	26 10	16 55	12 31	8 43	0 30	18 29	4 34	10 9	△	△	⚼		∠	⚺		□	⚼
21	28♌10	18 9	13 9	8 50	0 33	18 26	4 32	10D 9			△	□	⚺		□		
22	0♍ 9	19 23	13 48	8 57	0 35	18 24	4 31	10 9	□	□				☌			
23	2 7	20 36	14 26	9 4	0 37	18 22	4 29	10 9				⚹	☌			△	☍
24	4 5	21 50	15 4	9 10	0 39	18 19	4 28	10 9			□	∠		⚺	△	⚼	
25	6 1	23 4	15 43	9 17	0 41	18 17	4 27	10 9	⚹	⚹			⚺	∠	⚼		
26	7 56	24 17	16 21	9 23	0 43	18 15	4 25	10 10	∠	∠	⚹	⚺	∠				⚼
27	9 49	25 31	16 59	9 29	0 45	18 13	4 24	10 10	⚺	⚺	∠		⚹	⚹		☍	△
28	11 42	26 45	17 38	9 35	0 47	18 10	4 22	10 10			⚺	●			☍		
29	13 33	27 59	18 16	9 41	0 48	18 8	4 21	10 10	☌	☌			□	□			□
30	15 23	29♍12	18 54	9 47	0 50	18 6	4 20	10 11				⚺				⚼	
31	17♍11	0♎26	19♌32	9♊52	0♊51	18♒ 4	4♒19	10♐11	⚺		☌	∠	△	△	⚼	△	⚹

D M	Saturn Lat.	Saturn Dec.	Uranus Lat.	Uranus Dec.	Neptune Lat.	Neptune Dec.	Pluto Lat.	Pluto Dec.
	° ′	° ′	° ′	° ′	° ′	° ′	° ′	° ′
1	2S 5	18N 0	0S44	15S45	0N13	18S48	11N 2	11S 4
3	2 6	18 1	0 44	15 47	0 13	18 49	11 1	11 4
5	2 6	18 2	0 44	15 48	0 13	18 50	11 0	11 5
7	2 6	18 4	0 44	15 50	0 13	18 50	11 0	11 6
9	2 7	18 5	0 44	15 51	0 13	18 51	10 59	11 6
11	2 7	18 6	0 44	15 53	0 12	18 52	10 58	11 7
13	2 7	18 7	0 44	15 54	0 12	18 53	10 57	11 8
15	2 8	18 8	0 44	15 56	0 12	18 53	10 56	11 9
17	2 8	18 9	0 44	15 57	0 12	18 54	10 55	11 10
19	2 8	18 9	0 44	15 59	0 12	18 55	10 54	11 10
21	2 9	18 10	0 44	16 0	0 12	18 56	10 53	11 11
23	2 9	18 10	0 44	16 2	0 12	18 56	10 53	11 12
25	2 9	18 11	0 44	16 3	0 12	18 57	10 52	11 13
27	2 10	18 11	0 44	16 4	0 12	18 58	10 51	11 14
29	2 10	18 12	0 44	16 6	0 12	18 58	10 50	11 15
31	2S11	18N12	0S44	16S 7	0N12	18S59	10N49	11S16

Mutual Aspects

1 ☿∠♃. ☉P♄.
2 ☉△♇. ☿P♂.
3 ☉Q♄. 4 ☿⚼♇.
5 ♂P♃.
6 ♀□♄.
7 ☿⚹♄. ☿P♃.
8 ☿⚺♀. ♂☍♆. ☉P♅.
9 ☿☍♆.
10 ☿☌♂. ♀⚻♆. ☿P♂. ♀P♇.
11 ☉☍♅. ☿⚹♃.
12 ☉Q♃. ☿△♇. ♀⚺♂. ☿P♆.
13 ☿Q♄. ♀□♃. ♂⚹♃.
14 ♀□♇. ☿P♄.
15 ♀±♆.
16 ☿☍♅. ♂△♇. ♂P♆.
17 ☿Q♃. 18 ☿P♅.
20 ♂Q♄. ♂P♄. ♇Stat.
21 ♀⚻♅.
22 ☉☌☿. ☿□♄. ♀⚼♆.
23 ☉□♄. ♀⊥♂. ☉P♇.
24 ☿⚻♆. 25 ☿P♇.
26 ♀±♅. ☉P☿.
27 ☉⚻♆. ☿□♃. ☿±♆. ☿□♇.
29 ♀Q♇. ♂☍♅.
31 ☿⚻♅. ♀△♄. ♂P♅.

LAST QUARTER-Aug.22, 6h.51m. pm. (29°♉58′)

NEW MOON-Sep.27, 7h.53m. pm. (5°♎ 0′)

D M	D W	Sidereal Time	☉ Long.	☉ Dec.	☽ Long.	☽ Lat.	☽ Dec.	☽ Node	Midnight ☽ Long.	Midnight ☽ Dec.
		H. M. S.	° ′ ″	° ′	° ′ ″	° ′	° ′	° ′	° ′ ″	° ′
1	F	10 43 50	9 ♍ 20 46	8 N 4	19 ♎ 57 50	5 N 8	3 S 3	22 ♋ 7	26 ♎ 42 46	5 S 30
2	S	10 47 47	10 18 52	7 42	3 ♏ 21 11	5 4	7 52	22 4	9 ♏ 53 11	10 5
3	Su	10 51 43	11 16 59	7 20	16 19 2	4 45	12 10	22 1	22 39 5	14 5
4	M	10 55 40	12 15 8	6 58	28 53 47	4 12	15 49	21 58	5 ♐ 3 40	17 21
5	T	10 59 36	13 13 19	6 36	11 ♐ 9 18	3 28	18 41	21 55	17 11 20	19 47
6	W	11 3 33	14 11 31	6 13	23 10 23	2 36	20 40	21 52	29 7 9	21 19
7	Th	11 7 29	15 9 44	5 51	5 ♑ 2 15	1 38	21 43	21 48	10 ♑ 56 21	21 53
8	F	11 11 26	16 7 59	5 28	16 50 5	0 N36	21 47	21 45	22 44 3	21 28
9	S	11 15 22	17 6 16	5 6	28 38 49	0 S28	20 53	21 42	4 ♒ 34 54	20 5
10	Su	11 19 19	18 4 34	4 43	10 ♒ 32 49	1 31	19 3	21 39	16 32 57	17 48
11	M	11 23 16	19 2 54	4 20	22 35 42	2 30	16 21	21 36	28 41 22	14 42
12	T	11 27 12	20 1 15	3 57	4 ♓ 50 11	3 23	12 53	21 32	11 ♓ 2 22	10 55
13	W	11 31 9	20 59 38	3 34	17 18 0	4 7	8 49	21 29	23 37 11	6 36
14	Th	11 35 5	21 58 3	3 11	29 59 54	4 40	4 S17	21 26	6 ♈ 26 6	1 S55
15	F	11 39 2	22 56 30	2 48	12 ♈ 55 43	5 0	0 N30	21 23	19 28 37	2 N56
16	S	11 42 58	23 54 59	2 25	26 4 41	5 3	5 21	21 20	2 ♉ 43 45	7 44
17	Su	11 46 55	24 53 30	2 2	9 ♉ 25 41	4 51	10 2	21 17	16 10 21	12 14
18	M	11 50 51	25 52 3	1 39	22 57 38	4 22	14 17	21 13	29 47 26	16 10
19	T	11 54 48	26 50 39	1 15	6 ♊ 39 41	3 38	17 50	21 10	13 ♊ 34 19	19 16
20	W	11 58 45	27 49 16	0 52	20 31 18	2 41	20 26	21 7	27 30 36	21 17
21	Th	12 2 41	28 47 56	0 29	4 ♋ 32 10	1 33	21 49	21 4	11 ♋ 35 57	22 0
22	F	12 6 38	29 ♍ 46 38	0 N 5	18 41 50	0 S19	21 49	21 1	25 49 40	21 18
23	S	12 10 34	0 ♎ 45 23	0 S18	2 ♌ 59 13	0 N57	20 25	20 58	10 ♌ 10 9	19 12
24	Su	12 14 31	1 44 10	0 41	17 22 7	2 9	17 41	20 54	24 34 35	15 53
25	M	12 18 27	2 42 58	1 5	1 ♍ 47 0	3 14	13 51	20 51	8 ♍ 58 44	11 37
26	T	12 22 24	3 41 49	1 28	16 9 3	4 5	9 14	20 48	23 17 14	6 43
27	W	12 26 20	4 40 42	1 52	0 ♎ 22 34	4 41	4 N 9	20 45	7 ♎ 24 20	1 N32
28	Th	12 30 17	5 39 37	2 15	14 21 55	4 59	1 S 4	20 42	21 14 46	3 S37
29	F	12 34 14	6 38 34	2 38	28 2 26	5 0	6 7	20 38	4 ♏ 44 36	8 29
30	S	12 38 10	7 ♎ 37 33	3 S 2	11 ♏ 21 6	4 N44	10 S44	20 ♋ 35	17 ♏ 51 54	12 S50

D M	Mercury Lat.	Mercury Dec.	Mercury Dec.	Venus Lat.	Venus Dec.	Venus Dec.	Mars Lat.	Mars Dec.	Mars Dec.	Jupiter Lat.	Jupiter Dec.
	° ′	° ′	° ′	° ′	° ′	° ′	° ′	° ′	° ′	° ′	° ′
1	1 N12	5 N28	4 N 41	1 N 5	0 N20	0 S 11	1 N 10	15 N52	15 N 40	0 S 53	21 N 4
3	1 0	3 54	3 8	1 1	0 S 42	1 13	1 10	15 28	15 16	0 54	21 5
5	0 48	2 21	1 35	0 57	1 44	2 15	1 11	15 3	14 51	0 54	21 6
7	0 35	0 N49	0 N 3	0 53	2 45	3 16	1 11	14 39	14 26	0 54	21 7
9	0 21	0 S 42	1 S 27	0 49	3 47	4 18	1 11	14 14	14 1	0 54	21 8
11	0 N 6	2 12	2 56	0 45	4 48	5 19	1 12	13 48	13 35	0 54	21 9
13	0 S 9	3 39	4 23	0 40	5 49	6 20	1 12	13 22	13 9	0 54	21 10
15	0 24	5 5	5 48	0 35	6 50	7 20	1 13	12 56	12 43	0 55	21 11
17	0 39	6 29	7 10	0 30	7 50	8 20	1 13	12 30	12 17	0 55	21 11
19	0 55	7 51	8 30	0 25	8 49	9 19	1 13	12 3	11 50	0 55	21 12
21	1 11	9 9	9 48	0 19	9 48	10 17	1 14	11 36	11 23	0 55	21 12
23	1 26	10 25	11 2	0 14	10 46	11 14	1 14	11 9	10 56	0 55	21 12
25	1 41	11 38	12 14	0 8	11 42	12 10	1 14	10 42	10 28	0 55	21 12
27	1 56	12 48	13 22	0 N 3	12 38	13 6	1 14	10 14	10 1	0 55	21 12
29	2 10	13 54	14 S 26	0 S 3	13 33	14 S 0	1 15	9 47	9 N 33	0 56	21 12
31	2 S 23	14 S 56		0 S 9	14 S 26		1 N 15	9 N19		0 S 56	21 N12

FIRST QUARTER-Sep. 5, 4h.27m. pm. (13°♐ 24′)

FULL MOON-Sep.13, 7h.37m. pm. (21°♓18′)

D M	☿ Long.	♀ Long.	♂ Long.	♃ Long.	♄ Long.	♅ Long.	♆ Long.	♇ Long.	☉	☿	♀	♂	♃	♄	♅	♆	♇
	° ′	° ′	° ′	° ′	° ′	° ′	° ′	° ′									
1	18♍59	1♎39	20♌10	9♊58	0♊52	18♒ 1	4♒17	10♐11	∠	⚺		⚹	⚼	⚼	△		∠
2	20 45	2 53	20 49	10 3	0 53	17R 59	4R 16	10 12		∠	⚺					□	
3	22 30	4 7	21 27	10 8	0 54	17 57	4 15	10 12	⚹		∠	□			□		⚺
4	24 13	5 20	22 5	10 13	0 55	17 55	4 14	10 13		⚹				☍		⚹	
5	25 56	6 34	22 43	10 17	0 56	17 53	4 12	10 13	□		⚹		☍				☌
6	27 37	7 47	23 21	10 22	0 57	17 51	4 11	10 14		□		△			⚹	∠	
7	29♍17	9 1	23 59	10 26	0 57	17 49	4 10	10 14			□	⚼			∠	⚺	⚺
8	0♎56	10 15	24 37	10 30	0 58	17 47	4 9	10 15	△					⚼	⚺		
9	2 34	11 28	25 15	10 34	0 58	17 45	4 8	10 15	⚼	△			⚼	△		☌	∠
10	4 10	12 42	25 53	10 38	0 59	17 43	4 7	10 16			△		△				⚹
11	5 46	13 55	26 31	10 42	0 59	17 41	4 6	10 17		⚼		☍			☌		
12	7 20	15 9	27 9	10 45	0R 59	17 39	4 5	10 18			⚼		□	□		⚺	□
13	8 53	16 22	27 47	10 48	0 59	17 37	4 4	10 18	☍						⚺	∠	
14	10 26	17 36	28 25	10 52	0 58	17 35	4 3	10 19						⚹	∠	⚹	
15	11 57	18 49	29 3	10 54	0 58	17 33	4 2	10 20		☍	☍	⚼	⚹	∠	⚹		△
16	13 27	20 2	29♌41	10 57	0 58	17 32	4 1	10 21				△	∠	⚺			⚼
17	14 55	21 16	0♍18	11 0	0 57	17 30	4 0	10 22	⚼				⚺			□	
18	16 23	22 29	0 56	11 2	0 57	17 28	3 59	10 23	△						□		
19	17 50	23 43	1 34	11 4	0 56	17 26	3 58	10 24		⚼	⚼	□	☌	☌		△	☍
20	19 15	24 56	2 12	11 6	0 55	17 25	3 58	10 24		△	△				△	⚼	
21	20 40	26 9	2 50	11 8	0 54	17 23	3 57	10 25	□			⚹	⚺	⚺	⚼		
22	22 3	27 23	3 28	11 9	0 53	17 22	3 56	10 27		□		∠		∠			⚼
23	23 25	28 36	4 5	11 10	0 52	17 20	3 55	10 28	⚹		□	⚺	∠	⚹		☍	
24	24 46	29♎50	4 43	11 12	0 51	17 19	3 55	10 29	∠				⚹		☍		△
25	26 5	1♏ 3	5 21	11 12	0 50	17 17	3 54	10 30	⚺	⚹	⚹	☌		□			
26	27 23	2 16	5 59	11 13	0 48	17 16	3 53	10 31		∠	∠		□			⚼	□
27	28 40	3 29	6 36	11 14	0 47	17 14	3 53	10 32	☌	⚺	⚺	⚺		△	⚼	△	
28	29♎55	4 43	7 14	11 14	0 45	17 13	3 52	10 33					△	⚼	△		⚹
29	1♏ 9	5 56	7 52	11 14	0 43	17 12	3 52	10 35		☌		∠	⚼			□	∠
30	2♏21	7♏ 9	8♍29	11♊14	0♊41	17♒10	3♒51	10♐36	⚺		☌	⚹			□		⚺
				R													

D M	Saturn Lat.	Saturn Dec.	Uranus Lat.	Uranus Dec.	Neptune Lat.	Neptune Dec.	Pluto Lat.	Pluto Dec.
	° ′	° ′	° ′	° ′	° ′	° ′	° ′	° ′
1	2S11	18N12	0S44	16S 8	0N12	18S59	10N48	11S17
3	2 11	18 12	0 44	16 9	0 12	19 0	10 48	11 18
5	2 12	18 12	0 44	16 10	0 12	19 1	10 47	11 19
7	2 12	18 12	0 44	16 12	0 12	19 1	10 46	11 20
9	2 12	18 12	0 44	16 13	0 12	19 2	10 45	11 21
11	2 13	18 11	0 44	16 14	0 12	19 2	10 44	11 22
13	2 13	18 11	0 44	16 15	0 12	19 3	10 43	11 23
15	2 13	18 11	0 44	16 16	0 12	19 3	10 42	11 24
17	2 14	18 10	0 44	16 17	0 12	19 4	10 41	11 25
19	2 14	18 9	0 44	16 18	0 12	19 4	10 41	11 26
21	2 14	18 9	0 44	16 19	0 12	19 4	10 40	11 27
23	2 15	18 8	0 44	16 20	0 12	19 5	10 39	11 28
25	2 15	18 7	0 44	16 21	0 12	19 5	10 38	11 29
27	2 15	18 6	0 44	16 22	0 12	19 6	10 37	11 31
29	2 16	18 5	0 44	16 22	0 12	19 6	10 36	11 32
31	2S16	18N 4	0S44	16S23	0N12	19S 6	10N36	11S33

Mutual Aspects

1 ☿⚼♆.
2 ☉□♃. ☉±♆. ☉□♇. ☿⚺♂. ♀⚼♅.
3 ♀△♆.
4 ☿±♅. ♂Q♃. ♃☍♇.
5 ☿P♀. 6 ☿Q♇.
7 ♀∠♂.
8 ☿⊥♂. ☿△♄. ♀△♃. ♀⚹♇.
9 ☿⚼♅.
10 ☉∇♅. ☿△♆. ☉P♀.
11 ☉⚼♆. 12 ♄Stat.
13 ♀⚼♄. ☉P☿.
14 ☿△♃. ☿⚹♇. ♀△♅.
16 ☉±♅. 17 ☿∠♂.
18 ☿⚼♄. ♂□♄.
19 ☿△♅.
20 ♀±♄. ♀∠♇.
21 ☉Q♇. ♀⚼♃.
22 ♂P♇.
23 ☉△♄. ♂∇♆.
24 ☿±♄. ☿P♂. ♀P♂.
25 ☉⚼♅. ☿⚼♃. ☿∠♇. ♀∇♄. ☿P♇.
♀P♇.
26 ☉△♆. ☿P♀.
27 ♀□♆.
28 ♀±♃. ♀⊥♇.
29 ☿∇♄. ♃Stat.

LAST QUARTER-Sep.21, 1h.28m. am. (28°♊22′)

NEW MOON-Oct.27, 7h.58m. am. (4°♏12′)

D M	D W	Sidereal Time	☉ Long.	☉ Dec.	☽ Long.	☽ Lat.	☽ Dec.	☽ Node	Midnight ☽ Long.	Midnight ☽ Dec.
		H. M. S.	° ′ ″	° ′	° ′ ″	° ′	° ′	° ′	° ′ ″	° ′
1	Su	12 42 7	8♎36 34	3 S 25	24♏17 3	4 N13	14 S 45	20♋32	0♐36 48	16 S 28
2	M	12 46 3	9 35 37	3 48	6♐51 26	3 31	17 59	20 29	13 1 23	19 17
3	T	12 50 0	10 34 41	4 11	19 7 10	2 40	20 20	20 26	25 9 19	21 9
4	W	12 53 56	11 33 48	4 34	1♑8 27	1 43	21 43	20 23	7♑5 15	22 2
5	Th	12 57 53	12 32 56	4 57	13 0 23	0 N42	22 7	20 19	18 54 32	21 56
6	F	13 1 49	13 32 6	5 20	24 48 26	0 S 21	21 30	20 16	0♒42 44	20 50
7	S	13 5 46	14 31 17	5 43	6♒38 7	1 23	19 57	20 13	12 35 14	18 49
8	Su	13 9 43	15 30 31	6 6	18 34 42	2 21	17 30	20 10	24 37 3	15 58
9	M	13 13 39	16 29 46	6 29	0♓42 48	3 14	14 15	20 7	6♓52 21	12 21
10	T	13 17 36	17 29 3	6 52	13 6 5	3 59	10 19	20 4	19 24 15	8 9
11	W	13 21 32	18 28 22	7 14	25 47 0	4 33	5 51	20 0	2♈14 26	3 S 29
12	Th	13 25 29	19 27 43	7 37	8♈46 29	4 54	1 S 2	19 57	15 23 3	1 N27
13	F	13 29 25	20 27 6	7 59	22 3 55	5 0	3 N57	19 54	28 48 45	6 26
14	S	13 33 22	21 26 30	8 22	5♉37 13	4 49	8 51	19 51	12♉28 52	11 11
15	Su	13 37 18	22 25 58	8 44	19 23 17	4 21	13 23	19 48	26 20 0	15 25
16	M	13 41 15	23 25 27	9 6	3♊18 35	3 38	17 15	19 44	10♊18 36	18 51
17	T	13 45 12	24 24 58	9 28	17 19 43	2 41	20 10	19 41	24 21 36	21 11
18	W	13 49 8	25 24 32	9 50	1♋24 0	1 33	21 52	19 38	8♋26 42	22 13
19	Th	13 53 5	26 24 8	10 11	15 29 34	0 S 20	22 12	19 35	22 32 27	21 50
20	F	13 57 1	27 23 47	10 33	29 35 17	0 N54	21 7	19 32	6♌37 58	20 4
21	S	14 0 58	28 23 28	10 54	13♌40 25	2 5	18 43	19 29	20 42 30	17 5
22	Su	14 4 54	29♎23 11	11 15	27 44 4	3 8	15 12	19 25	4♍44 56	13 7
23	M	14 8 51	0♏22 56	11 36	11♍44 50	4 0	10 51	19 22	18 43 28	8 27
24	T	14 12 47	1 22 43	11 57	25 40 29	4 37	5 57	19 19	2♎35 30	3 N23
25	W	14 16 44	2 22 33	12 18	9♎28 4	4 57	0 N48	19 16	16 17 47	1 S 47
26	Th	14 20 41	3 22 25	12 38	23 4 14	5 0	4 S 19	19 13	29 47 1	6 47
27	F	14 24 37	4 22 18	12 59	6♏25 49	4 47	9 9	19 10	13♏0 21	11 23
28	S	14 28 34	5 22 14	13 19	19 30 25	4 18	13 28	19 6	25 55 56	15 22
29	Su	14 32 30	6 22 11	13 39	2♐16 54	3 37	17 4	19 3	8♐33 23	18 33
30	M	14 36 27	7 22 11	13 58	14 45 34	2 47	19 49	19 0	20 53 44	20 49
31	T	14 40 23	8♏22 12	14 S 18	26♐58 15	1 N49	21 S 35	18♋57	2♑59 32	22 S 6

D M	Mercury Lat.	Mercury Dec.		Venus Lat.	Venus Dec.		Mars Lat.	Mars Dec.		Jupiter Lat.	Jupiter Dec.
	° ′	° ′	° ′	° ′	° ′	° ′	° ′	° ′	° ′	° ′	° ′
1	2 S 23	14 S 56	15 S 26	0 S 9	14 S 26	14 S 52	1 N 15	9 N19	9 N 5	0 S 56	21 N12
3	2 36	15 54	16 21	0 15	15 18	15 44	1 15	8 50	8 36	0 56	21 12
5	2 48	16 47	17 12	0 21	16 9	16 34	1 15	8 22	8 8	0 56	21 12
7	2 58	17 35	17 56	0 27	16 58	17 22	1 16	7 54	7 39	0 56	21 11
9	3 6	18 16	18 34	0 33	17 45	18 8	1 16	7 25	7 11	0 56	21 10
11	3 13	18 50	19 4	0 39	18 31	18 53	1 16	6 56	6 42	0 56	21 10
13	3 17	19 16	19 26	0 45	19 15	19 36	1 16	6 27	6 13	0 56	21 9
15	3 18	19 33	19 37	0 51	19 57	20 17	1 17	5 58	5 44	0 57	21 8
17	3 14	19 39	19 37	0 57	20 36	20 56	1 17	5 29	5 15	0 57	21 7
19	3 6	19 31	19 22	1 3	21 14	21 32	1 17	5 0	4 46	0 57	21 6
21	2 53	19 9	18 51	1 9	21 49	22 6	1 17	4 31	4 16	0 57	21 5
23	2 32	18 30	18 3	1 14	22 23	22 38	1 17	4 2	3 47	0 57	21 3
25	2 5	17 33	16 58	1 20	22 53	23 8	1 17	3 32	3 18	0 57	21 2
27	1 31	16 19	15 38	1 25	23 21	23 34	1 18	3 3	2 48	0 57	21 0
29	0 52	14 54	14 S 9	1 31	23 47	23 S 59	1 18	2 34	2 N 19	0 57	20 59
31	0 S 10	13 S 25		1 S 36	24 S 10		1 N 18	2 N 4		0 S 57	20 N57

FIRST QUARTER-Oct. 5,10h.59m. am. (12°♑30′)

FULL MOON-Oct.13, 8h.53m. am. (20°♈19′)

EPHEMERIS]				OCTOBER	2000													21
D	☿	♀	♂	♃	♄	♅	♆	♇	Lunar Aspects									
M	Long.	Long.	Long.	Long.	Long.	Long.	Long.	Long.	☉	☿	♀	♂	♃	♄	♅	♆	♇
	° ′	° ′	° ′	° ′	° ′	° ′	° ′	° ′									
1	3♏32	8♏23	9♍ 7	11♊14	0♊39	17♒ 9	3♒51	10♐37	∠								
2	4 41	9 36	9 44	11R 13	0R 37	17R 8	3R 50	10 39	✱	⊻	⊻	□	☍	☍		✱	☌
3	5 47	10 49	10 22	11 12	0 35	17 7	3 50	10 40		∠					✱	∠	
4	6 52	12 2	11 0	11 12	0 33	17 6	3 49	10 41			∠				∠	⊻	
5	7 54	13 15	11 37	11 10	0 30	17 5	3 49	10 43	□	✱	✱	△		⚼	⊻		⊻
6	8 54	14 28	12 15	11 9	0 28	17 4	3 49	10 44				⚼	⚼	△			∠
7	9 51	15 42	12 52	11 8	0 25	17 3	3 49	10 46		□			△			☌	✱
8	10 45	16 55	13 30	11 6	0 23	17 2	3 48	10 47	△		□				☌		
9	11 36	18 8	14 7	11 4	0 20	17 1	3 48	10 49	⚼					□		⊻	
10	12 23	19 21	14 45	11 2	0 17	17 0	3 48	10 50		△		☍	□		⊻	∠	□
11	13 7	20 34	15 22	11 0	0 14	16 59	3 48	10 52		⚼	△			✱	∠		
12	13 46	21 47	15 59	10 57	0 11	16 59	3 48	10 54			⚼		✱	∠		✱	△
13	14 21	23 0	16 37	10 54	0 8	16 58	3 47	10 55	☍				∠		✱		⚼
14	14 50	24 13	17 14	10 52	0 5	16 57	3 47	10 57				⚼	⊻	⊻		□	
15	15 14	25 26	17 52	10 49	0♊ 2	16 57	3 47	10 58		☍	☍	△			□		
16	15 32	26 39	18 29	10 45	29♉58	16 56	3D 47	11 0	⚼					☌		△	
17	15 44	27 52	19 6	10 42	29 55	16 56	3 47	11 2				□	☌		△	⚼	☍
18	15 48	29♏ 4	19 44	10 38	29 51	16 55	3 48	11 4	△	⚼				⊻	⚼		
19	15R 45	0♐17	20 21	10 34	29 48	16 55	3 48	11 5		△	⚼	✱	⊻	∠			
20	15 33	1 30	20 58	10 30	29 44	16 55	3 48	11 7	□		△	∠	∠	✱		☍	⚼
21	15 13	2 43	21 36	10 26	29 40	16 54	3 48	11 9		□			✱		☍		△
22	14 44	3 56	22 13	10 22	29 37	16 54	3 48	11 11	✱		□	⊻		□			
23	14 6	5 8	22 50	10 17	29 33	16 54	3 48	11 13	∠	✱			□				□
24	13 20	6 21	23 27	10 12	29 29	16 54	3 49	11 15	⊻	∠		☌		△	⚼	⚼	
25	12 25	7 34	24 4	10 7	29 25	16 54	3 49	11 17		⊻	✱		△	⚼		△	✱
26	11 22	8 47	24 42	10 2	29 21	16 54	3 49	11 18			∠	⊻	⚼		△		∠
27	10 13	9 59	25 19	9 57	29 17	16D 54	3 50	11 20	☌	☌	⊻	∠				□	⊻
28	9 0	11 12	25 56	9 52	29 12	16 54	3 50	11 22							□		
29	7 43	12 25	26 33	9 46	29 8	16 54	3 51	11 24	⊻	⊻		✱		☍		✱	
30	6 26	13 37	27 10	9 40	29 4	16 54	3 51	11 26		∠	☌		☍		✱	∠	☌
31	5♏11	14♐50	27♍47	9♊34	28♉59	16♒54	3♒52	11♐28	∠			□			∠		

D	Saturn		Uranus		Neptune		Pluto	
M	Lat.	Dec.	Lat.	Dec.	Lat.	Dec.	Lat.	Dec.
	° ′	° ′	° ′	° ′	° ′	° ′	° ′	° ′
1	2S16	18N 4	0S44	16S23	0N12	19S 6	10N36	11S33
3	2 16	18 3	0 43	16 24	0 12	19 6	10 35	11 34
5	2 17	18 2	0 43	16 24	0 12	19 7	10 34	11 35
7	2 17	18 0	0 43	16 25	0 12	19 7	10 33	11 36
9	2 17	17 59	0 43	16 25	0 12	19 7	10 32	11 37
11	2 17	17 58	0 43	16 26	0 12	19 7	10 32	11 39
13	2 18	17 56	0 43	16 26	0 11	19 7	10 31	11 40
15	2 18	17 54	0 43	16 26	0 11	19 7	10 30	11 41
17	2 18	17 53	0 43	16 27	0 11	19 7	10 30	11 42
19	2 18	17 51	0 43	16 27	0 11	19 7	10 29	11 43
21	2 19	17 49	0 43	16 27	0 11	19 7	10 28	11 44
23	2 19	17 48	0 43	16 27	0 11	19 7	10 28	11 45
25	2 19	17 46	0 43	16 27	0 11	19 7	10 27	11 46
27	2 19	17 44	0 43	16 27	0 11	19 7	10 26	11 47
29	2 19	17 42	0 43	16 27	0 11	19 7	10 26	11 49
31	2S19	17N40	0S43	16S27	0N11	19S 6	10N25	11S50

Mutual Aspects

1 ☿□♆.
2 ☉⊻♀. ☉⊻♂. ☿±♃. ☿⊥♇. ♀✱♂. ♂±♆.
3 ☉✱♇. ♀∇♃. ♀⊻♇. ♂□♇.
4 ☉△♃. ♂□♃. ☿P♅.
6 ♀P♅.
8 ☉⚼♄. ☿∇♃. ☿⊻♇. ♀□♅. ☿P♄.
10 ☉△♅. ♀P♄.
11 ☉P♂.
12 ♀Q♆. ☿P♆.
13 ♃☍♇. ☿P♀. ♀P♆.
14 ♂∇♅. 15 ♆Stat.
16 ♂⚼♆.
17 ☉±♄.
18 ☉⚼♃. ☿Stat.
19 ☉⊥♂. ☉∠♇. ♀☍♄. ♀P♃.
21 ☿P♆.
22 ☉∇♄. ♀Q♂. ♀✱♆.
23 ♀Q♅. ♂±♅. ☉P♇.
25 ☿P♄.
26 ☉□♆. ☿⊻♇. ♅Stat.
27 ☉±♃. ☿⊻♀. ☿∠♂. ☿∇♃. ♀☍♃.
☿P♅.
28 ☉⊥♇. ♀☌♇.
29 ☉⊥♀.
30 ☉☌☿. ☿⊥♀. ☉P☿.
31 ☿⊥♇.

LAST QUARTER-Oct.20, 7h.59m. am. (27°♋14′)

NEW MOON-Nov.25,11h.11m. pm. (4°♐ 0′)

D M	D W	Sidereal Time	☉ Long.	☉ Dec.	☽ Long.	☽ Lat.	☽ Dec.	☽ Node	Midnight ☽ Long.	Midnight ☽ Dec.
		H. M. S.	° ′ ″	° ′	° ′ ″	° ′	° ′	° ′	° ′ ″	° ′
1	W	14 44 20	9 ♏ 22 15	14 S 37	8 ♑ 58 6	0 N 47	22 S 21	18 ♋ 54	14 ♑ 54 29	22 S 20
2	Th	14 48 16	10 22 19	14 56	20 49 18	0 S 16	22 5	18 50	26 43 12	21 35
3	F	14 52 13	11 22 25	15 15	2 ♒ 36 50	1 18	20 50	18 47	8 ♒ 30 54	19 52
4	S	14 56 10	12 22 33	15 33	14 26 5	2 17	18 41	18 44	20 23 4	17 17
5	Su	15 0 6	13 22 42	15 51	26 22 33	3 10	15 42	18 41	2 ♓ 25 11	13 57
6	M	15 4 3	14 22 53	16 9	8 ♓ 31 34	3 56	12 1	18 38	14 42 16	9 57
7	T	15 7 59	15 23 5	16 27	20 57 47	4 32	7 45	18 35	27 18 32	5 26
8	W	15 11 56	16 23 18	16 44	3 ♈ 44 49	4 56	3 S 2	18 31	10 ♈ 16 51	0 S 34
9	Th	15 15 52	17 23 34	17 1	16 54 43	5 5	1 N 57	18 28	23 38 22	4 N 29
10	F	15 19 49	18 23 50	17 18	0 ♉ 27 36	4 57	7 0	18 25	7 ♉ 22 7	9 27
11	S	15 23 45	19 24 9	17 35	14 21 27	4 31	11 49	18 22	21 25 2	14 3
12	Su	15 27 42	20 24 29	17 51	28 32 15	3 49	16 7	18 19	5 ♊ 42 21	17 57
13	M	15 31 39	21 24 51	18 7	12 ♊ 54 36	2 51	19 31	18 15	20 8 15	20 47
14	T	15 35 35	22 25 15	18 22	27 22 34	1 42	21 42	18 12	4 ♋ 36 52	22 17
15	W	15 39 32	23 25 40	18 38	11 ♋ 50 33	0 S 26	22 28	18 9	19 3 6	22 17
16	Th	15 43 28	24 26 8	18 53	26 14 4	0 N 51	21 44	18 6	3 ♌ 23 6	20 50
17	F	15 47 25	25 26 37	19 7	10 ♌ 29 57	2 4	19 36	18 3	17 34 26	18 4
18	S	15 51 21	26 27 8	19 22	24 36 23	3 9	16 18	18 0	1 ♍ 35 45	14 18
19	Su	15 55 18	27 27 41	19 36	8 ♍ 32 29	4 2	12 7	17 56	15 26 31	9 47
20	M	15 59 14	28 28 16	19 49	22 17 49	4 41	7 21	17 53	29 6 23	4 N 51
21	T	16 3 11	29 ♏ 28 52	20 2	5 ♎ 52 9	5 3	2 N 18	17 50	12 ♎ 35 3	0 S 15
22	W	16 7 8	0 ♐ 29 30	20 15	19 15 0	5 8	2 S 47	17 47	25 51 57	5 16
23	Th	16 11 4	1 30 10	20 28	2 ♏ 25 46	4 56	7 40	17 44	8 ♏ 56 22	9 58
24	F	16 15 1	2 30 52	20 40	15 23 41	4 30	12 9	17 41	21 47 38	14 10
25	S	16 18 57	3 31 34	20 51	28 8 10	3 50	16 0	17 37	4 ♐ 25 18	17 39
26	Su	16 22 54	4 32 19	21 3	10 ♐ 39 2	3 0	19 5	17 34	16 49 28	20 16
27	M	16 26 50	5 33 4	21 14	22 56 44	2 2	21 13	17 31	29 1 0	21 55
28	T	16 30 47	6 33 51	21 24	5 ♑ 2 33	0 N 59	22 22	17 28	11 ♑ 1 38	22 32
29	W	16 34 43	7 34 39	21 34	16 58 39	0 S 6	22 27	17 25	22 53 59	22 7
30	Th	16 38 40	8 ♐ 35 28	21 S 44	28 ♑ 48 6	1 S 10	21 S 32	17 ♋ 21	4 ♒ 41 30	20 S 43

D M	Mercury Lat.	Mercury Dec.		Venus Lat.	Venus Dec.		Mars Lat.	Mars Dec.		Jupiter Lat.	Jupiter Dec.
	° ′	° ′	° ′	° ′	° ′	° ′	° ′	° ′	° ′	° ′	° ′
1	0 N 10	12 S 42	12 S 1	1 S 38	24 S 20	24 S 30	1 N 18	1 N 50	1 N 35	0 S 57	20 N 56
3	0 48	11 24	10 52	1 43	24 39	24 47	1 18	1 20	1 5	0 57	20 54
5	1 21	10 25	10 4	1 48	24 55	25 2	1 18	0 51	0 36	0 57	20 52
7	1 46	9 49	9 39	1 52	25 8	25 14	1 18	0 N 22	0 N 7	0 57	20 50
9	2 4	9 35	9 36	1 57	25 19	25 23	1 18	0 S 8	0 S 22	0 57	20 48
11	2 15	9 42	9 52	2 0	25 26	25 28	1 18	0 37	0 51	0 56	20 46
13	2 20	10 6	10 24	2 4	25 30	25 31	1 18	1 6	1 20	0 56	20 44
15	2 20	10 44	11 7	2 7	25 32	25 31	1 18	1 35	1 49	0 56	20 41
17	2 16	11 32	11 58	2 10	25 30	25 28	1 18	2 4	2 18	0 56	20 39
19	2 9	12 26	12 55	2 13	25 26	25 23	1 18	2 33	2 47	0 56	20 37
21	2 0	13 25	13 55	2 16	25 19	25 14	1 19	3 1	3 16	0 56	20 34
23	1 49	14 26	14 57	2 18	25 8	25 2	1 19	3 30	3 44	0 55	20 32
25	1 37	15 28	15 58	2 19	24 55	24 48	1 18	3 58	4 13	0 55	20 29
27	1 24	16 29	16 59	2 20	24 39	24 30	1 18	4 27	4 41	0 55	20 27
29	1 10	17 29	17 S 58	2 21	24 21	24 S 10	1 18	4 55	5 S 9	0 55	20 24
31	0 N 56	18 S 27		2 S 22	23 S 59		1 N 18	5 S 23		0 S 54	20 N 22

FIRST QUARTER-Nov. 4, 7h.27m. am. (12°♒11′)

FULL MOON-Nov.11, 9h.15m. pm. (19°♉47′)

EPHEMERIS]				NOVEMBER 2000														23
D	☿	♀	♂	♃	♄	♅	♆	♇	Lunar Aspects									
M	Long.	Long.	Long.	Long.	Long.	Long.	Long.	Long.	☉	☿	♀	♂	♃	♄	♅	♆	♇
	° ′	° ′	° ′	° ′	° ′	° ′	° ′	° ′									
1	3♏59	16♐ 2	28♍24	9♊28	28♉55	16♒55	3♒52	11♐30	⚹	⚹				⚼		⚺	⚺
2	2R 55	17 15	29 1	9R 22	28R 50	16 55	3 53	11 32			⚺		⚼		⚺		∠
3	1 58	18 27	29♍38	9 16	28 46	16 55	3 53	11 34		□	∠	△		△		☌	
4	1 11	19 40	0♎15	9 9	28 41	16 56	3 54	11 37	□		⚹	⚼	△		☌		⚹
5	0 35	20 52	0 52	9 3	28 37	16 56	3 55	11 39		△				□			
6	0♏11	22 4	1 29	8 56	28 32	16 57	3 56	11 41					□			⚺	□
7	29♎59	23 17	2 6	8 49	28 27	16 57	3 56	11 43	△	⚼	□				⚺	∠	
8	29♎57	24 29	2 43	8 42	28 23	16 58	3 57	11 45	⚼			☍	⚹	⚹	∠	⚹	
9	0♏ 7	25 41	3 20	8 35	28 18	16 59	3 58	11 47					∠	∠	⚹		△
10	0D 27	26 53	3 57	8 28	28 13	16 59	3 59	11 49		☍	△			⚺		□	⚼
11	0 57	28 5	4 34	8 20	28 8	17 0	4 0	11 51	☍		⚼	⚼	⚺		□		
12	1 35	29♐17	5 11	8 13	28 4	17 1	4 1	11 54				△		☌		△	
13	2 22	0♑29	5 47	8 5	27 59	17 2	4 1	11 56		⚼			☌		△	⚼	☍
14	3 15	1 41	6 24	7 58	27 54	17 3	4 2	11 58		△	☍			⚺	⚼		
15	4 14	2 53	7 1	7 50	27 49	17 4	4 3	12 0	⚼			□	⚺	∠			
16	5 18	4 5	7 38	7 42	27 44	17 5	4 5	12 3	△				∠	⚹			⚼
17	6 27	5 17	8 14	7 35	27 39	17 6	4 6	12 5		□		⚹	⚹		☍	☍	△
18	7 40	6 29	8 51	7 27	27 34	17 7	4 7	12 7	□		⚼	∠		□			
19	8 56	7 40	9 28	7 19	27 30	17 8	4 8	12 9		⚹	△	⚺	□				□
20	10 15	8 52	10 4	7 11	27 25	17 9	4 9	12 12	⚹	∠				△		⚼	
21	11 36	10 3	10 41	7 3	27 20	17 11	4 10	12 14		⚺	□	☌	△	⚼	⚼	△	⚹
22	13 0	11 15	11 18	6 55	27 15	17 12	4 11	12 16	∠				⚼		△		
23	14 25	12 26	11 54	6 47	27 10	17 13	4 13	12 18	⚺							□	∠
24	15 52	13 38	12 31	6 38	27 5	17 15	4 14	12 21		☌	⚹	⚺			□		⚺
25	17 20	14 49	13 7	6 30	27 0	17 16	4 15	12 23	☌		∠	∠		☍		⚹	
26	18 49	16 1	13 44	6 22	26 55	17 18	4 17	12 25			⚺	⚹	☍				☌
27	20 18	17 12	14 20	6 14	26 51	17 19	4 18	12 28		⚺					⚹	∠	
28	21 49	18 23	14 56	6 6	26 46	17 21	4 19	12 30	⚺	∠					∠	⚺	
29	23 20	19 34	15 33	5 58	26 41	17 23	4 21	12 32			☌	□	⚼	⚼	⚺		⚺
30	24♏51	20♑45	16♎ 9	5♊49	26♉36	17♒24	4♒22	12♐35	∠	⚹				△		☌	∠

D	Saturn		Uranus		Neptune		Pluto	
M	Lat.	Dec.	Lat.	Dec.	Lat.	Dec.	Lat.	Dec.
	° ′	° ′	° ′	° ′	° ′	° ′	° ′	° ′
1	2S19	17N39	0S43	16S27	0N11	19S 6	10N25	11S50
3	2 19	17 37	0 43	16 26	0 11	19 6	10 25	11 51
5	2 19	17 35	0 42	16 26	0 11	19 6	10 24	11 52
7	2 19	17 33	0 42	16 26	0 11	19 5	10 24	11 53
9	2 19	17 31	0 42	16 25	0 11	19 5	10 23	11 54
11	2 19	17 29	0 42	16 25	0 11	19 5	10 23	11 55
13	2 19	17 27	0 42	16 24	0 11	19 4	10 22	11 56
15	2 19	17 25	0 42	16 23	0 11	19 4	10 22	11 57
17	2 19	17 23	0 42	16 23	0 11	19 3	10 21	11 58
19	2 19	17 21	0 42	16 22	0 11	19 3	10 21	11 59
21	2 19	17 19	0 42	16 21	0 11	19 2	10 21	12 0
23	2 19	17 17	0 42	16 20	0 11	19 2	10 20	12 1
25	2 18	17 14	0 42	16 19	0 11	19 1	10 20	12 1
27	2 18	17 12	0 42	16 18	0 11	19 1	10 20	12 2
29	2 18	17 11	0 42	16 17	0 11	19 0	10 20	12 3
31	2S18	17N 9	0S42	16S16	0N11	18S59	10N19	12S 4

Mutual Aspects

1 ☉∇♃. ☿⊥♂. ☿□♆.
2 ☿∠♀. ☿±♃. ♀⚹♅. ♂△♄. ☿P♇.
3 ☉⚺♇. ♀∠♆. ♂Q♇.
5 ☿⚺♂.
7 ♂⚼♅. ☉P♅.
8 ☿Stat. 9 ☉□♅.
10 ♂△♆.
11 ☉∠♂. ♀∇♄. ♀⊥♆. ☉P♄.
13 ☿±♃.
14 ☉Q♆. ♀∠♅.
15 ☿□♆.
16 ♀±♄. ♀⚺♆. ♂△♃.
17 ☿⊥♇. ☉P♆.
18 ☿∇♃. ☿P♇.
19 ☉☍♄. ♀∇♃.
20 ☿⚺♂. 21 ☿⚺♇.
22 ♀□♂. ♀⊥♅.
23 ♀±♃. ♀⚼♄. ♀⚺♇. ♂⚼♄. ☉P♃.
24 ♂⚹♇. 25 ☿□♅.
26 ☉⚹♆.
27 ☉Q♅. ☿⊥♂. ♀⚺♅. ☿P♅.
28 ☉☍♃. ☿Q♆. ♀⊥♇. ☿P♄.
30 ♀⚼♃.

LAST QUARTER-Nov.18, 3h.24m. pm. (26°♌36′)

NEW MOON-Dec.25, 5h.22m. pm. (4°♑14′)

D M	D W	Sidereal Time	☉ Long.	☉ Dec.	☽ Long.	☽ Lat.	☽ Dec.	☽ Node	Midnight ☽ Long.	Midnight ☽ Dec.
		H. M. S.	° ′ ″	° ′	° ′ ″	° ′	° ′	° ′	° ′ ″	° ′
1	F	16 42 37	9 ♐ 36 18	21 S 53	10 ♒ 34 44	2 S 11	19 S 41	17 ♋ 18	16 ♒ 28 22	18 S 26
2	S	16 46 33	10 37 9	22 2	22 23 1	3 6	16 59	17 15	28 19 20	15 21
3	Su	16 50 30	11 38 0	22 11	4 ♓ 17 56	3 54	13 34	17 12	10 ♓ 19 28	11 37
4	M	16 54 26	12 38 53	22 19	16 24 35	4 33	9 33	17 9	22 33 55	7 21
5	T	16 58 23	13 39 46	22 26	28 48 2	4 59	5 3	17 6	5 ♈ 7 30	2 S 40
6	W	17 2 19	14 40 40	22 34	11 ♈ 32 46	5 12	0 S 14	17 2	18 4 14	2 N 16
7	Th	17 6 16	15 41 35	22 40	24 42 11	5 10	4 N 46	16 59	1 ♉ 26 47	7 15
8	F	17 10 12	16 42 31	22 46	8 ♉ 18 4	4 50	9 42	16 56	15 15 52	12 3
9	S	17 14 9	17 43 27	22 52	22 19 55	4 12	14 17	16 53	29 29 45	16 21
10	Su	17 18 6	18 44 24	22 58	6 ♊ 44 46	3 18	18 11	16 50	14 ♊ 4 12	19 46
11	M	17 22 2	19 45 22	23 3	21 27 10	2 9	21 1	16 47	28 52 44	21 55
12	T	17 25 59	20 46 21	23 7	6 ♋ 19 52	0 S 51	22 26	16 43	13 ♋ 47 33	22 34
13	W	17 29 55	21 47 21	23 11	21 14 47	0 N 31	22 16	16 40	28 40 38	21 36
14	Th	17 33 52	22 48 22	23 15	6 ♌ 4 13	1 51	20 32	16 37	13 ♌ 24 51	19 9
15	F	17 37 48	23 49 23	23 18	20 41 52	3 2	17 28	16 34	27 54 48	15 32
16	S	17 41 45	24 50 26	23 20	5 ♍ 3 17	4 0	13 23	16 31	12 ♍ 7 5	11 4
17	Su	17 45 41	25 51 29	23 22	19 6 3	4 43	8 39	16 27	26 0 11	6 9
18	M	17 49 38	26 52 34	23 24	2 ♎ 49 29	5 8	3 N 36	16 24	9 ♎ 34 5	1 N 2
19	T	17 53 35	27 53 39	23 25	16 14 6	5 16	1 S 31	16 21	22 49 46	4 S 1
20	W	17 57 31	28 54 45	23 26	29 21 14	5 7	6 27	16 18	5 ♏ 48 46	8 47
21	Th	18 1 28	29 ♐ 55 52	23 26	12 ♏ 12 33	4 43	11 0	16 15	18 32 48	13 5
22	F	18 5 24	0 ♑ 57 0	23 26	24 49 46	4 5	15 0	16 12	1 ♐ 3 37	16 45
23	S	18 9 21	1 58 8	23 25	7 ♐ 14 35	3 16	18 17	16 8	13 22 50	19 37
24	Su	18 13 17	2 59 17	23 24	19 28 35	2 19	20 42	16 5	25 32 1	21 33
25	M	18 17 14	4 0 26	23 23	1 ♑ 33 20	1 16	22 9	16 2	7 ♑ 32 44	22 30
26	T	18 21 10	5 1 36	23 21	13 30 28	0 N 11	22 34	15 59	19 26 44	22 24
27	W	18 25 7	6 2 45	23 18	25 21 50	0 S 55	21 58	15 56	1 ♒ 16 3	21 17
28	Th	18 29 4	7 3 55	23 15	7 ♒ 9 41	1 58	20 23	15 53	13 3 6	19 15
29	F	18 33 0	8 5 5	23 12	18 56 40	2 56	17 55	15 49	24 50 48	16 25
30	S	18 36 57	9 6 15	23 8	0 ♓ 45 56	3 46	14 43	15 46	6 ♓ 42 35	12 53
31	Su	18 40 53	10 ♑ 7 25	23 S 3	12 ♓ 41 12	4 S 28	10 S 55	15 ♋ 43	18 ♓ 42 21	8 S 49

D M	Mercury Lat.	Mercury Dec.		Venus Lat.	Venus Dec.		Mars Lat.	Mars Dec.		Jupiter Lat.	Jupiter Dec.
	° ′	° ′	° ′	° ′	° ′	° ′	° ′	° ′	° ′	° ′	° ′
1	0 N 56	18 S 27	18 S 55	2 S 22	23 S 59	23 S 47	1 N 18	5 S 23	5 S 37	0 S 54	20 N 22
3	0 41	19 22	19 48	2 22	23 35	23 22	1 18	5 51	6 4	0 54	20 19
5	0 27	20 14	20 38	2 22	23 8	22 54	1 18	6 18	6 32	0 54	20 16
7	0 N 13	21 2	21 25	2 21	22 39	22 24	1 18	6 45	6 59	0 54	20 14
9	0 S 1	21 47	22 8	2 19	22 8	21 51	1 18	7 12	7 26	0 53	20 11
11	0 15	22 27	22 46	2 18	21 34	21 16	1 18	7 39	7 53	0 53	20 9
13	0 28	23 4	23 20	2 15	20 58	20 39	1 18	8 6	8 19	0 52	20 7
15	0 41	23 35	23 49	2 13	20 20	20 0	1 18	8 32	8 45	0 52	20 4
17	0 53	24 2	24 14	2 10	19 39	19 19	1 17	8 58	9 11	0 52	20 2
19	1 5	24 24	24 33	2 6	18 57	18 36	1 17	9 24	9 37	0 51	20 0
21	1 16	24 41	24 47	2 2	18 13	17 51	1 17	9 50	10 2	0 51	19 58
23	1 26	24 52	24 56	1 57	17 28	17 4	1 17	10 15	10 28	0 50	19 56
25	1 35	24 58	24 59	1 52	16 40	16 16	1 16	10 40	10 52	0 50	19 54
27	1 44	24 59	24 57	1 46	15 52	15 27	1 16	11 5	11 17	0 50	19 52
29	1 51	24 53	24 S 48	1 40	15 1	14 S 36	1 16	11 29	11 S 41	0 49	19 50
31	1 S 57	24 S 42		1 S 33	14 S 10		1 N 16	11 S 53		0 S 49	19 N 49

FIRST QUARTER-Dec. 4, 3h.55m. am. (12°♓18′)

FULL MOON-Dec.11, 9h. 3m. am. (19°♊38′)

D M	☿ Long.	♀ Long.	♂ Long.	♃ Long.	♄ Long.	♅ Long.	♆ Long.	♇ Long.
	° ′	° ′	° ′	° ′	° ′	° ′	° ′	° ′
1	26♏23	21♑56	16♎46	5♊41	26♉32	17♒26	4♒24	12♐37
2	27 55	23 7	17 22	5R 33	26R 27	17 28	4 25	12 39
3	29♏28	24 17	17 58	5 25	26 22	17 30	4 27	12 42
4	1♐ 0	25 28	18 34	5 17	26 18	17 32	4 28	12 44
5	2 33	26 38	19 11	5 9	26 13	17 34	4 30	12 46
6	4 6	27 49	19 47	5 1	26 9	17 36	4 31	12 49
7	5 38	28♑59	20 23	4 53	26 4	17 38	4 33	12 51
8	7 12	0♒ 9	20 59	4 45	26 0	17 40	4 35	12 53
9	8 45	1 19	21 35	4 37	25 55	17 42	4 36	12 55
10	10 18	2 29	22 11	4 30	25 51	17 44	4 38	12 58
11	11 51	3 39	22 47	4 22	25 47	17 46	4 40	13 0
12	13 25	4 49	23 23	4 14	25 43	17 48	4 42	13 2
13	14 58	5 59	23 59	4 7	25 38	17 51	4 43	13 5
14	16 31	7 8	24 35	4 0	25 34	17 53	4 45	13 7
15	18 5	8 17	25 11	3 52	25 30	17 55	4 47	13 9
16	19 39	9 27	25 46	3 45	25 26	17 58	4 49	13 12
17	21 13	10 36	26 22	3 38	25 23	18 0	4 51	13 14
18	22 47	11 44	26 58	3 31	25 19	18 3	4 53	13 16
19	24 21	12 53	27 34	3 24	25 15	18 5	4 54	13 18
20	25 55	14 2	28 9	3 18	25 11	18 8	4 56	13 21
21	27 30	15 10	28 45	3 11	25 8	18 10	4 58	13 23
22	29♐ 4	16 19	29 21	3 5	25 4	18 13	5 0	13 25
23	0♑39	17 27	29♎56	2 58	25 1	18 15	5 2	13 27
24	2 15	18 35	0♏32	2 52	24 58	18 18	5 4	13 30
25	3 50	19 42	1 7	2 46	24 54	18 21	5 6	13 32
26	5 25	20 50	1 42	2 41	24 51	18 23	5 8	13 34
27	7 1	21 57	2 18	2 35	24 48	18 26	5 10	13 36
28	8 37	23 5	2 53	2 29	24 45	18 29	5 12	13 38
29	10 14	24 12	3 28	2 24	24 42	18 32	5 14	13 41
30	11 51	25 18	4 4	2 19	24 39	18 35	5 16	13 43
31	13♑28	26♒25	4♏39	2♊14	24♉37	18♒38	5♒19	13♐45

Lunar Aspects

D M	☉	☿	♀	♂	♃	♄	♅	♆	♇
1	⚹				△				⚹
2			⊻	△		□	☌		
3		□	∠	⚼	□			⊻	
4	□						⊻	∠	□
5		△	⚹		⚹	⚹	∠	⚹	
6	△					∠	⚹		△
7	⚼	⚼	□	☍	∠	⊻			⚼
8					⊻			□	
9						☌	□		
10		☍	△	⚼	☌			△	☍
11	☍		⚼	△		⊻	△	⚼	
12					⊻	∠	⚼		
13				□	∠	⚹			⚼
14	⚼	⚼	☍		⚹			☍	△
15	△	△		⚹		□	☍		
16				∠	□				
17		□				△		⚼	□
18	□		⚼	⊻	△		⚼	△	
19			△		⚼	⚼	△		⚹
20	⚹	⚹		☌				□	∠
21	∠	∠	□				□		⊻
22		⊻		⊻		☍			
23	⊻				☍			⚹	
24			⚹	∠			⚹	∠	☌
25	●	☌	∠	⚹			∠	⊻	
26					⚼	⚼	⊻		⊻
27			⊻			△			∠
28	⊻	⊻		□	△			☌	
29	∠		☌			□	☌		⚹
30		∠		△	□			⊻	
31	⚹	⚹					⊻		□

D M	Saturn Lat.	Saturn Dec.	Uranus Lat.	Uranus Dec.	Neptune Lat.	Neptune Dec.	Pluto Lat.	Pluto Dec.
	° ′	° ′	° ′	° ′	° ′	° ′	° ′	° ′
1	2S18	17N 9	0S42	16S16	0N11	18S59	10N19	12S 4
3	2 18	17 7	0 42	16 15	0 11	18 59	10 19	12 5
5	2 17	17 5	0 42	16 14	0 11	18 58	10 19	12 5
7	2 17	17 3	0 41	16 12	0 11	18 57	10 19	12 6
9	2 17	17 1	0 41	16 11	0 11	18 56	10 19	12 7
11	2 16	17 0	0 41	16 10	0 11	18 56	10 19	12 7
13	2 16	16 58	0 41	16 8	0 10	18 55	10 19	12 8
15	2 16	16 57	0 41	16 7	0 10	18 54	10 19	12 9
17	2 15	16 55	0 41	16 5	0 10	18 53	10 19	12 9
19	2 15	16 54	0 41	16 4	0 10	18 52	10 19	12 10
21	2 14	16 52	0 41	16 2	0 10	18 51	10 19	12 10
23	2 14	16 51	0 41	16 1	0 10	18 50	10 19	12 11
25	2 13	16 50	0 41	15 59	0 10	18 49	10 19	12 11
27	2 13	16 49	0 41	15 57	0 10	18 48	10 19	12 12
29	2 12	16 48	0 41	15 55	0 10	18 48	10 19	12 12
31	2S12	16N47	0S41	15S53	0N10	18S47	10N19	12S12

Mutual Aspects

1 ☿☍♄.
2 ♂△♅. ☿P♆.
4 ☉☌♇.
5 ♀△♄. ☿P♃.
6 ☿⚹♆. ♀∠♇. ♂⚼♃.
7 ☿∠♂. ☿☍♃. ☿Q♅. ♂±♄. ☉P♀.
9 ☉⚹♅. ♃△♆.
10 ☿P♀. 11 ☉∠♆.
12 ☿☌♇. ♀△♃. ♀☌♆.
14 ☉P☿.
15 ☿⚹♅. ♂∇♄.
16 ☿∠♆. ♀P♃.
17 ☉∇♄. 18 ☉⚹♂.
19 ☉∠♀. ♀⚹♇. ♂±♃. ♀P♆.
20 ☉⊥♆. ☿∇♄. ♂∠♇.
22 ☉±♄. ☿⚹♂. ☿⊥♆.
23 ☿±♄.
24 ☉∇♃. ☉∠♅. ☿∇♃. ♀☌♅.
25 ☉☌☿. ☿∠♅. ♀P♄.
26 ☉⊻♆. ☿⊻♆.
27 ☿∠♀. ♂∇♃. ♀P♅.
28 ☿±♃.
29 ☉±♃. ☿⚼♄. ♀□♄.
30 ☿⊥♅. ♀Q♇.
31 ☉⚼♄. ☿⊻♇.

LAST QUARTER-Dec.18, 0h.41m. am. (26°♍24′)

JANUARY

D	☉ ° ′ ″	☽ ° ′ ″	☽Dec. ° ′	☿ ° ′	♀ ° ′	♂ ′
1	1 01 10	11 57 26	3 26	1 34	1 13	47
2	1 01 10	11 51 56	2 50	1 34	1 13	47
3	1 01 11	11 49 22	2 07	1 34	1 13	47
4	1 01 11	11 49 17	1 17	1 35	1 13	47
5	1 01 11	11 51 19	0 23	1 35	1 13	47
6	1 01 11	11 55 15	0 34	1 35	1 13	47
7	1 01 10	12 01 01	1 30	1 36	1 13	47
8	1 01 10	12 08 45	2 22	1 36	1 13	47
9	1 01 10	12 18 40	3 08	1 37	1 13	47
10	1 01 09	12 31 03	3 47	1 37	1 13	46
11	1 01 09	12 46 07	4 17	1 37	1 13	46
12	1 01 08	13 03 58	4 36	1 38	1 13	46
13	1 01 08	13 24 19	4 45	1 38	1 13	46
14	1 01 07	13 46 26	4 41	1 39	1 13	46
15	1 01 06	14 09 01	4 20	1 39	1 13	46
16	1 01 05	14 30 09	3 41	1 40	1 13	46
17	1 01 05	14 47 31	2 41	1 40	1 13	46
18	1 01 04	14 58 49	1 23	1 41	1 13	46
19	1 01 03	15 02 11	0 06	1 41	1 13	46
20	1 01 03	14 56 50	1 34	1 42	1 13	46
21	1 01 02	14 43 12	2 50	1 42	1 13	46
22	1 01 01	14 22 53	3 47	1 43	1 14	46
23	1 01 01	13 58 13	4 23	1 43	1 14	46
24	1 01 00	13 31 47	4 39	1 44	1 14	46
25	1 00 59	13 05 53	4 39	1 44	1 14	46
26	1 00 59	12 42 24	4 28	1 44	1 14	46
27	1 00 58	12 22 33	4 07	1 45	1 14	46
28	1 00 58	12 07 06	3 38	1 45	1 14	46
29	1 00 57	11 56 19	3 02	1 45	1 14	46
30	1 00 56	11 50 07	2 20	1 45	1 14	46
31	1 00 56	11 48 13	1 32	1 45	1 14	46

FEBRUARY

D	☉ ° ′ ″	☽ ° ′ ″	☽Dec. ° ′	☿ ° ′	♀ ° ′	♂ ′
1	1 00 55	11 50 09	0 39	1 44	1 14	46
2	1 00 54	11 55 22	0 18	1 43	1 14	46
3	1 00 53	12 03 13	1 15	1 42	1 14	46
4	1 00 52	12 13 07	2 10	1 41	1 14	46
5	1 00 51	12 24 29	2 59	1 40	1 14	46
6	1 00 49	12 36 51	3 41	1 38	1 14	46
7	1 00 48	12 49 54	4 13	1 35	1 14	46
8	1 00 47	13 03 23	4 34	1 32	1 14	46
9	1 00 45	13 17 12	4 44	1 28	1 14	46
10	1 00 44	13 31 15	4 40	1 24	1 14	46
11	1 00 42	13 45 24	4 21	1 19	1 14	46
12	1 00 40	13 59 17	3 47	1 14	1 14	46
13	1 00 39	14 12 18	2 55	1 07	1 14	46
14	1 00 37	14 23 30	1 48	1 00	1 14	46
15	1 00 35	14 31 41	0 27	0 52	1 14	46
16	1 00 34	14 35 35	0 58	0 44	1 14	46
17	1 00 32	14 34 03	2 18	0 35	1 14	46
18	1 00 30	14 26 30	3 24	0 25	1 14	46
19	1 00 29	14 13 03	4 11	0 16	1 14	45
20	1 00 27	13 54 39	4 38	0 05	1 14	45
21	1 00 26	13 32 54	4 47	0 05	1 14	45
22	1 00 24	13 09 43	4 41	0 15	1 14	45
23	1 00 23	12 47 07	4 22	0 24	1 14	45
24	1 00 21	12 26 47	3 54	0 33	1 14	45
25	1 00 20	12 10 05	3 18	0 41	1 14	45
26	1 00 18	11 57 52	2 36	0 49	1 14	45
27	1 00 17	11 50 40	1 48	0 54	1 14	45
28	1 00 16	11 48 36	0 56	0 59	1 14	45
29	1 00 14	11 51 30	0 00	1 02	1 14	45

MARCH

D	☉ ° ′ ″	☽ ° ′ ″	☽Dec. ° ′	☿ ° ′	♀ ° ′	♂ ′
1	1 00 12	11 58 58	0 58	1 03	1 14	45
2	1 00 11	12 10 18	1 54	1 03	1 14	45
3	1 00 09	12 24 37	2 46	1 01	1 14	45
4	1 00 07	12 40 48	3 33	0 58	1 14	45
5	1 00 06	12 57 38	4 10	0 54	1 14	45
6	1 00 04	13 13 56	4 36	0 49	1 14	45
7	1 00 02	13 28 38	4 49	0 44	1 14	45
8	1 00 00	13 41 00	4 48	0 38	1 14	45
9	0 59 58	13 50 44	4 31	0 31	1 14	45
10	0 59 55	13 57 57	3 58	0 25	1 14	45
11	0 59 53	14 03 03	3 08	0 18	1 14	45
12	0 59 51	14 06 31	2 03	0 12	1 14	45
13	0 59 49	14 08 42	0 47	0 05	1 14	45
14	0 59 47	14 09 35	0 34	0 01	1 14	44
15	0 59 44	14 08 52	1 52	0 07	1 14	44
16	0 59 42	14 05 53	3 00	0 12	1 14	44
17	0 59 40	13 59 56	3 53	0 18	1 14	44
18	0 59 38	13 50 28	4 29	0 23	1 14	44
19	0 59 36	13 37 25	4 46	0 28	1 14	44
20	0 59 34	13 21 14	4 48	0 32	1 14	44
21	0 59 32	13 03 00	4 35	0 36	1 14	44
22	0 59 30	12 44 07	4 11	0 40	1 14	44
23	0 59 28	12 26 07	3 37	0 44	1 14	44
24	0 59 26	12 10 31	2 55	0 48	1 14	44
25	0 59 24	11 58 32	2 07	0 51	1 14	44
26	0 59 23	11 51 05	1 14	0 54	1 14	44
27	0 59 21	11 48 48	0 18	0 57	1 14	44
28	0 59 19	11 51 57	0 39	1 00	1 14	44
29	0 59 17	12 00 29	1 35	1 03	1 14	44
30	0 59 15	12 14 00	2 29	1 05	1 14	44
31	0 59 14	12 31 43	3 18	1 08	1 14	44

APRIL

D	☉ ° ′ ″	☽ ° ′ ″	☽Dec. ° ′	☿ ° ′	♀ ° ′	♂ ′
1	0 59 12	12 52 23	4 00	1 10	1 14	44
2	0 59 10	13 14 20	4 33	1 12	1 14	44
3	0 59 08	13 35 38	4 53	1 14	1 14	44
4	0 59 06	13 54 14	4 59	1 16	1 14	44
5	0 59 04	14 08 28	4 48	1 18	1 14	43
6	0 59 02	14 17 19	4 18	1 20	1 14	43
7	0 59 00	14 20 41	3 29	1 22	1 14	43
8	0 58 57	14 19 21	2 23	1 24	1 14	43
9	0 58 55	14 14 33	1 06	1 26	1 14	43
10	0 58 53	14 07 42	0 16	1 27	1 14	43
11	0 58 50	13 59 56	1 35	1 29	1 14	43
12	0 58 48	13 51 52	2 44	1 31	1 14	43
13	0 58 46	13 43 36	3 38	1 32	1 14	43
14	0 58 43	13 34 51	4 17	1 34	1 14	43
15	0 58 41	13 25 09	4 40	1 36	1 14	43
16	0 58 39	13 14 03	4 47	1 37	1 14	43
17	0 58 37	13 01 27	4 41	1 39	1 14	43
18	0 58 35	12 47 35	4 22	1 41	1 14	43
19	0 58 33	12 33 06	3 53	1 42	1 14	43
20	0 58 32	12 18 59	3 13	1 44	1 14	43
21	0 58 30	12 06 21	2 27	1 46	1 14	43
22	0 58 28	11 56 20	1 34	1 47	1 14	43
23	0 58 27	11 49 57	0 38	1 49	1 14	43
24	0 58 25	11 48 05	0 20	1 51	1 14	43
25	0 58 23	11 51 20	1 16	1 52	1 14	42
26	0 58 22	12 00 02	2 10	1 54	1 14	42
27	0 58 20	12 14 12	3 00	1 56	1 14	42
28	0 58 19	12 33 23	3 44	1 57	1 14	42
29	0 58 17	12 56 38	4 21	1 59	1 14	42
30	0 58 15	13 22 21	4 48	2 01	1 14	42

MAY

D	☉	☽	☽Dec.	☿	♀	♂
	° ′ ″	° ′ ″	° ′	° ′	° ′	′
1	0 58 14	13 48 19	5 02	2 02	1 14	42
2	0 58 12	14 11 55	5 01	2 04	1 14	42
3	0 58 11	14 30 31	4 40	2 05	1 14	42
4	0 58 09	14 42 07	3 57	2 06	1 14	42
5	0 58 07	14 45 48	2 54	2 08	1 14	42
6	0 58 05	14 42 02	1 35	2 09	1 14	42
7	0 58 04	14 32 19	0 08	2 09	1 14	42
8	0 58 02	14 18 44	1 17	2 10	1 14	42
9	0 58 00	14 03 17	2 31	2 11	1 14	42
10	0 57 58	13 47 33	3 29	2 11	1 14	42
11	0 57 56	13 32 28	4 10	2 11	1 14	42
12	0 57 54	13 18 24	4 35	2 10	1 14	42
13	0 57 52	13 05 21	4 45	2 10	1 14	42
14	0 57 51	12 53 01	4 42	2 09	1 14	42
15	0 57 49	12 41 10	4 28	2 07	1 14	42
16	0 57 47	12 29 39	4 03	2 06	1 14	42
17	0 57 46	12 18 33	3 27	2 04	1 14	41
18	0 57 45	12 08 13	2 44	2 02	1 14	41
19	0 57 43	11 59 12	1 53	2 00	1 14	41
20	0 57 42	11 52 12	0 57	1 58	1 14	41
21	0 57 41	11 48 02	0 01	1 55	1 14	41
22	0 57 40	11 47 26	0 58	1 53	1 14	41
23	0 57 39	11 51 07	1 53	1 50	1 14	41
24	0 57 38	11 59 37	2 43	1 47	1 14	41
25	0 57 37	12 13 14	3 27	1 44	1 14	41
26	0 57 36	12 31 55	4 05	1 41	1 14	41
27	0 57 35	12 55 09	4 34	1 38	1 14	41
28	0 57 34	13 21 47	4 54	1 35	1 14	41
29	0 57 33	13 49 56	5 01	1 32	1 14	41
30	0 57 32	14 17 02	4 52	1 29	1 14	41
31	0 57 31	14 40 07	4 22	1 26	1 14	41

JUNE

D	☉	☽	☽Dec.	☿	♀	♂
	° ′ ″	° ′ ″	° ′	° ′	° ′	′
1	0 57 31	14 56 24	3 29	1 23	1 14	41
2	0 57 30	15 03 57	2 14	1 20	1 14	41
3	0 57 29	15 02 14	0 45	1 17	1 14	41
4	0 57 28	14 52 10	0 48	1 13	1 14	41
5	0 57 26	14 35 46	2 13	1 10	1 14	41
6	0 57 25	14 15 31	3 20	1 07	1 14	41
7	0 57 24	13 53 45	4 07	1 03	1 14	41
8	0 57 23	13 32 17	4 35	1 00	1 14	41
9	0 57 22	13 12 20	4 46	0 56	1 14	41
10	0 57 21	12 54 32	4 45	0 53	1 14	40
11	0 57 20	12 39 04	4 32	0 49	1 14	40
12	0 57 19	12 25 51	4 09	0 45	1 14	40
13	0 57 18	12 14 43	3 37	0 41	1 14	40
14	0 57 17	12 05 28	2 56	0 37	1 14	40
15	0 57 17	11 58 00	2 08	0 33	1 14	40
16	0 57 16	11 52 21	1 14	0 29	1 14	40
17	0 57 15	11 48 43	0 17	0 24	1 14	40
18	0 57 15	11 47 25	0 42	0 20	1 14	40
19	0 57 15	11 48 54	1 37	0 15	1 14	40
20	0 57 14	11 53 37	2 28	0 11	1 14	40
21	0 57 14	12 02 04	3 13	0 06	1 14	40
22	0 57 14	12 14 38	3 51	0 02	1 14	40
23	0 57 14	12 31 29	4 21	0 03	1 14	40
24	0 57 14	12 52 28	4 42	0 07	1 14	40
25	0 57 14	13 16 59	4 53	0 12	1 14	40
26	0 57 14	13 43 47	4 50	0 16	1 14	40
27	0 57 14	14 10 56	4 32	0 20	1 14	40
28	0 57 14	14 35 54	3 52	0 24	1 14	40
29	0 57 14	14 55 50	2 50	0 27	1 14	40
30	0 57 14	15 08 14	1 28	0 30	1 14	40

JULY

D	☉	☽	☽Dec.	☿	♀	♂
	° ′ ″	° ′ ″	° ′	° ′	° ′	′
1	0 57 14	15 11 24	0 07	0 33	1 14	40
2	0 57 14	15 05 06	1 41	0 35	1 14	40
3	0 57 13	14 50 24	3 01	0 36	1 14	40
4	0 57 13	14 29 28	3 59	0 37	1 14	40
5	0 57 13	14 04 54	4 36	0 37	1 14	40
6	0 57 13	13 39 14	4 52	0 37	1 14	40
7	0 57 12	13 14 31	4 52	0 36	1 14	40
8	0 57 12	12 52 09	4 40	0 34	1 14	40
9	0 57 12	12 33 00	4 18	0 32	1 14	39
10	0 57 12	12 17 25	3 46	0 29	1 14	39
11	0 57 12	12 05 23	3 07	0 26	1 14	39
12	0 57 12	11 56 44	2 21	0 22	1 14	39
13	0 57 12	11 51 09	1 29	0 18	1 14	39
14	0 57 13	11 48 19	0 32	0 13	1 14	39
15	0 57 13	11 47 58	0 26	0 08	1 14	39
16	0 57 13	11 49 57	1 23	0 03	1 14	39
17	0 57 14	11 54 11	2 16	0 02	1 14	39
18	0 57 14	12 00 46	3 03	0 08	1 14	39
19	0 57 15	12 09 50	3 42	0 14	1 14	39
20	0 57 16	12 21 35	4 12	0 19	1 14	39
21	0 57 16	12 36 12	4 34	0 25	1 14	39
22	0 57 17	12 53 44	4 45	0 31	1 14	39
23	0 57 18	13 13 59	4 45	0 37	1 14	39
24	0 57 19	13 36 23	4 32	0 42	1 14	39
25	0 57 20	13 59 48	4 02	0 48	1 14	39
26	0 57 21	14 22 37	3 12	0 54	1 14	39
27	0 57 22	14 42 42	2 02	0 59	1 14	39
28	0 57 23	14 57 39	0 35	1 05	1 14	39
29	0 57 24	15 05 22	0 59	1 10	1 14	39
30	0 57 25	15 04 24	2 28	1 15	1 14	39
31	0 57 25	14 54 35	3 41	1 20	1 14	39

AUGUST

D	☉	☽	☽Dec.	☿	♀	♂
	° ′ ″	° ′ ″	° ′	° ′	° ′	′
1	0 57 26	14 36 56	4 30	1 25	1 14	39
2	0 57 27	14 13 35	4 57	1 30	1 14	39
3	0 57 27	13 47 09	5 03	1 34	1 14	39
4	0 57 28	13 20 12	4 53	1 38	1 14	39
5	0 57 29	12 54 55	4 31	1 42	1 14	39
6	0 57 30	12 32 50	4 00	1 46	1 14	39
7	0 57 31	12 14 54	3 20	1 49	1 14	39
8	0 57 31	12 01 31	2 34	1 52	1 14	39
9	0 57 32	11 52 42	1 43	1 55	1 14	39
10	0 57 33	11 48 12	0 47	1 57	1 14	39
11	0 57 34	11 47 34	0 12	1 58	1 14	39
12	0 57 35	11 50 16	1 09	2 00	1 14	39
13	0 57 36	11 55 45	2 04	2 01	1 14	39
14	0 57 37	12 03 27	2 54	2 02	1 14	39
15	0 57 39	12 12 53	3 35	2 02	1 14	38
16	0 57 40	12 23 42	4 08	2 02	1 14	38
17	0 57 41	12 35 40	4 31	2 02	1 14	38
18	0 57 43	12 48 41	4 44	2 01	1 14	38
19	0 57 45	13 02 47	4 45	2 01	1 14	38
20	0 57 46	13 18 00	4 33	2 00	1 14	38
21	0 57 48	13 34 15	4 06	1 59	1 14	38
22	0 57 50	13 51 15	3 22	1 58	1 14	38
23	0 57 52	14 08 20	2 21	1 57	1 14	38
24	0 57 53	14 24 22	1 04	1 56	1 14	38
25	0 57 55	14 37 44	0 24	1 55	1 14	38
26	0 57 57	14 46 35	1 52	1 54	1 14	38
27	0 57 58	14 49 09	3 12	1 52	1 14	38
28	0 58 00	14 44 17	4 13	1 51	1 14	38
29	0 58 02	14 31 50	4 52	1 50	1 14	38
30	0 58 03	14 12 47	5 09	1 49	1 14	38
31	0 58 05	13 49 08	5 07	1 47	1 14	38

SEPTEMBER

D	☉ ° ′ ″	☽ ° ′ ″	☽Dec. ° ′	☿ ° ′	♀ ° ′	♂ ′
1	0 58 06	13 23 20	4 49	1 46	1 14	38
2	0 58 08	12 57 51	4 18	1 45	1 14	38
3	0 58 09	12 34 45	3 39	1 44	1 14	38
4	0 58 11	12 15 31	2 52	1 42	1 14	38
5	0 58 12	12 01 05	1 59	1 41	1 14	38
6	0 58 13	11 51 51	1 03	1 40	1 14	38
7	0 58 15	11 47 50	0 04	1 39	1 14	38
8	0 58 17	11 48 44	0 54	1 38	1 14	38
9	0 58 18	11 54 00	1 50	1 37	1 14	38
10	0 58 20	12 02 53	2 42	1 35	1 14	38
11	0 58 21	12 14 29	3 27	1 34	1 13	38
12	0 58 23	12 27 49	4 04	1 33	1 13	38
13	0 58 25	12 41 53	4 32	1 32	1 13	38
14	0 58 27	12 55 49	4 47	1 31	1 13	38
15	0 58 29	13 08 58	4 51	1 30	1 13	38
16	0 58 31	13 21 00	4 41	1 29	1 13	38
17	0 58 33	13 31 57	4 15	1 28	1 13	38
18	0 58 35	13 42 03	3 33	1 27	1 13	38
19	0 58 38	13 51 37	2 35	1 26	1 13	38
20	0 58 40	14 00 53	1 23	1 24	1 13	38
21	0 58 42	14 09 40	0 01	1 23	1 13	38
22	0 58 44	14 17 22	1 25	1 22	1 13	38
23	0 58 47	14 22 54	2 44	1 21	1 13	38
24	0 58 49	14 24 54	3 50	1 20	1 13	38
25	0 58 51	14 22 02	4 37	1 18	1 13	38
26	0 58 53	14 13 31	5 05	1 17	1 13	38
27	0 58 55	13 59 21	5 13	1 15	1 13	38
28	0 58 57	13 40 30	5 03	1 14	1 13	38
29	0 58 59	13 18 41	4 38	1 12	1 13	38
30	0 59 01	12 55 57	4 01	1 10	1 13	38

OCTOBER

D	☉ ° ′ ″	☽ ° ′ ″	☽Dec. ° ′	☿ ° ′	♀ ° ′	♂ ′
1	0 59 03	12 34 23	3 14	1 09	1 13	38
2	0 59 05	12 15 44	2 21	1 07	1 13	38
3	0 59 06	12 01 18	1 23	1 05	1 13	38
4	0 59 08	11 51 56	0 23	1 02	1 13	38
5	0 59 10	11 48 03	0 36	1 00	1 13	38
6	0 59 12	11 49 42	1 34	0 57	1 13	38
7	0 59 13	11 56 35	2 27	0 54	1 13	37
8	0 59 15	12 08 06	3 15	0 51	1 13	37
9	0 59 17	12 23 17	3 56	0 47	1 13	37
10	0 59 19	12 40 55	4 28	0 44	1 13	37
11	0 59 21	12 59 29	4 49	0 39	1 13	37
12	0 59 23	13 17 26	4 59	0 35	1 13	37
13	0 59 25	13 33 18	4 54	0 30	1 13	37
14	0 59 27	13 46 04	4 32	0 24	1 13	37
15	0 59 29	13 55 18	3 52	0 18	1 13	37
16	0 59 32	14 01 09	2 55	0 11	1 13	37
17	0 59 34	14 04 17	1 42	0 04	1 13	37
18	0 59 36	14 05 34	0 20	0 03	1 13	37
19	0 59 38	14 05 43	1 05	0 11	1 13	37
20	0 59 41	14 05 08	2 24	0 20	1 13	37
21	0 59 43	14 03 40	3 31	0 29	1 13	37
22	0 59 45	14 00 46	4 21	0 38	1 13	37
23	0 59 47	13 55 39	4 54	0 47	1 13	37
24	0 59 50	13 47 35	5 09	0 55	1 13	37
25	0 59 52	13 36 10	5 07	1 03	1 13	37
26	0 59 54	13 21 35	4 50	1 09	1 13	37
27	0 59 56	13 04 36	4 19	1 14	1 13	37
28	0 59 58	12 46 28	3 36	1 17	1 13	37
29	0 59 59	12 28 40	2 45	1 17	1 13	37
30	1 00 01	12 12 41	1 47	1 15	1 13	37
31	1 00 03	11 59 51	0 46	1 11	1 13	37

NOVEMBER

D	☉ ° ′ ″	☽ ° ′ ″	☽Dec. ° ′	☿ ° ′	♀ ° ′	♂ ′
1	1 00 04	11 51 12	0 16	1 05	1 12	37
2	1 00 06	11 47 32	1 15	0 57	1 12	37
3	1 00 08	11 49 15	2 09	0 47	1 12	37
4	1 00 09	11 56 29	2 58	0 36	1 12	37
5	1 00 11	12 09 01	3 41	0 24	1 12	37
6	1 00 12	12 26 13	4 16	0 13	1 12	37
7	1 00 14	12 47 02	4 43	0 01	1 12	37
8	1 00 15	13 09 54	4 59	0 10	1 12	37
9	1 00 17	13 32 53	5 03	0 20	1 12	37
10	1 00 18	13 53 50	4 50	0 30	1 12	37
11	1 00 20	14 10 48	4 17	0 38	1 12	37
12	1 00 22	14 22 21	3 24	0 46	1 12	37
13	1 00 24	14 27 58	2 12	0 53	1 12	37
14	1 00 26	14 27 59	0 46	0 59	1 12	37
15	1 00 27	14 23 30	0 44	1 04	1 12	37
16	1 00 29	14 15 53	2 08	1 09	1 12	37
17	1 00 31	14 06 26	3 18	1 13	1 12	37
18	1 00 33	13 56 05	4 11	1 16	1 12	37
19	1 00 35	13 45 21	4 45	1 19	1 12	37
20	1 00 36	13 34 19	5 03	1 21	1 12	37
21	1 00 38	13 22 52	5 05	1 24	1 12	37
22	1 00 40	13 10 45	4 53	1 25	1 11	37
23	1 00 41	12 57 55	4 28	1 27	1 11	37
24	1 00 43	12 44 29	3 52	1 28	1 11	37
25	1 00 44	12 30 52	3 04	1 29	1 11	36
26	1 00 46	12 17 42	2 09	1 30	1 11	36
27	1 00 47	12 05 49	1 08	1 30	1 11	36
28	1 00 48	11 56 06	0 06	1 31	1 11	36
29	1 00 49	11 49 27	0 55	1 31	1 11	36
30	1 00 50	11 46 38	1 51	1 32	1 11	36

DECEMBER

D	☉ ° ′ ″	☽ ° ′ ″	☽Dec. ° ′	☿ ° ′	♀ ° ′	♂ ′
1	1 00 51	11 48 18	2 42	1 32	1 11	36
2	1 00 52	11 54 54	3 25	1 32	1 11	36
3	1 00 52	12 06 40	4 01	1 33	1 11	36
4	1 00 53	12 23 27	4 30	1 33	1 11	36
5	1 00 54	12 44 44	4 50	1 33	1 10	36
6	1 00 55	13 09 25	4 59	1 33	1 10	36
7	1 00 56	13 35 52	4 56	1 33	1 10	36
8	1 00 56	14 01 51	4 35	1 33	1 10	36
9	1 00 57	14 24 51	3 54	1 33	1 10	36
10	1 00 58	14 42 25	2 50	1 33	1 10	36
11	1 00 59	14 52 42	1 25	1 33	1 10	36
12	1 01 00	14 54 55	0 10	1 33	1 10	36
13	1 01 01	14 49 26	1 44	1 34	1 09	36
14	1 01 02	14 37 38	3 05	1 34	1 09	36
15	1 01 03	14 21 25	4 05	1 34	1 09	36
16	1 01 03	14 02 47	4 44	1 34	1 09	36
17	1 01 04	13 43 26	5 03	1 34	1 09	36
18	1 01 05	13 24 37	5 07	1 34	1 09	36
19	1 01 06	13 07 08	4 56	1 34	1 09	36
20	1 01 07	12 51 18	4 33	1 35	1 08	36
21	1 01 08	12 37 13	4 00	1 35	1 08	36
22	1 01 08	12 24 49	3 17	1 35	1 08	36
23	1 01 09	12 14 00	2 25	1 35	1 08	35
24	1 01 09	12 04 45	1 27	1 35	1 08	35
25	1 01 10	11 57 08	0 25	1 36	1 08	35
26	1 01 10	11 51 23	0 37	1 36	1 07	35
27	1 01 10	11 47 51	1 35	1 36	1 07	35
28	1 01 10	11 46 59	2 27	1 36	1 07	35
29	1 01 10	11 49 17	3 12	1 37	1 07	35
30	1 01 10	11 55 16	3 49	1 37	1 07	35
31	1 01 10	12 05 21	4 17	1 37	1 06	35

d	h m			PHENOMENA, 2000
Jan.				
2	6 29	pm	☿	in Aphelion
3	5 00	am	⊕	in Perihelion
4	0 36	pm	☽	in Apogee
6	9 41	am	☽	Max. Dec.20°S.57′
13	3 38	pm	☽	on Equator
19	10 30	pm	☽	Max. Dec.20°N.57′
19	10 54	pm	☽	in Perigee
21	4 40	am	◗	Total Eclipse
26	5 57	am	☽	on Equator
Feb.				
1	1 26	am	☽	in Apogee
2	4 36	pm	☽	Max. Dec.20°S.56′
5	1 03	pm	●	Partial Eclipse
9	8 59	pm	☽	on Equator
11	2 21	am	☿	in ☊
15	1 00	am	☿	Gt. Elong.18°E.
15	6 07	pm	☿	in Perihelion
16	7 45	am	☽	Max. Dec.20°N.58′
16	5 24	pm	♀	in ☋
17	2 40	am	☽	in Perigee
22	3 25	pm	☽	on Equator
28	8 48	pm	☽	in Apogee
29	11 54	pm	☽	Max. Dec.21°S. 1′
Mar.				
8	2 47	am	☽	on Equator
14	2 01	pm	☽	Max. Dec.21°N. 6′
14	11 47	pm	☽	in Perigee
20	7 35	am	☉	Enters ♈,Equinox
20	9 28	am	☿	in ☋
21	0 36	am	☽	on Equator
22	1 13	pm	♀	in Aphelion
25	2 16	pm	♂	in ☊
27	5 19	pm	☽	in Apogee
28	7 44	am	☽	Max. Dec.21°S.13′
28	9 00	pm	☿	Gt. Elong.28°W.
30	5 44	pm	☿	in Aphelion
Apr.				
4	10 46	am	☽	on Equator
8	9 58	pm	☽	in Perigee
10	7 17	pm	☽	Max. Dec.21°N.21′
17	8 37	am	☽	on Equator
24	0 22	pm	☽	in Apogee
24	3 51	pm	☽	Max. Dec.21°S.29′
May				
1	8 45	pm	☽	on Equator
6	8 58	am	☽	in Perigee
8	2 05	am	☽	Max. Dec.21°N.35′
9	1 36	am	☿	in ☊
13	5 22	pm	☿	in Perihelion
14	3 22	pm	☽	on Equator
21	11 41	pm	☽	Max. Dec.21°S.40′
22	3 49	am	☽	in Apogee
29	7 06	am	☽	on Equator
Jun.				
3	1 12	pm	☽	in Perigee
4	11 23	am	☽	Max. Dec.21°N.43′
8	8 50	pm	♀	in ☊
9	1 00	pm	☿	Gt. Elong.24°E.
10	9 37	pm	☽	on Equator
16	8 44	am	☿	in ☋
18	6 48	am	☽	Max. Dec.21°S.45′
18	0 43	pm	☽	in Apogee
21	1 48	am	☉	Enters ♋,Solstice
25	4 06	pm	☽	on Equator
26	5 00	pm	☿	in Aphelion

d	h m			PHENOMENA, 2000
Jul.				
1	7 20	pm	●	Partial Eclipse
1	10 10	pm	☽	in Perigee
1	10 17	pm	☽	Max. Dec.21°N.45′
4	0 00	am	⊕	in Aphelion
8	4 25	am	☽	on Equator
12	8 47	pm	♀	in Perihelion
15	1 09	pm	☽	Max. Dec.21°S.44′
15	3 17	pm	☽	in Apogee
16	1 55	pm	◗	Total Eclipse
22	10 50	pm	☽	on Equator
27	9 00	am	☿	Gt. Elong.20°W.
29	8 57	am	☽	Max. Dec.21°N.45′
30	7 38	am	☽	in Perigee
31	2 25	am	●	Partial Eclipse
Aug.				
4	0 26	pm	☽	on Equator
5	0 52	am	☿	in ☊
9	4 38	pm	☿	in Perihelion
11	7 15	pm	☽	Max. Dec.21°S.45′
11	10 14	pm	☽	in Apogee
19	4 01	am	☽	on Equator
25	5 45	pm	☽	Max. Dec.21°N.49′
27	1 50	pm	☽	in Perigee
31	9 36	pm	☽	on Equator
Sep.				
8	1 48	am	☽	Max. Dec.21°S.53′
8	0 30	pm	☽	in Apogee
12	8 00	am	☿	in ☋
15	9 31	am	☽	on Equator
22	0 11	am	☽	Max. Dec.22°N. 0′
22	4 18	pm	☿	in Aphelion
22	5 28	pm	☉	Enters ♎,Equinox
24	8 13	am	☽	in Perigee
28	7 05	am	☽	on Equator
28	10 12	am	♀	in ☋
Oct.				
5	9 21	am	☽	Max. Dec.22°S. 7′
6	7 01	am	☽	in Apogee
6	10 00	am	☿	Gt. Elong.26°E.
12	5 00	pm	☽	on Equator
19	5 32	am	☽	Max. Dec.22°N.15′
19	10 01	pm	☽	in Perigee
25	3 44	pm	☽	on Equator
Nov.				
1	0 09	am	☿	in ☊
1	5 45	pm	☽	Max. Dec.22°S.23′
2	6 07	am	♀	in Aphelion
2	9 08	pm	♂	in Aphelion
3	3 32	am	☽	in Apogee
5	3 56	pm	☿	in Perihelion
9	2 42	am	☽	on Equator
14	11 10	pm	☽	in Perigee
15	6 00	am	☿	Gt. Elong.19°W.
15	0 09	pm	☽	Max. Dec.22°N.28′
21	10 49	pm	☽	on Equator
29	2 11	am	☽	Max. Dec.22°S.33′
30	11 44	pm	☽	in Apogee
Dec.				
6	1 07	pm	☽	on Equator
9	7 15	am	☿	in ☋
12	9 31	pm	☽	Max. Dec.22°N.34′
12	10 28	pm	☽	in Perigee
19	4 50	am	☽	on Equator
19	3 34	pm	☿	in Aphelion
21	1 37	pm	☉	Enters ♑,Solstice
25	5 22	pm	●	Partial Eclipse
26	9 38	am	☽	Max. Dec.22°S.35′
28	3 16	pm	☽	in Apogee

JANUARY

Day	Aspect	Time	
1 S	☽✱☉	5am 34	G
	♀±♃	5 35	
	☽☍♄	6 10	B
	☽⊻♇	8 16	g
	☉△♄	0pm 37	
	☽□♅	2 59	B
	☽P♇	3 14	D
	☽∠☿	8 12	b
	☽P♄	11 29	B
2 SU	♂Q♄	1am 3	
	☽P♂	2 18	B
	☿⊻♆	8 33	
	♀Q♅	1pm 45	
	☽∠☉	2 27	b
	☉⊻♇	2 27	
	☽□♂	7 28	B
	♀✱♆	9 16	
3 M	☽✱♆	4am 7	G
	☽☌♀	4 52	G
	☽⊻☿	7 1	g
	☽P♅	10 15	B
	♂P♄	0pm 27	
	☽⚻♃	6 30	b
	☽☌♇	8 54	D
	☽⊻☉	11 41	g
4 TU	☽✱♅	3am 50	G
	♀P♆	9 1	
	☽∠♆	10 38	b
	☽P♆	10 38	D
	☽P♀	10 55	G
5 W	☽⚻♄	0 56	b
	☽△♃	1 6	G
	☽∠♅	10 25	b
	☽✱♂	0pm 36	G
	☽⊻♆	5 11	g
6 TH	☽⊻♀	0am 41	g
	☿⊥♅	1 26	
	☉⊻♅	2 4	
	☽☌☿	5 13	G
	☽△♄	7 18	G
	☽⊻♇	9 56	g
	☽⊻♅	4pm 54	g
	☽☌☉	6 14	D
	☿△♄	8 42	
	☽∠♂	9 3	b
7 F	☽∠♀	10am 22	b
	☽□♃	2pm 0	B
	☽∠♇	4 12	b
	♂P♇	4 39	
	☿⊻♇	5 6	
	☽P♀	7 56	G
8 S	☽⊻♂	5am 13	g
	☽☌♆	5 44	D
	☽P♆	8 34	D
	♂⊻♆	1pm 46	
	☉⊥♇	4 33	
	♀∇♄	4 51	
	☽□♄	7 22	B
	☽✱♀	7 39	G
	☽✱♇	10 10	G
	♀⚻♃	11 48	
9 SU	☽⊻☿	2am 28	g
	☽☌♅	5 4	B
	☽P♅	8 39	B
	☽⊻☉	11 34	g
	♀☌♇	9pm 14	
	☿⊻♅	10 50	

Day	Aspect	Time	
10 M	☽✱♃	1am 41	G
	☽∠☿	0pm 12	b
	☽⊻♆	4 48	g
	☽P♄	5 6	B
	☽∠☉	7 22	b
	☽☌♂	8 2	B
11 TU	☽P♇	0am 54	D
	☽✱♄	5 47	G
	☽∠♃	6 46	b
	☽P♂	7 31	B
	☽□♇	8 38	B
	☽□♀	0pm 19	B
	☿⊥♇	0 39	
	☽⊻♅	3 23	g
	☽P♃	4 20	G
	☽✱☿	9 5	G
	☽∠♆	9 29	b
12 W	☽✱☉	2am 23	G
	☉∠♂	3 8	
	♄ Stat	4 59	
	☽∠♄	10 4	b
	☽⊻♃	11 12	g
	☽∠♅	7pm 33	b
	♀✱♅	9 32	
13 TH	☽✱♆	1am 28	G
	☽⊻♂	7 54	g
	☽⊻♄	1pm 38	g
	♀±♄	2 54	
	☽△♇	4 28	G
	☽✱♅	10 57	G
14 F	☽△♀	1am 23	G
	☽□☿	11 41	B
	☽∠♂	0pm 27	b
	☽□☉	1 34	B
	☽☌♃	5 47	G
	☽⚻♇	7 12	b
	☉P♀	9 50	
	☿∠♂	11 4	
15 S	☽⚻♀	6am 21	b
	☽□♆	7 3	B
	☽P♃	1pm 26	G
	☽P♂	1 52	B
	♀∠♆	2 31	
	☽✱♂	4 4	G
	☽☌♄	6 23	B
	☉⊥♀	6 36	
	♂P♃	7 27	
16 SU	☉☌☿	1am 19	
	☽P♇	2 41	D
	☽□♅	3 22	B
	☿⊥♀	4 27	
	☽P♄	9 42	B
	☿□♃	4pm 26	
	♂⊥♆	5 4	
	☽△☉	8 51	G
	☽⊻♃	9 14	g
	☽△☿	9 50	G
17 M	☿∠♇	2am 47	
	☉□♃	2 51	
	☽△♆	9 38	G
	♂✱♄	10 28	
	☽P♅	0pm 18	B
	☉∠♇	7 20	
	☽⊻♄	8 19	g
	☽□♂	8 51	B
	☽∠♃	10 0	b
	☽☍♇	11 2	B
	☽⚻☉	11 18	b
18	☽⚻☿	1am 33	b

Day	Aspect	Time	
TU	☽△♅	5 2	G
	☽P♆	8 16	D
	☽⚻♆	10 4	b
	☽☍♀	3pm 55	B
	☽∠♄	8 32	b
	♂∠♃	9 53	
	☽✱♃	10 21	G
19 W	☽P☉	3am 51	G
	☽⚻♅	5 14	b
	♂□♇	4pm 6	
	☿P♀	4 23	
	☽✱♄	8 32	G
	☽△♂	11 38	G
20 TH	☽□♃	10 36	B
	☽⚻♇	11 17	b
	☽P☉	11 57	G
21 F	☽⚻♂	0am 55	b
	♀⚻♄	1 3	
	☽•☉	4 40	B
	☿☌♆	6 5	
	☽☍♆	10 18	B
	☽☍☿	10 50	B
	☽P♆	0pm 58	D
	☽□♄	8 45	B
	☽⚻♀	10 30	b
	☽△♇	11 34	G
22 S	♀△♃	4am 58	
	☽☍♅	5 48	B
	☽P♅	9 13	B
	☽△♃	11pm 53	G
23 SU	☽△♀	1am 30	G
	♀⊥♆	4 42	
	☽P♄	10 47	B
	☽P♇	6pm 11	D
	☽△♄	10 48	G
24 M	☽⚻♃	1am 29	b
	☽□♇	1 48	B
	☽P♃	5 39	G
	☽☍♂	7 47	B
	☽⚻☉	1pm 24	b
	☽⚻♆	1 45	b
	☉☌♆	6 8	
	☿⊥♂	7 7	
	♂⊻♅	9 42	
	☽P♂	10 8	B
25 TU	☽⚻☿	0am 58	b
	☽⚻♄	1 1	b
	☿□♄	1 18	
	☽□♀	10 30	B
	☽⚻♅	11 9	b
	☽△♆	4pm 33	G
	☉P♆	5 6	
	♀∠♅	5 58	
	☽△☉	6 20	G
26 W	☿✱♇	1am 55	
	♃⚻♇	3 19	
	☿P♆	4 18	
	☽✱♇	7 27	G
	☽△☿	8 17	G
	☉P☿	1pm 39	
	☽△♅	2 48	G
27 TH	☽P♂	10am 46	B
	☽∠♇	11 45	b
	☽☍♃	11 59	B
	☿Q♃	10pm 14	
	☽⚻♂	11 42	b
28 F	☽✱♀	0am 36	G
	☽□♆	1 6	B
	♀⊻♆	5 48	

Day	Aspect	Time	
	☽□☉	7 57	B
	☿☌♅	9 55	
	☽P♃	10 43	G
	☽☍♄	1pm 31	B
	☽⊻♇	4 58	g
	☽P♇	10 45	D
	♂∠♆	11 27	
29 S	☽□♅	0am 56	B
	☽□☿	3 23	B
	☽△♂	7 11	G
	☽P♄	7 58	B
	☽∠♀	9 27	b
30 SU	☿P♅	9 55	
	☽P☿	0pm 36	G
	☽✱♆	0 55	G
	☽P♅	1 12	B
	☽⊻♀	7 6	g
	☿⊻♂	11 18	
	☽P☉	11 39	G
31 M	☽✱☉	1am 28	G
	☉□♄	5 15	
	☽☌♇	5 17	D
	☽⚻♃	6 18	b
	☽✱♅	1pm 39	G
	☽P♆	2 40	D
	☽∠♆	7 28	b
	☽□♂	11 58	B

FEBRUARY

Day	Aspect	Time	
1 TU	☽✱☿	2am 22	G
	☽⚻♄	8 21	b
	☽∠☉	10 49	b
	☽△♃	1pm 8	G
	♂⊥♃	3 16	
	☽∠♅	8 17	b
	☉✱♇	11 0	
2 W	☿Q♇	1am 30	
	☽⊻♆	2 2	g
	♂⊥♅	8 3	
	♀⊥♅	10 25	
	♀△♄	1pm 7	
	☽∠☿	2 2	b
	♀Q♂	2 2	
	☽△♄	2 52	G
	☽☌♀	3 4	G
	☽⊻♇	6 18	g
	☽⊻☉	8 3	g
3 TH	☽⊻♅	2am 46	g
	☿∠♀	0pm 31	
	☽✱♂	4 48	G
	♀⊻♇	10 45	
4 F	☽∠♇	0am 25	b
	☽⊻☿	1 10	g
	☽□♃	2 16	B
	☉P♅	2 17	
	☿✱♃	9 31	
	☽☌♆	2pm 22	D
	☿Q♄	3 2	
	☽P♆	6 3	D
	☿P♄	6 10	
5 S	☽∠♂	0am 32	b
	☽□♄	2 52	B
	☽✱♇	6 6	G
	☽⊻♀	9 32	g
	☽•●	1pm 3	D
	☽☌♅	2 28	B
	☽P♅	6 58	B
	☽P☉	11 23	G
6	☉Q♃	3am 54	

Day	Aspect	Time	
SU	☉☌♅	7 14	
	☽⊻♂	7 38	g
	☽✱♃	1pm 34	G
	♂∠♄	3 59	
	☽∠♀	5 42	b
	☿P♇	6 29	
	☽☌☿	8 52	G
	☽P♄	8 55	B
7 M	☽⊻♆	0am 43	g
	☽P♇	6 42	D
	☽P☿	9 35	G
	☽✱♄	0pm 47	G
	♀⊻♅	1 10	
	☽P♃	2 58	G
	☽□♇	3 47	B
	♃Q♅	4 22	
	☽∠♃	6 22	b
8 TU	☽⊻♅	0am 0	g
	☽✱♀	1 5	G
	☽⊻☉	3 17	g
	☿⊻♆	3 48	
	☽∠♆	5 3	b
	☿P♃	0pm 38	
	☽∠♄	4 54	b
	☽☌♂	7 46	B
	♀⊥♇	9 42	
	☽⊻♃	10 34	g
9 W	☽∠♅	3am 54	b
	☽✱♆	8 48	G
	☽∠☉	9 19	b
	☽⊻☿	0pm 33	g
	☽P♂	2 36	B
	☽⊻♄	8 26	g
	☽△♇	11 11	G
10 TH	☽P♂	2am 32	B
	☽✱♅	7 14	G
	☽□♀	1pm 37	B
	☽✱☉	2 39	G
	☽∠☿	6 54	b
11 F	☽⚻♇	2am 4	b
	☽⊻♂	5 14	g
	☽☌♃	5 19	G
	♂⊻♃	6 59	
	☽P☿	1pm 17	G
	☽□♆	2 40	B
12 S	☽✱☿	0am 18	G
	☽☌♄	1 56	B
	☽P♃	2 29	G
	☽P♇	8 40	D
	☽∠♂	9 2	b
	☿⊥♆	10 0	
	☽□♅	0pm 20	B
	☽P♄	6 23	B
	☿✱♄	6 28	
	☽P☉	10 13	G
	☉⊻♀	11 6	
	☽□☉	11 21	B
	☽△♀	11 22	G
13 SU	☽⊻♃	9am 58	g
	☽✱♂	0pm 17	G
	☽P♅	3 47	B
	☽△♆	6 33	G
	☿□♇	11 23	
14 M	☉Q♇	1am 3	
	☽⚻♀	3 19	b
	☽⊻♄	5 30	g
	☽☍♇	7 47	B
	☽□☿	8 28	B
	☽∠♃	11 37	b

	☽ P ♆	1pm 25	D
	☽ △ ♅	3 34	G
	☉ P ♄	3 47	
	☽ ⚼ ♆	7 51	b
15	♂ ∠ ♅	1am 45	
TU	☽ △ ☉	5 51	G
	☽ ∠ ♄	6 41	b
	☽ ✱ ♃	0pm 55	G
	☽ ⚼ ♅	4 38	b
	☽ □ ♂	5 24	B
	☽ P ♀	5 33	G
16	♀ ∠ ♇	7am 29	
W	☽ ✱ ♄	7 37	G
	☽ ⚼ ☉	8 32	b
	☽ △ ☿	1pm 46	G
	☿ ∠ ♃	6 46	
17	☽ P ♀	4am 32	G
TH	☽ ⚼ ♇	10 24	b
	☽ ☍ ♀	0pm 51	B
	☉ ⊥ ♂	2 28	
	☽ □ ♃	2 56	B
	☽ ⚼ ☿	3 42	b
	☽ △ ♂	9 31	G
	☽ ☍ ♆	10 21	B
18	☽ P ♆	1am 53	D
F	☽ □ ♄	9 12	B
	☽ △ ♇	11 7	G
	♂ ✱ ♆	2pm 7	
	♀ □ ♃	5 4	
	☽ ☍ ♅	7 5	B
	☉ Q ♄	10 39	
	☽ P ♅	11 19	B
	☽ ⚼ ♂	11 40	b
19	♂ ⊥ ♄	10am 16	
S	☉ P ♇	2pm 1	
	☽ ☍ ☉	4 27	B
	☽ △ ♃	5 15	G
	☿ ∠ ♀	5 48	
	☽ P ♄	6 28	B
20	☽ P ♇	4am 59	D
SU	☉ ✱ ♃	5 57	
	☽ P ☉	6 18	G
	☽ P ♃	8 7	G
	☽ △ ♄	11 39	G
	☽ □ ♇	1pm 26	B
	☽ ⚼ ♃	7 0	b
	☽ ☍ ☿	8 59	B
	☽ ⚼ ♀	11 11	b
21	☉ P ♃	1am 23	
M	☽ ⚼ ♆	2 1	b
	☿ Stat	0pm 46	
	☽ ⚼ ♄	1 40	b
	☿ P ♂	8 42	
22	☽ ⚼ ♅	0am 8	b
TU	☽ P ♂	2 3	B
	☽ P ☿	2 37	G
	☽ △ ♀	4 2	G
	☽ △ ♆	4 24	G
	♀ ☌ ♆	8 6	
	☽ ☍ ♂	9 19	B
	☽ ✱ ♇	6pm 9	G
23	☽ △ ♅	3am 15	G
W	☽ P ☿	3 43	G
	☽ ⚼ ☉	5 19	b
	☽ P ♂	6 56	B
	☽ ∠ ♇	9pm 48	b
24	☿ ∠ ♃	4am 19	
TH	☽ ⚼ ☿	4 57	b
	☽ ☍ ♃	4 59	B
	♀ P ♆	5 3	
	☽ △ ☉	11 45	G
	☽ □ ♆	11 46	B
	☉ ⊻ ♆	0pm 6	
	☽ □ ♀	5 15	B
	☽ P ☉	6 40	G
25	☽ ☍ ♄	0am 52	B
F	☽ ⊻ ♇	2 22	g
	☽ P ♃	4 38	G
	☽ P ♇	6 10	D
	☽ △ ☿	8 33	G
	☽ □ ♅	0pm 18	B
	☽ P ♄	7 32	B
	☿ ⊥ ♀	11 7	
26	☽ ⚼ ♂	3am 38	b
S	☽ P ♅	4pm 6	B
	☽ ✱ ♆	10 41	G
27	☽ □ ☉	3am 53	B
SU	☽ P ♀	8 38	G
	☽ ✱ ♀	11 6	G
	☽ △ ♂	11 39	G
	☽ ☌ ♇	1pm 54	D
	☽ □ ☿	4 43	B
	☽ P ♆	6 17	D
	☽ ⚼ ♃	10 56	b
	♀ ✱ ♂	11 29	
28	☽ ✱ ♅	0am 28	G
M	♀ □ ♄	2 57	
	☽ ∠ ♆	5 4	b
	♂ ⊻ ♄	5 25	
	♀ ✱ ♇	2pm 6	
	♃ P ♇	2 49	
	☽ ⚼ ♄	7 17	b
	☿ ⊻ ♀	8 21	
	☽ ∠ ♀	9 4	b
	♂ △ ♇	11 35	
29	☿ ⊻ ♂	2am 11	
TU	☿ □ ♇	4 7	
	☽ △ ♃	5 53	G
	☽ ∠ ♅	7 5	b
	☽ ⊻ ♆	11 37	g
	☿ ✱ ♄	3pm 6	
	☽ ✱ ☉	10 21	G
MARCH			
1	☽ ✱ ☿	1am 1	G
W	☽ △ ♄	1 56	G
	☽ ⊻ ♇	2 48	g
	☽ □ ♂	4 38	B
	☽ ⊻ ♀	7 2	g
	☽ ⊻ ♅	1pm 35	g
	☿ ⊥ ♆	2 11	
	☉ ☌ ☿	3 10	
	☉ ⊥ ♆	4 17	
2	☽ ∠ ☿	4am 46	b
TH	☽ ∠ ☉	7 18	b
	☽ ∠ ♇	8 58	b
	☽ □ ♃	7pm 13	B
	☉ ✱ ♄	8 19	
	☽ ☌ ♆	11 59	D
3	☉ □ ♇	3am 25	
F	☽ P ♆	4 57	D
	☽ ⊻ ☿	8 6	g
	☿ ⊥ ♂	10 50	
	☽ □ ♄	2pm 6	B
	☽ ✱ ♇	2 34	G
	☽ ⊻ ☉	3 32	g
	☽ ✱ ♂	8 8	G
4	♀ ☌ ♅	0am 39	
S	☽ ☌ ♅	1 9	B
	☽ • ♀	1 12	G
	♀ P ♅	5 10	
	☽ P ♅	6 36	B
	☽ P ♀	6 47	G
	☉ P ♂	2pm 16	
	☽ P ♄	11 48	B
5	☽ ∠ ♂	2am 41	b
SU	☽ ✱ ♃	6 6	G
	☽ ⊻ ♆	9 53	g
	☽ P ♃	11 45	G
	☽ ☌ ☿	1pm 19	G
	☽ P ♇	2 22	D
	☉ P ☿	3 12	
	☽ ✱ ♄	11 32	G
	☽ □ ♇	11 37	B
6	☽ ☌ ☉	5am 17	D
M	♂ Q ♆	5 57	
	☽ ⊻ ♂	8 21	g
	☽ ⊻ ♅	9 53	g
	☽ ∠ ♃	10 24	b
	♄ ⊽ ♇	11 56	
	☽ ∠ ♆	1pm 44	b
	☽ ⊻ ♀	3 35	g
	☽ P ♂	4 8	B
	☽ P ☿	6 37	G
	♀ Q ♃	8 32	
7	☽ P ☉	0am 20	G
TU	☽ ∠ ♄	3 10	b
	♂ ✱ ♅	1pm 6	
	☽ ∠ ♅	1 12	b
	☽ ⊻ ♃	2 1	g
	☿ ⊻ ♆	3 1	
	☽ ⊻ ☿	4 49	g
	☽ ✱ ♆	4 55	G
	☽ ∠ ♀	9 25	b
8	☽ △ ♇	5am 57	G
W	☽ ⊻ ♄	6 13	g
	☽ ⊻ ☉	3pm 39	g
	☽ ✱ ♅	3 58	G
	☽ ☌ ♂	5 25	B
	☽ ∠ ☿	6 6	b
	☉ ⊻ ♅	8 20	
9	☿ ∠ ♂	0am 26	
TH	☽ P ☉	0 50	G
	☽ ✱ ♀	2 34	G
	☽ ⚼ ♇	8 20	b
	♀ Q ♇	8 21	
	☿ ✱ ♃	11 5	
	☉ ∠ ♃	3pm 31	
	☽ P ☿	5 3	G
	☽ P ♂	5 16	B
	☽ ✱ ☿	7 13	G
	☽ ☌ ♃	7 41	G
	☽ ∠ ☉	7 56	b
	☽ □ ♆	9 49	B
10	☿ P ♂	1am 35	
F	♀ P ♄	4 23	
	☽ ☌ ♄	10 58	B
	☽ P ♇	0pm 46	D
	☽ P ♃	5 24	G
	☽ □ ♅	8 20	B
	☉ ∠ ♆	10 48	
	☽ ✱ ☉	11 50	G
11	☽ ⊻ ♂	0am 29	g
S	☽ P ♀	1 8	G
	☽ P ♄	3 23	B
	☽ □ ♀	11 31	B
	☽ P ♅	4pm 49	B
	☽ □ ☿	9 18	B
12	☽ ⊻ ♃	0am 3	g
SU	☽ △ ♆	1 31	G
	☽ ∠ ♂	3 37	b
	☉ ⊻ ♂	9 37	
	☽ ☍ ♇	1pm 47	B
	☽ ⊻ ♄	2 43	g
	☽ P ♆	3 19	D
	☽ △ ♅	11 48	G
13	☽ ∠ ♃	1am 59	b
M	☽ ⚼ ♆	3 7	b
	☽ ✱ ♂	6 34	G
	☽ □ ☉	6 59	B
	☽ ∠ ♄	4pm 24	b
	♀ P ♃	6 14	
	☽ △ ♀	7 33	G
	☽ △ ☿	11 38	G
14	☽ ⚼ ♅	1am 22	b
TU	☽ ✱ ♃	3 51	G
	☽ ✱ ♄	6pm 1	G
	♀ Q ♄	7 54	
	☿ Stat	8 39	
	☽ ⚼ ♀	11 25	b
15	☽ ⚼ ☿	1am 0	b
W	☉ ⊥ ♅	4 22	
	♇ Stat	11 55	
	☽ □ ♂	0pm 16	B
	☽ △ ☉	1 43	G
	☽ ⚼ ♇	6 10	b
	☿ ☌ ♀	6 23	
16	♀ P ♇	7am 20	
TH	☽ □ ♃	7 28	B
	☽ ☍ ♆	7 36	B
	☿ P ♂	9 17	
	☽ P ♆	0pm 45	D
	☽ ⚼ ☉	5 6	b
	♃ □ ♆	5 15	
	☽ △ ♇	7 37	G
	☽ □ ♄	9 16	B
17	☽ ☍ ♅	6am 0	B
F	☽ P ♅	11 25	B
	☽ △ ♂	6pm 7	G
	☽ P ♄	10 45	B
18	♀ ⊻ ♆	5am 43	
S	☽ ☍ ☿	6 33	B
	☽ P ♃	6 53	G
	☽ ☍ ♀	11 24	B
	☽ △ ♃	11 28	G
	♀ ✱ ♃	0pm 20	
	☽ P ♇	2 51	D
	♀ P ♂	5 17	
	☽ P ♂	8 17	B
	☽ P ♀	8 49	G
	☽ ⚼ ♂	9 21	b
	☽ P ☿	10 23	G
	☽ □ ♇	11 2	B
19	☽ △ ♄	1am 6	G
SU	☉ ∠ ♄	10 33	
	☿ P ♀	11 4	
	☽ ⚼ ♆	0pm 58	b
	☽ ⚼ ♃	1 54	b
20	☽ ⚼ ♄	3am 32	b
M	☽ ☍ ☉	4 44	B
	♂ ⚼ ♇	4 47	
	☽ ⚼ ♅	0pm 19	b
	☽ △ ♆	3 29	G
	☽ P ☉	11 19	G
21	☉ ⊥ ♃	2am 7	
TU	☽ P ☉	2 8	G
	☽ ✱ ♇	3 58	G
	☽ △ ♅	3pm 25	G
	♃ ± ♇	3 52	
	☽ ⚼ ☿	4 42	b
22	☽ ⚼ ♀	3am 18	b
W	☽ ∠ ♇	7 22	b
	♂ P ♇	9 13	
	☽ ☍ ♂	10 26	B
	☽ P ♀	8pm 42	G
	☽ △ ☿	9 54	G
	☽ □ ♆	10 30	B
23	☽ ☍ ♃	0am 45	B
TH	♀ ⊥ ♆	4 44	
	☽ P ☿	5 3	G
	☿ ⊻ ♆	9 27	
	☽ △ ♀	10 26	G
	☽ ⊻ ♇	11 33	g
	☽ P ♇	1pm 23	D
	☽ ☍ ♄	2 47	B
	☽ P ♂	3 32	B
	♀ □ ♇	9 52	
	☽ ⚼ ☉	10 30	b
	☽ □ ♅	11 53	B
24	☽ P ♃	1am 11	G
F	☽ P ♄	9 6	B
	☉ ∠ ♅	4pm 42	
	☽ P ♅	7 38	B
	♂ Q ♅	9 40	
25	☽ △ ☉	6am 24	G
S	☽ ✱ ♆	8 40	G
	♀ ✱ ♄	10 31	
	☽ □ ☿	11 45	B
	☿ ✱ ♃	4pm 33	
	☽ P ♆	10 1	D
	☽ ☌ ♇	10 16	D
26	☽ □ ♀	3am 52	B
SU	☽ ⚼ ♂	7 19	b
	☉ ✱ ♆	10 38	
	☽ ✱ ♅	11 26	G
	☽ ∠ ♆	2pm 47	b
	☽ ⚼ ♃	6 41	b
27	☽ ⚼ ♄	8am 48	b
M	☽ △ ♂	3pm 41	G
	☽ ∠ ♅	5 57	b
	☽ ⊻ ♆	9 15	g
28	☽ □ ☉	0am 21	B
TU	☽ △ ♃	1 42	G
	☽ ✱ ☿	5 16	G
	☽ ⊻ ♇	10 57	g
	☽ △ ♄	3pm 34	G
	☉ ⊻ ♃	8 49	
	☽ ✱ ♀	11 43	G
29	☽ ⊻ ♅	0am 30	g
W	♀ ⊻ ♅	7 24	
	♀ ∠ ♂	8 56	
	☽ ∠ ☿	2pm 24	b
	☉ ⊥ ♄	3 15	
	☽ ∠ ♇	5 15	b
30	☿ ⊥ ♆	7am 16	
TH	☽ □ ♂	8 13	B
	☽ ∠ ♀	9 18	b
	☽ ☌ ♆	9 51	D
	♀ ∠ ♆	2pm 51	
	☽ □ ♃	3 13	B
	☽ P ♆	5 9	D
	☽ ✱ ☉	6 7	G
	☿ □ ♇	10 25	
	☽ ✱ ♇	11 2	G
	☽ ⊻ ☿	11 6	g

Day	Aspect	Time	
31	☽□♄	4am 5	B
F	♂P♃	11 51	
	♂□♆	0pm 11	
	☽☌♅	0 19	B
	☉P♀	0 35	
	☽⚺♀	5 58	g
	☽P♅	7 20	B
APRIL			
1	☽∠☉	1am 48	b
S	☽P♄	3 1	B
	☽P♂	7 36	B
	☽P♃	8 33	G
	♂±♇	9 14	
	☽⚺♆	7pm 55	g
	☽⚹♂	9 46	G
2	☽P♇	0am 19	D
SU	☽⚹♃	1 54	G
	☉△♇	6 18	
	♀∠♃	7 3	
	☽□♇	8 12	B
	☽⚺☉	8 21	g
	☿⚹♄	10 19	
	☽⚹♄	1pm 29	G
	☽☌☿	1 46	G
	☽⚺♅	8 53	g
	☽P☿	10 5	G
	☽∠♆	11 36	b
3	☽∠♂	2am 58	b
M	☽∠♃	5 50	b
	☽☌♀	7 44	G
	☽P☉	7 46	G
	♀⊥♅	8 2	
	☽∠♄	4pm 49	b
	☽P♀	9 15	G
	☽∠♅	11 50	b
4	☽⚹♆	2am 26	G
TU	☽⚺♂	7 9	g
	☽⚺♃	8 54	g
	♂P♄	0pm 6	
	☽△♇	1 53	G
	☽☌☉	6 12	D
	☽⚺♄	7 21	g
	☽P♀	9 45	G
5	☽⚺☿	0am 22	g
W	☽⚹♅	2 4	G
	☉P☿	11 7	
	☉⚺♄	0pm 30	
	☽⚼♇	3 42	b
	☽P☿	4 36	G
	☽⚺♀	5 16	g
	☽P☉	5 36	G
	☿⚺♅	7 13	
6	☽∠☿	4am 34	b
TH	☽□♆	6 9	B
	♂☌♃	6 41	
	☽☌♃	1pm 9	G
	☽☌♂	1 23	B
	☽P♇	6 6	D
	☽∠♀	9 2	b
	☿∠♆	9 44	
	☽☌♄	10 50	B
7	☽⚺☉	1am 4	g
F	☽□♅	5 4	B
	☽⚹☿	8 24	G
	☽P♃	10 58	G
	☽P♄	2pm 35	B
	☽P♂	6 51	B
	☽P♅	7 17	B

Day	Aspect	Time	
	♀∠♄	7 51	
	☉Q♆	8 25	
8	☽⚹♀	0am 33	G
S	♂P♅	1 21	
	☽∠☉	4 2	b
	☽△♆	8 33	G
	☽⚺♃	4pm 15	g
	☽P♆	5 42	D
	☽⚺♂	6 20	g
	☽☍♇	7 17	B
9	☽⚺♄	1am 29	g
SU	☽⚹☉	7 0	G
	☽△♅	7 25	G
	☽⚼♆	9 42	b
	♂⊽♇	0pm 52	
	☉⚹♅	1 9	
	☽□☿	4 1	B
	☽∠♃	5 49	b
	☽∠♂	8 51	b
10	☽∠♄	2am 55	b
M	☿⊥♅	7 22	
	☽□♀	7 38	B
	☽⚼♅	8 43	b
	☿∠♃	1pm 7	
	☽⚹♃	7 34	G
	♀∠♅	8 29	
	☽⚹♂	11 33	G
11	☽⚹♄	4am 32	G
TU	♀⊥♃	6 0	
	☽□☉	1pm 30	B
	♀⚹♆	10 45	
	☽⚼♇	11 19	b
12	☽△☿	0am 45	G
W	☽☍♆	2pm 15	B
	☽△♀	3 45	G
	☽P♆	9 43	D
	☽□♃	11 49	B
13	☽△♇	1am 8	G
TH	☽⚼☿	5 45	b
	☽□♂	5 50	B
	☿∠♂	7 16	
	☽□♄	8 33	B
	☽P♂	0pm 1	B
	☽☍♅	2 3	B
	☿P♀	3 26	
	☽⚼♀	8 20	b
	☽P♅	9 9	B
	☽△☉	9 14	G
14	☽P♄	0am 5	B
F	☽P♃	2 16	G
	☿∠♄	9 1	
	☽P♇	11pm 9	D
15	☽⚼☉	1am 37	b
S	☽△♃	5 15	G
	☽□♇	5 36	B
	☽P☉	6 4	G
	☽△♂	1pm 26	G
	☽△♄	1 45	G
	♂☌♄	8 28	
	☽⚼♆	9 14	b
	♀⊥♄	10 4	
	♀⊥♂	11 56	
16	♃⊽♇	0am 41	
SU	☽⚼♃	8 28	b
	☿∠♅	8 32	
	☽P♀	3pm 25	G
	☽⚼♄	4 53	b
	☽⚼♂	5 50	b
	☽⚼♅	10 2	b

Day	Aspect	Time	
	☽☍☿	11 52	B
17	♀△♇	0am 9	
M	☽△♆	0 15	G
	☿⚹♆	2 55	
	♀⚺♃	6 2	
	☽P☿	6 51	G
	☉⚼♇	7 58	
	☿⊥♃	10 30	
	☽P☿	10 58	G
	☽⚹♇	11 28	G
	☽☍♀	0pm 39	B
18	☽△♅	1am 30	G
TU	☽P♀	6 3	G
	☽∠♇	3pm 5	b
	☽☍☉	5 41	B
	☉P♇	6 13	
19	☽□♆	7am 45	B
W	☽⚺♇	7pm 18	g
	☽P♇	8 10	D
	☽☍♃	9 9	B
	☽P☉	10 42	G
20	♂□♅	2am 59	
TH	☽☍♄	5 20	B
	☿⊥♄	8 14	
	☽□♅	10 11	B
	☽☍♂	10 36	B
	☿△♇	6pm 20	
	☽P♃	10 42	G
	☽P♄	11 23	B
21	☽P♅	0am 19	B
F	☽⚼☿	1 8	b
	♀⚺♄	8 2	
	☽⚼♀	11 3	b
	☿⚺♃	1pm 26	
	☽⚹♆	5 44	G
	♀Q♆	6 40	
	♂P♆	8 5	
22	☽P♆	2am 48	D
S	☽P♂	3 25	B
	☉Q♅	5 11	
	☽☌♇	5 40	D
	☽△☿	11 45	G
	☽⚼☉	4pm 16	b
	☽△♀	8 14	G
	☽⚹♅	9 25	G
	☿⊥♂	9 33	
	☽∠♆	11 39	b
23	♀⚹♅	7am 54	
SU	♃P♄	1pm 21	
	☽⚼♃	3 37	b
	♃P♅	5 7	
	♄P♅	8 8	
	☽⚼♄	11 26	b
24	☿⚺♄	0am 6	
M	☽△☉	1 14	G
	☿Q♆	3 8	
	☽∠♅	3 48	b
	☽⚺♆	6 0	g
	☽⚼♂	9 46	b
	☽⚺♇	6pm 7	g
	☽△♃	10 43	G
25	☿⚹♅	4am 29	
TU	☽△♄	6 16	G
	☽⚺♅	10 21	g
	☽□☿	11 26	B
	☽□♀	4pm 7	B
	☽△♂	6 12	G
26	☽∠♇	0am 32	b
W	☉±♇	9 19	

Day	Aspect	Time	
	☉□♆	11 35	
	☽P♂	6pm 36	B
	☽☌♆	6 52	D
	☽□☉	7 30	B
27	☽P♆	5am 0	D
TH	☽⚹♇	6 38	G
	☽□♃	0pm 26	B
	♀⚺♂	0 33	
	☽□♄	7 12	B
	☽☌♅	10 39	B
28	☿⚺♂	2am 50	
F	☽P♃	5 3	G
	☽P♄	6 15	B
	☽P♅	7 40	B
	☽□♂	9 44	B
	☽⚹☿	10 33	G
	☽⚹♀	10 44	G
	☿☌♀	1pm 27	
	☽P☉	2 20	G
	☿⚼♇	8 6	
	♀⚼♇	11 54	
29	☽⚺♆	5am 38	g
S	☿P♀	8 17	
	☽⚹☉	11 5	G
	☽P♇	11 22	D
	☽□♇	4pm 37	B
	☽∠♀	6 25	b
	☽P☿	6 38	G
	☽P♀	7 26	G
	☽∠☿	8 21	b
	☽⚹♃	11 14	G
30	☽⚹♄	5am 4	G
SU	☽⚺♅	7 48	g
	☽∠♆	9 37	b
	☽∠☉	5pm 3	b
	☽⚹♂	9 13	G
MAY			
1	☽⚺♀	0am 43	g
M	☽∠♃	3 3	b
	☽⚺☿	4 36	g
	☿P♇	6 58	
	☽∠♄	8 26	b
	☽∠♅	10 52	b
	☿Q♅	10 54	
	☽⚹♆	0pm 34	G
	☉P♅	1 58	
	☽⚺☉	9 46	g
	☽△♇	10 41	G
2	☽∠♂	1am 11	b
TU	☽⚺♃	5 51	g
	☉⊽♇	10 20	
	☽⚺♄	10 50	g
	☽⚹♅	0pm 59	G
	☉P♄	8 3	
	♀P♇	9 12	
3	☽⚼♇	0am 21	b
W	☽⚺♂	4 9	g
	♀Q♅	5 59	
	☿±♇	6 21	
	☿□♆	9 31	
	☽☌♀	9 37	G
	☽□♆	3pm 53	B
	☽☌☿	4 57	G
4	☽P♇	2am 12	D
TH	☽☌☉	4 12	D
	☽P♀	5 19	G
	☉P♃	6 13	
	☽☌♃	9 5	G

Day	Aspect	Time	
	☽☌♄	1pm 27	B
	☽□♅	3 7	B
	☽P☿	5 44	G
5	☽P♅	1am 45	B
F	☽P♄	4 42	B
	☽P♃	7 17	G
	☽☌♂	8 8	B
	☽P☉	8 54	G
	☽⚺♀	3pm 27	g
	☽△♆	5 5	G
	☽P♆	11 46	D
6	☿⊽♇	2am 12	
S	☽☍♇	2 16	B
	☽⚺☿	2 17	g
	♀±♇	4 13	
	☽⚺☉	8 36	g
	☿P♅	9 22	
	☽⚺♃	10 47	g
	♀□♆	10 57	
	☽⚺♄	2pm 45	g
	☽△♅	4 1	G
	☽⚼♆	5 28	b
	☽∠♀	6 4	b
7	☿P♄	1am 40	
SU	☽P♂	6 18	B
	☽∠☿	6 53	b
	☽∠☉	10 48	b
	☽⚺♂	11 27	g
	☽∠♃	11 40	b
	☽∠♄	3pm 28	b
	☽⚼♅	4 34	b
	☿P♃	4 43	
	☽⚹♀	8 52	G
8	☉☌♃	4am 8	
M	☽⚹☿	11 54	G
	♆Stat	0pm 31	
	☽⚹♃	0 51	G
	☽⚹☉	1 19	G
	☽∠♂	1 28	b
	☽⚹♄	4 31	G
	☽P♂	5 14	B
	☿☌♃	6 53	
9	☉P☿	3am 9	
TU	☉☌☿	3 50	
	☽⚼♇	4 14	b
	☽⚹♂	3pm 58	G
	☽☍♆	8 10	B
	☿☌♄	8 11	
10	☿□♅	0am 46	
W	☽□♀	3 57	B
	☽△♇	5 39	G
	☽P♆	5 45	D
	☽P☿	6 52	G
	☿P♆	11 6	
	☽P☉	11 8	G
	☽□♃	4pm 35	B
	☉☌♄	7 45	
	☽□♄	8 0	B
	☽□☉	8 0	B
	☽☍♅	8 31	B
	☽P♃	8 33	G
	♀⊽♇	11 1	
11	☽□☿	0am 11	B
TH	☽P♄	0 32	B
	☉□♅	3 16	
	☽P♅	5 13	B
	☽P♀	9 2	G
	☽□♂	10pm 44	B
12	☽P♇	6am 26	D

Day	Aspect	Time	
F	☽□♇	10 5	B
	☽△♀	1pm 41	G
	♀P♅	8 43	
	☽△♃	10 31	G
13	☉P♆	1am 10	
S	☽△♄	1 37	G
	☽⚼♆	3 8	b
	♂△♆	4 54	
	☽△☉	5 17	G
	♄□♅	8 34	
	☽△☿	3pm 57	G
	☽⚼♀	7 36	b
14	☽⚼♃	2am 18	b
SU	☽⚼♅	5 2	b
	☽⚼♄	5 14	b
	☽△♆	6 30	G
	☽△♂	7 57	G
	☽⚼☉	10 53	b
	☽✱♇	4pm 34	G
15	☽⚼☿	1am 6	b
M	♀P♄	1 33	
	☽△♅	8 55	G
	☽⚼♂	1pm 27	b
	☽∠♇	8 35	b
16	☿P♂	0 3	
TU	☽□♆	2 45	B
17	☽⊻♇	1am 6	g
W	☽P♇	2 27	D
	☿△♆	9 10	
	♀P♃	9 36	
	♀☌♃	10 30	
	☽☍♃	4pm 54	B
	☽☍♀	5 28	B
	☽□♅	6 11	B
	☽☍♄	7 14	B
18	♀□♅	0am 39	
TH	☽P♅	6 9	B
	☽☍☉	7 34	B
	♀☌♄	0pm 56	
	☽P♄	1 30	B
	☽P♃	8 16	G
19	☽P♀	0am 24	G
F	☽✱♆	1 3	G
	☽P♆	8 56	D
	☽☍☿	9 14	B
	☽☍♂	9 37	B
	☽☌♇	11 40	D
	☿☌♂	0pm 26	
	☿☍♇	11 41	
20	☽P☉	3am 13	G
S	☽✱♅	5 30	G
	☽∠♆	6 57	b
	♃□♅	1pm 16	
	♂☍♇	8 25	
21	☽∠♅	11am 48	b
SU	☽⚼♃	0pm 15	b
	☽⊻♆	1 15	g
	☽⚼♄	1 50	b
	♀P♆	5 41	
	☽⚼♀	9 25	b
22	☽⊻♇	0am 1	g
M	☽⚼☉	9 44	b
	☽⊻♅	6pm 20	g
	☽△♃	7 24	G
	☽△♄	8 42	G
23	☽∠♇	6am 29	b
TU	☽△♀	7 31	G
	☽⚼♂	10 13	b
	☽P☉	10 19	G
	☽△☉	6pm 57	G
	☽⚼☿	10 0	b
24	☽☌♆	2am 12	D
W	☽P♀	6 15	G
	☽✱♇	0pm 49	G
	☽P♆	2 41	D
	☿△♅	4 23	
	☽△♂	6 26	G
25	☽P♃	0am 15	G
TH	☿⚼♆	1 26	
	☽☌♅	6 59	B
	☿⊻♃	7 17	
	♅Stat	8 15	
	☽P♄	8 36	B
	☽□♃	9 13	B
	☽△☿	9 31	G
	☽□♄	9 56	B
	☿⊻♄	0pm 35	
	☽P♅	5 45	B
26	☽□♀	2am 34	B
F	☽□☉	11 55	B
	☽⊻♆	1pm 46	g
	☽P♇	9 37	D
	☽□♇	11 49	B
27	☽□♂	8am 39	B
S	☉△♆	11 38	
	☽⊻♅	5pm 7	g
	☽∠♆	6 20	b
	☽✱♃	8 19	G
	☽✱♄	8 29	G
28	☽□☿	4am 17	B
SU	♃☌♄	4pm 4	
	☽✱♀	5 19	G
	☽∠♅	8 43	b
	☽✱♆	9 52	G
29	☽∠♄	0am 13	b
M	☽∠♃	0 17	b
	☽✱☉	0 33	G
	☽△♇	7 7	G
	☿⊥♄	10 7	
	☿⊥♃	11 34	
	☽✱♂	6pm 18	G
	☽∠♀	10 37	b
	☽✱♅	11 15	G
30	☽⊻♄	2am 53	g
TU	☽⊻♃	3 9	g
	☽∠☉	4 55	b
	☽⚼♇	9 14	b
	☿±♆	11 28	
	☽✱☿	4pm 18	G
	♀△♆	6 4	
	☽∠♂	9 22	b
31	☽□♆	1am 54	B
W	☽⊻♀	2 38	g
	☽⊻☉	8 8	g
	☽P♇	0pm 19	D
	☽∠☿	8 11	b
	☽⊻♂	11 30	g
JUNE			
1	☽□♅	1am 39	B
TH	☽☌♄	5 30	B
	☽☌♃	6 8	G
	☽P♅	11 51	B
	☉☍♇	6pm 17	
	☽P♄	8 47	B
	☽⊻☿	11 6	g
2	☽△♆	2am 53	G
F	☽P♃	5 29	G
	☽☌♀	8 1	G
	☽P♆	9 45	D
	☽☍♇	11 3	B
	☽☌☉	0pm 14	D
	♂△♅	9 35	
3	☽△♅	1am 50	G
S	☽☌♂	2 3	B
	☽⚼♆	2 48	b
	☿⚼♅	5 57	
	☽⊻♄	6 1	g
	☽⊻♃	6 59	g
	☿⊼♆	4pm 59	
	♂⚼♆	6 39	
	♀☍♇	8 30	
4	☽⚼♅	1am 43	b
SU	☽☌☿	3 36	G
	☽∠♄	6 8	b
	☽∠♃	7 16	b
	☽⊻♀	0pm 7	g
	☽⊻☉	3 20	g
5	☽⊻♂	4am 19	g
M	☽✱♄	6 27	G
	☽✱♃	7 48	G
	☽⚼♇	10 57	b
	☿∠♄	1pm 35	
	☽∠♀	2 32	b
	☽∠☉	5 18	b
6	☽☍♆	3am 12	B
TU	☽∠♂	6 1	b
	☽⊻☿	8 36	g
	☿∠♃	11 9	
	☽△♇	11 33	G
	☽P♆	1pm 55	D
	☽P♃	4 30	G
	☽✱♀	5 34	G
	☽✱☉	7 52	G
7	☽P♄	2am 27	B
W	☽☍♅	3 13	B
	☽✱♂	8 23	G
	☽□♄	8 35	B
	☽□♃	10 22	B
	☽∠☿	11 57	b
	☽P♅	0pm 48	B
	♂⊻♄	1 4	
	☿⊼♇	10 22	
8	☽P♇	1 45	D
TH	☽□♇	2 40	B
	☽✱☿	4 2	G
9	☽□♀	2am 16	B
F	☽□☉	3 29	B
	☽⚼♆	8 18	b
	☽△♄	1pm 29	G
	☿P♂	3 33	
	☽□♂	3 36	B
	☽△♃	3 48	G
	☉P♀	7 20	
	♂⊻♃	9 26	
10	☽⚼♅	10am 26	b
S	☽△♆	11 29	G
	☽⚼♄	5pm 5	b
	☽⚼♃	7 42	b
	☽✱♇	8 43	G
11	☽□☿	2am 33	B
SU	☉△♅	8 12	
	♀△♅	8 43	
	☿±♅	10 2	
	☉☌♀	10 31	
	☽△♅	2pm 18	G
	☽△☉	2 48	G
	☽△♀	2 54	G
	♀⚼♆	7 40	
	☉⚼♆	10 15	
12	☽∠♇	0am 48	b
M	☽△♂	2 15	G
	☿P♀	10 52	
	☽□♆	7pm 54	B
	☽⚼☉	9 44	b
	☉P☿	10 10	
	☽⚼♀	10 35	b
13	♃P♆	3am 0	
TU	☽⊻♇	5 31	g
	☽P♇	8 28	D
	☽⚼♂	8 43	b
	☽△☿	3pm 40	G
	☽□♅	11 55	B
14	☽☍♄	7am 58	B
W	☽☍♃	11 31	B
	☽P♅	1pm 4	B
	♀⊻♄	4 49	
	☿±♇	6 15	
	☽⚼☿	10 53	b
15	☽P♄	2am 47	B
TH	☽✱♆	6 38	G
	☽P♆	4pm 11	D
	☽☌♇	4 31	D
	☽P♃	5 25	G
	☉⊻♄	6 23	
16	☽✱♅	11am 31	G
F	♀⊻♃	0pm 1	
	☽∠♆	0 38	b
	♂±♆	6 56	
	☽☍☉	10 27	B
17	☽☍♀	1am 50	B
S	☽☍♂	7 31	B
	☽∠♅	5pm 49	b
	☽⊻♆	6 56	g
18	☽P☿	0am 53	G
SU	☽⚼♄	3 10	b
	☽⊻♇	4 58	g
	☽⚼♃	7 39	b
	♂⊥♄	8 46	
	☉⊻♃	9 19	
	☽☍☿	9pm 28	B
19	☽⊻♅	0am 16	g
M	♀±♆	0 55	
	☽P☿	3 19	G
	☽△♄	10 0	G
	☽∠♇	11 26	b
	☽△♃	2pm 46	G
20	♀⊥♄	2am 19	
TU	☽☌♆	7 51	D
	☽P♃	5pm 49	G
	☽✱♇	5 49	G
	☽P♆	9 24	D
21	☽⚼☉	1am 50	b
W	☉±♆	4 9	
	☽⚼♀	7 46	b
	☽⚼♂	8 20	b
	☽P♄	9 44	B
	☽☌♅	0pm 58	B
	♀☌♂	7 27	
	☽□♄	11 12	B
22	☽P♅	0am 36	B
TH	☽□♃	4 25	B
	☽△☉	10 26	G
	♀⊥♃	10 43	
	☽△♂	4pm 0	G
	☽△♀	5 3	G
	☽⚼☿	5 39	b
	☽⊻♆	7 50	g
	☉⊥♄	10 1	
23	☽□♇	5am 28	B
F	☽P♇	5 39	D
	♂⊥♃	5 40	
	☿Stat	8 33	
	♀⚼♅	9 33	
	♀⊼♆	8pm 12	
	☽△☿	10 50	G
	☽⊻♅	11 51	g
24	☽∠♆	0am 55	b
S	☽✱♄	10 14	G
	☽✱♃	3pm 40	G
	♂⚼♅	4 33	
25	☽□☉	1am 0	B
SU	☽∠♅	4 6	b
	☽□♂	4 45	B
	☽✱♆	5 8	G
	☽□♀	8 38	B
	♂⊼♆	11 56	
	☽△♇	2pm 10	G
	☽∠♄	2 26	b
	☽∠♃	7 53	b
26	☽□☿	5am 59	B
M	☽✱♅	7 23	G
	☉⊥♃	0pm 39	
	☽⚼♇	5 5	b
	☽⊻♄	5 36	g
	☉⚼♅	6 3	
	☽⊻♃	11 4	g
27	☉⊼♆	7am 48	
TU	☿P♃	10 32	
	☽□♆	10 39	B
	☽✱☉	10 52	G
	☽✱♂	1pm 4	G
	♀⊼♇	6 27	
	☽✱♀	7 6	G
	☽P♇	10 33	D
28	♀∠♄	3am 41	
W	☽✱☿	8 51	G
	☽□♅	11 5	B
	☽∠☉	2pm 4	b
	☽∠♂	3 37	b
	☽☌♄	9 6	B
	☽∠♀	10 34	b
	☽P♅	11 32	B
29	☽☌♃	2am 34	G
TH	☽∠☿	8 57	b
	☽△♆	0pm 38	G
	☽P♄	0 46	B
	☽⊻☉	4 21	g
	☽⊻♂	5 19	g
	☽☍♇	8 33	B
	☽P♆	9 41	D
	☽P☿	10 40	G
30	☽⊻♀	1am 8	g
F	☽P♃	3 58	G
	☽⊻☿	8 26	g
	☽△♅	11 47	G
	☽⚼♆	0pm 41	b
	♀±♅	1 53	
	☿P♆	3 5	
	☽⊻♄	9 49	g
JULY			
1	☽⊻♃	3am 26	g
S	♀∠♃	7 13	
	☽⚼♅	11 32	b

Day	Aspect	Time	
	☉☌♂	3pm 50	
	☽☌♂	7 16	B
	☽●●	7 20	D
	☽∠♄	9 42	b
2 SU	☽∠♃	3am 27	b
	☽☌♀	4 56	G
	☽☌☿	6 23	G
	☉⚻♇	8 30	
	♀±♇	1pm 27	
	♂⚻♇	3 35	
	☿☌♀	5 39	
	☽⚼♇	7 52	b
	☽⚹♄	9 36	G
3 M	☿±♇	3am 11	
	☽⚹♃	3 34	G
	☽☍♆	11 55	B
	☉∠♄	1pm 30	
	☽P♃	3 15	G
	☽△♇	7 48	G
	☽⊻♂	9 10	g
	☽⊻☉	10 17	g
	☽P♆	10 42	D
4 TU	☽P☿	2am 21	G
	☽⊻☿	4 31	g
	☽P♄	7 3	B
	☽⊻♀	9 12	g
	☽☍♅	11 11	B
	♂∠♄	1pm 22	
	☿∠♃	1 44	
	☽P♅	8 44	B
	☽□♄	10 26	B
	☽∠♂	10 48	b
5 W	☽∠☉	0am 30	b
	☽∠☿	4 10	b
	☽□♃	5 0	B
	♀⚻♅	8 25	
	☽∠♀	0pm 19	b
	☽□♇	9 15	B
	☽P♇	9 57	D
	☉±♅	10 17	
6 TH	☽⚹♂	1am 12	G
	☽⚹☉	3 34	G
	☽⚹☿	4 25	G
	☉☌☿	11 35	
	☽⚼♆	2pm 32	b
	☽⚹♀	4 25	G
7 F	☽△♄	1am 57	G
	☽△♃	9 21	G
	☿±♅	9 55	
	☉P♀	0pm 45	
	☿☌♂	2 8	
	☽⚼♅	3 54	b
	☽△♆	4 59	G
	♂±♅	5 40	
8 S	☽⚹♇	1am 52	G
	☽⚼♄	5 3	b
	☽□☿	7 15	B
	☽□♂	8 59	B
	☉±♇	0pm 10	
	☽□☉	0 53	B
	☽⚼♃	0 55	b
	☉∠♃	1 39	
	☽△♅	7 13	G
9 SU	☽□♀	4am 10	B
	☽∠♇	5 32	b
	♀⚼♇	6pm 10	
10 M	☽□♆	0am 34	B
	☿∠♄	2 41	
	☽⊻♇	10 3	g

Day	Aspect	Time	
	☽△☿	1pm 26	G
	☽P♇	2 51	D
	☽△♂	8 54	G
11 TU	☽△☉	2am 37	G
	☽□♅	4 22	B
	♀⚹♄	11 8	
	♂±♇	11 10	
	☽⚼☿	5pm 42	b
	☽☍♄	7 36	B
	☽△♀	8 29	G
	☽P♅	8 58	B
12 W	☉⚻♅	0am 31	
	☽⚼♂	4 8	b
	☽☍♃	4 52	B
	☽⚼☉	10 49	b
	☽⚹♆	11 14	G
	☽P♄	2pm 37	B
	☽P☿	7 10	G
	☽☌♇	9 9	D
	♂∠♃	10 52	
13 TH	☽P♆	0am 4	D
	☽⚼♀	5 53	b
	☽P♃	1pm 39	G
	☽⚹♅	4 3	G
	☽∠♆	5 20	b
14 F	☽P♀	8am 36	G
	☽P☉	9pm 13	G
	☽∠♅	10 22	b
	☽⊻♆	11 41	g
15 S	☽⊻♇	9am 48	g
	☽☍☿	9 59	B
	☽⚼♄	3pm 4	b
	♀⚹♃	8 33	
16 SU	☽⚼♃	1am 21	b
	☿⚻♇	2 1	
	☽☍♂	4 27	B
	☽⊻♅	4 48	g
	♂⚻♅	10 29	
	☽P☉	1pm 8	G
	☽•☍☉	1 55	B
	☽∠♇	4 15	b
	☽△♄	9 48	G
	☿P♆	10 4	
17 M	☽P♀	6am 55	G
	☽△♃	8 18	G
	☽P♃	10 48	G
	☽☍♀	11 48	B
	☽☌♆	0pm 30	D
	☿Stat	1 20	
	☉⚼♇	6 21	
	♀☍♆	6 30	
	☽⚹♇	10 35	G
18 TU	☽P☿	0am 7	G
	☽P♆	1 52	D
	♀P♃	4 35	
	☽P♄	10 41	B
	☿⚻♇	3pm 5	
	☽☌♅	5 17	B
19 W	☽P♅	4am 42	B
	☽⚼☿	4 48	b
	☽□♄	10 37	B
	☽□♃	9pm 22	B
20 TH	☽⊻♆	0am 24	g
	☽⚼♂	4 6	b
	☽□♇	10 16	B
	☽△☿	10 59	G
	☽P♇	11 21	D
	☿P♀	1pm 27	
	☽⚼☉	3 46	b

Day	Aspect	Time	
21 F	☉⚹♄	0am 38	
	☽⊻♅	4 18	g
	☽∠♆	5 39	b
	☽△♂	10 57	G
	☽⚼♇	2pm 58	b
	♀△♇	6 50	
	☽⚹♄	9 34	G
	☽△☉	11 8	G
	♀Q♄	11 52	
22 S	☽⚹♃	8am 18	G
	☽∠♅	8 55	b
	☽⚹♆	10 15	G
	♀P♆	10 19	
	☉P♃	10 22	
	☽△♇	7pm 44	G
	☿⊻♀	8 18	
	☽□☿	10 16	B
	☽△♀	10 24	G
23 SU	☽∠♄	2am 0	b
	☽∠♃	0pm 39	b
	☽⚹♅	0 47	G
	☉P☿	4 51	
	☽□♂	10 11	B
	☽⚼♇	11 20	b
24 M	☽⊻♄	5am 37	g
	☽□☉	11 2	B
	☽⊻♃	4pm 9	g
	☽□♆	5 9	B
	♂⚼♇	9 15	
	♀P♄	10 26	
25 TU	☽⚹☿	7am 9	G
	☽P♇	7 12	D
	☽□♀	10 2	B
	☿±♅	4pm 17	
	☽□♅	6 4	B
	☿P♃	6 13	
26 W	☽⚹♂	5am 37	G
	☿∠♄	7 20	
	☽☌♄	10 20	B
	☽P♅	10 24	B
	☽∠☿	10 31	b
	☽⚹☉	6pm 52	G
	☽☌♃	8 35	G
	☽P♀	8 46	G
	☽△♆	8 47	G
27 TH	☽P♄	2am 4	B
	☽☍♇	5 18	B
	♀Q♃	7 0	
	☽∠♂	7 59	b
	☽P♆	8 52	D
	♃△♆	11 23	
	☽P☉	11 38	G
	☽⊻☿	1pm 13	g
	☽⚹♀	5 29	G
	☽△♅	8 18	G
	☽∠☉	9 28	b
	☽⚼♆	9 33	b
	☉☍♆	10 49	
28 F	☽P♃	0am 28	G
	☉⚹♃	1 41	
	☽P☿	4 18	G
	☽⊻♂	9 40	g
	☽⊻♄	0pm 9	g
	☿±♇	5 50	
	☉P♆	7 14	
	☽∠♀	8 2	b
	☽⚼♅	8 32	b
	☽P♂	9 46	B
	☽⊻♃	10 15	g

Day	Aspect	Time	
	☽⊻☉	11 24	g
29 S	♀☍♅	2am 0	
	☽∠♄	0pm 20	b
	☽●☿	5 19	G
	☽⊻♀	10 8	g
	☽∠♃	10 28	b
	☽P♂	11 57	B
30 SU	☽⚼♇	5am 53	b
	☽P☿	9 47	G
	☽●♂	11 47	B
	☽⚹♄	0pm 18	G
	☽P♃	4 5	G
	♀P♅	6 44	
	☽☍♆	9 30	B
	☽⚹♃	10 34	G
31 M	♂⚹♄	1am 21	
	☽●●	2 25	D
	☽△♇	5 43	G
	☿⚻♅	7 11	
	☽P♆	7 50	D
	☽P☉	1pm 13	G
	☽P♄	2 8	B
	☽☍♅	8 6	B
	☽⊻☿	9 23	g
	AUGUST		
1 TU	☉P♄	0am 33	
	☽●♀	2 14	G
	☽P♅	5 5	B
	☽P♀	9 0	G
	☽□♄	0pm 34	B
	☽⊻♂	2 0	g
	☿∠♃	2 59	
	☽□♃	11 25	B
2 W	☽∠☿	0am 12	b
	☿P♂	1 18	
	☉△♇	5 53	
	☽□♇	6 14	B
	☽⊻☉	6 16	g
	☽P♇	7 2	D
	☽∠♂	3pm 52	b
	☽⚼♆	10 32	b
3 TH	☽⚹☿	4am 3	G
	☽⊻♀	8 24	g
	☽∠☉	9 14	b
	☽△♄	2pm 50	G
	☉Q♄	3 55	
	☽⚹♂	6 33	G
	☽⚼♅	10 40	b
4 F	☽△♆	0am 9	G
	☽△♃	2 41	G
	☽⚹♇	9 20	G
	☿⚼♇	9 59	
	☽∠♀	1pm 1	b
	☽⚹☉	1 16	G
	☽⚼♄	5 13	b
5 S	☽△♅	1am 8	G
	☽⚼♃	5 42	b
	♂P♃	8 29	
	☽∠♇	0pm 16	b
	☽□☿	4 3	B
	☽⚹♀	6 56	G
6 SU	☽□♂	3am 10	B
	☽□♆	6 15	B
	♀□♄	1pm 25	
	☽⊻♇	4 12	g
	☽P♇	10 12	D
7 M	☽□☉	1am 2	B
	☿P♃	2 20	

Day	Aspect	Time	
	☿⚹♄	3 20	
	☽P♀	7 27	G
	☽□♅	9 2	B
8 TU	☽P♅	5 37	B
	☽☍♄	6 17	B
	☽P☉	7 5	G
	☿⊻♀	7 34	
	☽□♀	10 40	B
	☽△☿	10 51	G
	♂☍♆	2pm 4	
	☽⚹♆	4 7	G
	☽△♂	4 15	G
	☽☍♃	8 41	B
	☉P♅	10 19	
9 W	☽P♄	0am 18	B
	☽☌♇	2 44	D
	☽P♆	7 57	D
	☽△☉	5pm 13	G
	☽P♂	8 2	B
	☽⚹♅	8 15	G
	☽P☿	8 27	G
	☿☍♆	8 33	
	☽∠♆	10 7	b
	☽⚼☿	10 25	b
10 TH	☽⚼♂	0am 2	b
	☿P♂	1 43	
	☽P♃	7 31	G
	☿☌♂	0pm 37	
	☿P♇	3 22	
	♀⚻♆	3 27	
11 F	☽⚼☉	2am 18	b
	☽∠♅	2 33	b
	☽⊻♆	4 29	g
	☉☍♅	5 20	
	☿⚹♃	5 44	
	☽△♀	6 2	G
	☽⊻♇	3pm 26	g
12 S	☉Q♃	0am 25	
	☽⚼♄	1 29	b
	☽⊻♅	8 59	g
	☿△♇	2pm 14	
	☽⚼♀	4 6	b
	☽⚼♃	4 55	b
	☿P♆	4 56	
	☽∠♇	9 55	b
	♀⊻♂	11 58	
13 SU	♀□♃	0am 50	
	♂⚹♃	1 50	
	☽P♃	5 50	G
	☽△♄	8 4	G
	☿Q♄	2pm 28	
	☽☌♆	5 16	D
	☽△♃	11 37	G
14 M	☽☍♂	0am 35	B
	☽P♂	2 27	B
	☽⚹♇	4 12	G
	☽P♆	6 3	D
	☿P♄	7 54	
	☽☍☿	11 53	B
	☽P♄	1pm 35	B
	☽P☿	2 58	G
	☽☌♅	9 17	B
	♀□♇	11 55	
15 TU	☽☍☉	5am 13	B
	☽P♅	8 1	B
	♀±♆	10 13	
	☽□♄	8pm 17	B
	☽P☉	11 47	G
16	♂P♆	1am 12	

Day	Aspect	Time	
W	☽⊻♆	4 51	g
	☽□♃	11 47	B
	☽□♇	3pm 35	B
	☽P♇	3 58	D
	☿☍♅	6 43	
	♂△♇	7 34	
	☽☍♀	7 58	B
17	☽⊻♅	7am 56	g
TH	☽∠♆	9 56	b
	☽P♀	10 40	G
	☿Q♃	3pm 9	
	☽⚼♂	9 51	b
18	☿P♅	4am 16	
F	☽⚹♄	6 31	G
	☽∠♅	0pm 28	b
	☽⚹♆	2 27	G
	☽⚼☿	8 32	b
	☽⚹♃	9 48	G
19	☽△♇	0am 52	G
S	☽⚼☉	3 18	b
	☽△♂	3 41	G
	☽∠♄	10 47	b
	☽⚹♅	4pm 26	G
20	☽∠♃	1am 55	b
SU	☽⚼♇	4 39	b
	☽△☿	5 31	G
	♂P♄	7 22	
	☽△☉	9 14	G
	♂Q♄	11 40	
	☽P♀	0pm 24	G
	☽⊻♄	2 27	g
	☽⚼♀	5 31	b
	☽□♆	9 46	B
	♇Stat	10 44	
21	☽⊻♃	5am 25	g
M	☽□♂	1pm 17	B
	☽P♇	1 46	D
	☽P☉	5 24	G
	♀∇♅	5 28	
	☽□♅	10 35	B
	☽△♀	11 7	G
22	☉☌☿	1am 5	
TU	☽P☿	2 7	G
	♀⚼♆	2pm 34	
	☿□♄	5 23	
	☽P♅	6 51	B
	☽□☉	6 51	B
	☽☌♄	7 57	B
	☽□☿	8 22	B
23	☽△♆	2am 43	G
W	♀⊥♂	4 59	
	☽P♂	6 20	B
	☽☌♃	10 33	G
	☽P♄	10 38	B
	☉□♄	11 16	
	☽☍♇	0pm 27	B
	☉P♇	2 38	
	☽P♆	5 7	D
	☽⚹♂	8 8	G
24	☽△♅	2am 23	G
TH	☽⚼♆	4 19	b
	☽□♀	7 57	B
	☽P♃	3pm 45	G
	☿∇♆	4 46	
	☽∠♂	10 35	b
	☽⊻♄	11 7	g
25	☿P♇	0am 37	
F	☽⚹☉	1 36	G
	☽⚼♅	3 29	b

Day	Aspect	Time	
	☽⚹☿	7 22	G
	☽⊻♃	1pm 24	g
	☽∠♄	11 58	b
26	☽⊻♂	0am 31	g
S	☽∠☉	4 6	b
	☉P☿	6 2	
	♀±♅	11 9	
	☽∠☿	11 44	b
	☽∠♃	2pm 10	b
	☽⚹♀	2 11	G
	☽⚼♇	3 25	b
	☽P♃	6 50	G
27	☽⚹♄	0am 28	G
SU	☽⊻☉	6 13	g
	☽☍♆	6 25	B
	☿□♃	7 31	
	☉∇♆	9 14	
	☽⚹♃	2pm 41	G
	☽⊻☿	3 40	g
	☽△♇	3 45	G
	☿□♇	4 23	
	☽∠♀	4 43	b
	☽P♆	4 45	D
	☿±♆	7 16	
	☽P♄	10 57	B
28	☽☌♂	3am 28	B
M	☽☍♅	4 44	B
	☽P♂	9 40	B
	☽P♅	1pm 23	B
	☽⊻♀	7 14	g
29	☽□♄	1am 12	B
TU	♂☍♅	7 22	
	☽☌☉	10 19	D
	☽□♃	3pm 46	B
	♀Q♇	3 51	
	☽P♇	4 18	D
	☽□♇	4 33	B
	☽☌☿	11 33	G
30	☽P☉	3am 55	G
W	☽⊻♂	6 43	g
	☽⚼♆	7 41	b
	☽P☿	1pm 7	G
31	☽☌♀	1am 21	G
TH	☽△♄	2 58	G
	♂P♅	5 39	
	☽⚼♅	6 45	b
	☽△♆	8 52	G
	☽∠♂	9 7	b
	☽⊻☉	4pm 7	g
	☽P♀	6 17	G
	☽△♃	6 27	G
	☽⚹♇	6 56	G
	♀△♄	8 21	
	☿∇♅	11 24	
SEPTEMBER			
1	☽P♀	0am 20	G
F	☽⚼♄	4 48	b
	☽△♅	8 36	G
	☽⊻☿	10 0	g
	☽⚹♂	0pm 23	G
	☿⚼♆	4 7	
	☽∠☉	8 22	b
	☽⚼♃	8 56	b
	☽∠♇	9 17	b
	☽P☿	10 9	G
2	☉□♃	4am 46	
S	☉□♇	9 1	
	☉±♆	10 51	

Day	Aspect	Time	
	☽⊻♀	11 4	g
	☽P☉	11 14	G
	☿⊻♂	1pm 19	
	☽□♆	1 40	B
	♀⚼♅	1 57	
	☽∠☿	5 3	b
3	☽⊻♇	0am 35	g
SU	☽⚹☉	1 50	G
	☽P♇	6 50	D
	♀△♆	2pm 36	
	☽□♅	3 4	B
	☽∠♀	5 50	b
	☽□♂	10 13	B
4	☽⚹☿	1am 34	G
M	☿±♅	7 48	
	☽P♂	8 15	B
	♃☍♇	10 53	
	☽P♅	2pm 35	B
	☽☍♄	3 56	B
	♂Q♃	5 45	
	☽⚹♆	10 21	G
5	☽⚹♀	1am 56	G
TU	☽P♄	7 27	B
	☽☌♇	10 9	D
	☽☍♃	10 17	B
	☽P♆	3pm 21	D
	☽□☉	4 27	B
	☿P♀	11 40	
6	☽⚹♅	1am 21	G
W	☽∠♆	4 1	b
	☽△♂	0pm 22	G
	☽P♃	7 50	G
	☿Q♇	8 47	
	☽□☿	10 26	B
7	☽∠♅	7am 30	b
TH	☽⊻♆	10 14	g
	♀∠♂	10 38	
	☽⚼♂	8pm 29	b
	☽□♀	9 2	B
	☽⊻♇	10 35	g
8	☿⊥♂	4am 28	
F	☽⚼♄	10 14	b
	☽△☉	10 27	G
	♀⚹♇	0pm 4	
	☿△♄	0 27	
	☽⊻♅	1 55	g
	♀△♃	5 29	
9	☽∠♇	5am 7	b
S	☽⚼♃	5 44	b
	☽P♃	7 22	G
	☿⚼♅	2pm 40	
	☽△♄	4 42	G
	☽⚼☉	7 37	b
	☽△☿	9 10	G
	☽☌♆	11 5	D
10	☉∇♅	3am 19	
SU	☿△♆	11 9	
	☽⚹♇	11 26	G
	☽P♆	0pm 10	D
	☽△♃	0 11	G
	☽△♀	4 47	G
	☽P♄	8 26	B
	☉P♀	11 17	
11	☽☌♅	2am 17	B
M	☽⚼☿	7 50	b
	☽P♅	0pm 52	B
	☉⚼♆	1 11	
	☽☍♂	8 9	B
12	☽⚼♀	1am 50	b

Day	Aspect	Time	
TU	☽□♄	4 29	B
	☽P♂	7 12	B
	☽⊻♆	10 32	g
	♄Stat	11 33	
	☽P♇	9pm 17	D
	☽□♇	10 34	B
	☽□♃	11 30	B
13	♀⚼♄	4am 21	
W	☉P☿	10 6	
	☽⊻♅	0pm 36	g
	☽∠♆	3 21	b
	☽☍☉	7 37	B
14	☽P♀	2am 28	G
TH	☿⚹♇	10 18	
	☽P☿	11 36	G
	♀△♅	11 53	
	☽⚹♄	1pm 50	G
	☽∠♅	4 50	b
	☽P☉	6 6	G
	☿△♃	7 3	
	☽⚹♆	7 33	G
15	☽△♇	7am 12	G
F	☽⚹♃	8 16	G
	☽☍☿	9 57	B
	☽⚼♂	2pm 9	b
	☽∠♄	5 35	b
	☽⚹♅	8 28	G
	☽P☉	10 30	G
	☽☍♀	11 54	B
16	☉±♅	2am 41	
S	☽⚼♇	10 40	b
	☽∠♃	11 46	b
	☽P☿	2pm 34	G
	☽△♂	6 50	G
	☽⊻♄	8 49	g
	☽P♀	11 10	G
17	☽□♆	2am 18	B
SU	☽⚼☉	0pm 54	b
	☽⊻♃	2 48	g
	☽P♇	7 31	D
	☿∠♂	11 2	
18	☽P♂	0am 53	B
M	☽□♅	2 19	B
	☿⚼♄	4 49	
	♂□♄	0pm 18	
	☽△☉	5 31	G
19	☽P♅	0am 54	B
TU	☽☌♄	2 1	B
	☽□♂	2 41	B
	☽⚼☿	4 32	b
	☿△♅	5 38	
	☽△♆	7 19	G
	☽P♄	2pm 29	B
	☽⚼♀	3 55	b
	☽☍♇	6 30	B
	☽☌♃	7 40	G
	☽P♆	10 9	D
20	☽△♅	6am 39	G
W	☽⚼♆	9 19	b
	☽△☿	9 34	G
	♀±♄	11 44	
	☽△♀	8pm 19	G
	♀∠♇	9 25	
	☽P♃	10 33	G
21	☽□☉	1am 28	B
TH	☉Q♇	2 40	
	☽⊻♄	5 49	g
	☽⚼♅	8 20	b
	☽⚹♂	8 57	G

Day	Aspect	Time	
	♀⚼♃	11 22	
	☽⊻♃	11pm 13	g
22	♂P♇	3am 48	
F	☽∠♄	7 16	b
	☽∠♂	11 35	b
	☽□☿	6pm 15	B
	☽⚼♇	11 22	b
23	☽∠♃	0am 34	b
S	☽P♃	1 27	G
	☽□♀	3 58	B
	♂∇♆	5 49	
	☽⚹☉	8 0	G
	☽⚹♄	8 28	G
	☽☍♆	1pm 34	B
	☽⊻♂	1 56	g
	☉△♄	2 44	
24	☽△♇	0am 30	G
SU	☽P♆	1 2	D
	♀P♂	1 31	
	☽⚹♃	1 42	G
	☽P♄	8 43	B
	☿P♂	8 50	
	☽∠☉	10 52	b
	☽☍♅	11 54	B
	☿±♄	1pm 34	
	☽P♅	9 7	B
25	♀P♇	0am 46	
M	☿∠♇	1 9	
	☽⚹☿	1 33	G
	☉⚼♅	1 42	
	☿P♇	5 53	
	♀∇♄	7 45	
	☽□♄	10 25	B
	☽⚹♀	10 40	G
	☽⊻☉	1pm 40	g
	☿⚼♃	2 15	
	☽☌♂	6 13	B
	☽P♀	10 29	G
	☽P☿	10 32	G
26	☽P♇	0am 38	D
TU	☿P♀	0 54	
	☽□♇	2 33	B
	☽□♃	3 44	B
	☽∠☿	5 4	b
	☽P♂	5 33	B
	☽∠♀	2pm 3	b
	☽⚼♆	4 36	b
	☉△♆	4 40	
27	☽⊻☿	8am 49	g
W	☽△♄	0pm 41	G
	☽⚼♅	3 10	b
	☽⊻♀	5 49	g
	☽△♆	5 58	G
	♀□♆	7 34	
	☽☌☉	7 53	D
	☽P☉	9 48	G
	☽⊻♂	11 7	g
28	☽⚹♇	5am 24	G
TH	☽△♃	6 35	G
	♀⊥♇	8 54	
	☽⚼♄	2pm 24	b
	☽△♅	4 57	G
	☽P☉	5 58	G
	♀±♃	10 15	
29	☽∠♂	2am 24	b
F	☿∇♄	3 40	
	☽∠♇	7 38	b
	☽⚼♃	8 48	b
	♃Stat	0pm 51	

Day	Aspect	h	m	
	☽☌☿	6	6	G
	☽□♆	10	24	B
30 S	☽☌♀	3am	35	G
	☽⊻☉	4	40	g
	☽P♂	5	51	B
	☽✱♂	6	31	G
	☽⊻♇	10	37	g
	☽P♇	4pm	29	D
	☽□♅	10	42	B
OCTOBER				
1 SU	☽P♀	9am	42	G
	☽∠☉	10	37	b
	☽P☿	1pm	28	G
	☿□♆	6	27	
	☽P♅	11	23	B
2 M	☽☍♄	0am	3	B
	☽✱♆	6	11	G
	☽⊻☿	7	22	g
	☿⊥♇	11	17	
	☉⊻♀	11	45	
	☽P♄	0pm	37	B
	♂±♆	3	40	
	☽✱☉	5	46	G
	♀✱♂	5	50	
	☽□♂	5	54	B
	☽⊻♀	5	54	g
	☽☌♇	7	22	D
	☽☍♃	8	28	B
	☉⊻♂	9	51	
	☽P♆	10	16	D
	☿±♃	11	32	
3 TU	☽✱♅	8am	3	G
	♀⊻♇	9	0	
	☽∠♆	11	26	b
	☉✱♇	2pm	12	
	☽∠☿	3	38	b
	♀⊽♃	7	38	
	♂□♇	11	55	
4 W	☽P♃	0am	49	G
	☽∠♀	2	50	b
	☉△♃	3	8	
	☽∠♅	1pm	55	b
	☿P♅	2	36	
	☽⊻♆	5	24	g
	♂□♃	7	28	
5 TH	☽✱☿	0am	40	G
	☽⊻♇	7	20	g
	☽△♂	9	2	G
	☽□☉	10	59	B
	☽✱♀	0pm	34	G
	☽⚼♄	5	4	b
	☽⊻♅	8	16	g
6 F	♀P♅	3am	4	
	☽∠♇	1pm	54	b
	☽⚼♃	2	44	b
	☽⚼♂	5	14	b
	☽P♃	6	18	G
	☽△♄	11	28	G
7 S	☽☌♆	6am	17	D
	☽□☿	7pm	2	B
	☽✱♇	8	21	G
	☽△♃	9	3	G
	☽P♆	9	8	D
8 SU	☽△☉	5am	19	G
	☽P♄	7	40	B
	☽□♀	8	18	B
	☽P☿	8	39	G
	☽☌♅	8	55	B
	☉⚼♄	9	1	
	☽P♀	0pm	56	G
	☿⊻♇	1	5	
	♀□♅	2	19	
	☿P♄	4	7	
	☽P♅	8	33	B
	☿⊽♃	9	23	
9 M	☽□♄	11am	16	B
	☽⚼☉	1pm	40	b
	☽⊻♆	6	2	g
10 TU	☉△♅	0am	28	
	♀P♄	1	39	
	☽P♇	4	23	D
	☽□♇	7	39	B
	☽□♃	8	3	B
	☽△☿	10	33	G
	☽☍♂	3pm	18	B
	☽⊻♅	7	26	g
	☽∠♆	10	51	b
11 W	☉P♂	0am	11	
	☽△♀	1	9	G
	☽P☉	5	21	G
	☽P♂	6	5	B
	☽⚼☿	4pm	35	b
	☽✱♄	8	16	G
	☽∠♅	11	32	b
12 TH	☽✱♆	2am	52	G
	☽⚼♀	7	59	b
	♀Q♆	0pm	14	
	☽△♇	3	52	G
	☽✱♃	3	57	G
	☿P♆	4	50	
	☽∠♄	11	36	b
13 F	☽✱♅	2am	52	G
	♀P♆	3	14	
	♃☍♇	8	24	
	☽☍☉	8	53	B
	☿P♀	3pm	25	
	☽∠♃	6	49	b
	☽⚼♇	6	53	b
	☽P♂	11	35	B
14 S	♂⊽♅	1am	20	
	☽⊻♄	2	17	g
	☽⚼♂	5	46	b
	☽□♆	8	47	B
	☽P☉	9	22	G
	☽⊻♃	9pm	8	g
15 SU	☽P♇	2am	39	D
	☽☍☿	4	36	B
	☽□♅	7	46	B
	☽△♂	9	14	G
	♆Stat	2pm	20	
	☽☍♀	11	26	B
16 M	☽☌♄	6am	17	B
	☽P♅	6	31	B
	☽△♆	0pm	50	G
	☽P♄	4	35	B
	☽⚼☉	9	26	b
	♂⚼♆	11	52	
17 TU	☉±♄	0am	35	
	☽☌♃	0	42	G
	☽☍♇	1	13	B
	☽P♆	2	15	D
	☽P☿	6	55	G
	☽△♅	11	19	G
	☽⚼♆	2pm	30	b
	☽□♂	3	10	B
	☽P♀	5	36	G
	☽P♃	10	58	G
18 W	☽△☉	1am	1	G
	☽⊻♄	9	23	g
	☽⚼☿	10	58	b
	☽⚼♅	0pm	53	b
	☿Stat	1	41	
	☉⚼♃	5	9	
19 TH	♀P♃	1am	30	
	♀☍♄	2	46	
	☽⊻♃	3	40	g
	☉∠♇	4	14	
	☉⊥♂	8	36	
	☽∠♄	10	49	b
	☽⚼♀	11	37	b
	☽△☿	0pm	25	G
	☽✱♂	8	39	G
20 F	☽∠♃	5am	5	b
	☽⚼♇	6	5	b
	☽P♀	6	46	G
	☽□☉	7	59	B
	☽✱♄	0pm	15	G
	☽P♃	0	24	G
	☽△♀	3	34	G
	☽☍♆	7	10	B
	☽∠♂	11	22	b
21 S	☽✱♃	6am	30	G
	☽△♇	7	41	G
	☽P☿	8	5	G
	☽P♆	8	41	D
	☽□☿	2pm	33	B
	☿P♆	2	49	
	☽☍♅	5	31	B
	☽P♄	6	49	B
22 SU	☽⊻♂	2am	8	g
	☽P♅	4	12	B
	♀✱♆	9	31	
	☽✱☉	3pm	2	G
	☽□♄	3	12	B
	☉⊽♄	5	5	
	♀Q♂	11	33	
	☽□♀	11	36	B
23 M	♀Q♅	7am	13	
	☽P♇	7	19	D
	☽P☉	8	22	G
	☽□♃	9	30	B
	☽□♇	11	5	B
	♂±♅	2pm	30	
	☽✱☿	3	51	G
	☽∠☉	6	44	b
	☉P♇	10	32	
24 TU	☽⚼♆	0am	9	b
	☽☌♂	7	59	B
	☽∠☿	4pm	20	b
	☽△♄	6	34	G
	☽⊻☉	10	40	g
	☽P♂	10	41	B
	☽⚼♅	10	47	b
25 W	☿P♄	1am	42	
	☽△♆	2	8	G
	☽✱♀	8	21	G
	☽△♃	1pm	8	G
	☽✱♇	3	10	G
	☽⊻☿	4	49	g
	☽⚼♄	8	38	b
26 TH	☽△♅	1am	3	G
	☽P♂	7	22	B
	☿⊻♇	1pm	22	
	☽∠♀	1	23	b
	☽⊻♂	3	2	g
	♅Stat	3	26	
	☽⚼♃	3	29	b
	☽∠♇	5	47	b
	☉□♆	10	54	
27 F	☉±♃	2am	41	
	☿P♅	7	17	
	☽□♆	7	17	B
	☽☌☉	7	58	D
	☿∠♂	10	48	
	♀☍♃	11	17	
	☿⊻♀	2pm	20	
	☿⊽♃	5	54	
	☽☌☿	6	20	G
	☽⊻♀	7	8	g
	☽∠♂	7	25	b
	☽⊻♇	8	58	g
28 S	☽P♇	2am	20	D
	☽□♅	7	10	B
	☽P☉	11	2	G
	☉⊥♇	0pm	2	
	♀☌♇	3	32	
	☽P☿	11	29	G
29 SU	☽✱♂	0am	37	G
	☽☍♄	6	4	B
	☽P♅	7	30	B
	☉⊥♀	7	31	
	☽✱♆	2pm	59	G
	☽P♄	4	53	B
	☽⊻☉	8	29	g
	☽⊻☿	9	25	g
30 M	☿⊥♀	0am	35	
	☉☌☿	2	9	
	☽☍♃	2	13	B
	☽P♆	5	2	D
	☽☌♇	5	32	D
	☽☌♀	9	33	G
	☉P☿	4pm	7	
	☽✱♅	4	11	G
	☽∠♆	8	0	b
	☽∠☿	11	50	b
31 TU	☽P♃	1am	49	G
	☽∠☉	4	14	b
	☿⊥♇	6	25	
	☽□♂	1pm	43	B
	☽∠♅	9	50	b
NOVEMBER				
1 W	☽⊻♆	1am	45	g
	☽✱☿	2	53	G
	☿⊥♂	6	21	
	☽✱☉	0pm	53	G
	☉⊽♃	2	10	
	☿□♆	2	29	
	☽⊻♇	5	8	g
	☽⚼♄	9	56	b
2 TH	☿±♃	0am	21	
	☽⊻♀	3	55	g
	☽⊻♅	4	4	g
	♀✱♅	5	25	
	♂△♄	5	41	
	☿P♇	6pm	26	
	☽⚼♃	7	9	b
	☿∠♀	7	14	
	☽∠♇	11	40	b
3 F	☽△♄	4am	13	G
	☽△♂	5	37	G
	♂Q♇	9	17	
	☽□☿	10	46	B
	☽P♃	11	4	G
	☽∠♀	1pm	54	b
	☽☌♆	2	36	D
	☉⊻♇	4	59	
	♀∠♆	8	48	
4 S	☽△♃	1am	24	G
	☽✱♇	6	16	G
	☽□☉	7	27	B
	☽P♆	8	2	D
	☽⚼♂	1pm	45	b
	☽☌♅	5	3	B
	☽P♄	9	31	B
	☽✱♀	11	44	G
5 SU	☿⊻♂	6am	5	
	☽P♅	6	40	B
	☽P☉	11	2	G
	☽□♄	4pm	26	B
	☽△☿	8	4	G
6 M	☽⊻♆	2am	58	g
	☽□♃	0pm	47	B
	☽P♇	0	52	D
	☽□♇	6	10	B
7 TU	☽P☿	0am	10	G
	☽△☉	0	22	G
	☽⚼☿	0	40	b
	☽⊻♅	4	20	g
	♂⚼♅	6	6	
	☽∠♆	8	8	b
	☉P♅	10	18	
	☽□♀	4pm	51	B
8 W	☽✱♄	2am	4	G
	☿Stat	2	28	
	☽⚼☉	7	15	b
	☽∠♅	8	42	b
	☽☍♂	10	0	B
	☽✱♆	0pm	23	G
	☽✱♃	9	2	G
9 TH	☉□♅	1am	57	
	☽P♂	2	33	B
	☽△♇	2	43	G
	☽P♂	2	52	B
	☽∠♄	5	31	b
	☽✱♅	0pm	7	G
	☽∠♃	11	48	b
10 F	☽△♀	5am	7	G
	☽⚼♇	5	36	b
	☽⊻♄	8	6	g
	☽☍☿	0pm	0	B
	♂△♆	1	14	
	☽□♆	6	8	B
11 S	☽P☿	0am	56	G
	☽⊻♃	1	46	g
	☉P♄	4	1	
	☽⚼♀	9	37	b
	♀⊥♆	10	7	
	☽P♇	0pm	30	D
	♀⊽♄	1	1	
	☽□♅	4	31	B
	☽☍☉	9	15	B
	☽⚼♂	9	16	b
	☉∠♂	9	47	
12 SU	☽☌♄	11am	12	B
	☽P♅	1pm	50	B
	☽P♄	8	40	B
	☽△♆	9	10	G
	☽△♂	11	37	G
13 M	☽P☉	0am	18	G
	☽☌♃	4	3	G
	☿±♃	5	9	
	☽P♆	8	24	D
	☽☍♇	10	22	B

	☽△♅	6pm 51	G
	☽⚼☿	7 51	b
	☽⚼♆	10 10	b
	☽P♃	11 23	G
14	☉Q♆	2am 48	
TU	☽⚺♄	0pm 52	g
	♀∠♅	7 18	
	☽⚼♅	7 45	b
	☽☍♀	7 47	B
	☽△☿	10 25	G
15	☽□♂	3am 38	B
W	☽⚺♃	5 24	g
	☽⚼☉	5 54	b
	☿□♆	7 58	
	☽∠♄	1pm 37	b
16	♀±♄	5am 30	
TH	☽∠♃	6 9	b
	☽△☉	8 46	G
	♀⚺♆	11 50	
	☽⚼♇	1pm 21	b
	☽✱♄	2 30	G
	♂△♃	2 38	
17	☽☍♆	1am 11	B
F	☽P♃	1 51	G
	☿⊥♇	4 13	
	☽□☿	4 33	B
	☉P♆	5 33	
	☽✱♃	7 7	G
	☽✱♂	8 0	G
	☽△♇	2pm 41	G
	☽P☉	3 42	G
	☽P♆	4 32	D
	☽☍♅	11 12	B
18	☽P♄	4am 58	B
S	☽⚼♀	6 9	b
	☿∇♃	8 14	
	☽∠♂	10 39	b
	☽P♅	11 30	B
	☿P♇	0pm 14	
	☽□☉	3 24	B
	☽□♄	5 3	B
19	♀∇♃	5am 33	
SU	☽□♃	9 54	B
	☽△♀	10 21	G
	☽P☿	10 26	G
	☽P♇	0pm 41	D
	☉☍♄	0 42	
	☽✱☿	0 45	G
	☽⚺♂	1 40	g
	☽□♇	6 18	B
20	☿⚺♂	6am 7	
M	☽⚼♆	6 28	b
	☽∠☿	5pm 46	b
	☽△♄	8 57	G
	☽✱☉	11 45	G
21	☽⚼♅	5am 26	b
TU	☽P♂	8 46	B
	☽△♆	8 58	G
	☽△♃	2pm 5	G
	☽□♀	8 12	B
	☽☌♂	9 0	B
	☿⚺♇	11 7	
	☽✱♇	11 24	G
	☽⚺☿	11 26	g
	☽⚼♄	11 28	b
22	☽∠☉	4am 40	b
W	☽△♅	8 18	G
	♀⊥♅	11 0	
	♀□♂	1pm 43	

	☽P♂	2 24	B
	☽⚼♃	4 46	b
23	☽∠♇	2am 36	b
TH	♀⚼♄	6 49	
	♀⚺♇	9 12	
	☽⚺☉	10 9	g
	☽□♆	3pm 17	B
	♀±♃	6 4	
	☉P♃	7 17	
	♂⚼♄	9 14	
24	♂✱♇	5am 3	
F	☽⚺♇	6 18	g
	☽⚺♂	6 22	g
	☽✱♀	8 23	G
	☽P♇	11 16	D
	☽☌☿	1pm 0	G
	☽□♅	3 28	B
25	☽P☿	7am 43	G
S	☽☍♄	9 52	B
	☿□♅	11 2	
	☽∠♂	11 58	b
	☽P♅	2pm 12	B
	☽∠♀	3 32	b
	☽P♄	8 50	B
	☽☌☉	11 11	D
	☽✱♆	11 42	G
26	☽☍♃	3am 50	B
SU	☉✱♆	5 38	
	☽P♆	11 27	D
	☽☌♇	3pm 27	D
	☽✱♂	6 17	G
	☽⚺♀	11 31	g
27	☽✱♅	0am 57	G
M	☽P♃	2 3	G
	☿P♅	3 48	
	☽∠♆	4 50	b
	☽⚺☿	6 6	g
	☉Q♅	6 29	
	☽P☉	0pm 5	G
	☿⊥♂	0 42	
	♀⚺♅	2 40	
28	☉☍♃	2am 12	
TU	☽∠♅	6 37	b
	☽⚺♆	10 34	g
	♀⊥♇	2pm 29	
	☽⚺☉	3 20	g
	☽∠☿	4 4	b
	☿Q♆	8 10	
	☿P♄	9 41	
29	☽⚼♄	1am 24	b
W	☽⚺♇	3 1	g
	☽□♂	8 57	B
	☽⚺♅	0pm 49	g
	☽☌♀	5 49	G
	☽⚼♃	7 58	b
30	☽∠☉	0am 25	b
TH	☽✱☿	2 47	G
	☽△♄	7 34	G
	☽P☉	8 50	G
	☽∠♇	9 30	b
	♀⚼♃	1pm 21	
	☽☌♆	11 22	D
DECEMBER			
1	☽△♃	2am 8	G
F	☽P♃	4 23	G
	☽✱☉	9 50	G
	☿☍♄	2pm 7	
	☽✱♇	4 10	G

	☽P♆	6 53	D
	☽P☿	10 6	G
2	☽△♂	1am 16	G
S	☽☌♅	2 0	B
	☽P♄	10 52	B
	☽⚺♀	1pm 38	g
	☿P♆	3 50	
	♂△♅	4 18	
	☽P♅	5 32	B
	☽□♄	8 10	B
3	☽□☿	0am 51	B
SU	☽⚼♂	9 12	b
	☽⚺♆	0pm 18	g
	☽□♃	2 12	B
	☽P♇	9 16	D
	☽∠♀	11 1	b
4	☽□☉	3am 55	B
M	☽□♇	4 44	B
	☉☌♇	2pm 3	
	☽⚺♅	2 12	g
	☽∠♆	6 0	b
5	♀△♄	3am 54	
TU	☽P♂	5 52	B
	☽✱♄	7 5	G
	☽✱♀	7 26	G
	☿P♃	2pm 28	
	☽∠♅	7 10	b
	☽△☿	8 7	G
	☽✱♆	10 50	G
	☽✱♃	11 55	G
6	☽∠♄	11am 15	b
W	♀∠♇	11 54	
	☽△♇	2pm 21	G
	☽△☉	6 16	G
	☿✱♆	6 49	
	♂⚼♃	7 44	
	☽✱♅	11 10	G
7	♂±♄	0am 57	
TH	☿☍♃	1 10	
	☽∠♃	3 23	b
	☽⚼☿	3 42	b
	☽☍♂	3 50	B
	☿∠♂	5 23	
	☉P♀	11 2	
	☿Q♅	11 47	
	☽⚺♄	2pm 26	g
	☽⚼♇	5 38	b
	☽□♀	8 22	B
	☽P♂	10 3	B
	☽⚼☉	11 32	b
8	☽□♆	5am 30	B
F	☽⚺♃	5 52	g
9	☽P♇	0 17	D
S	☽□♅	4 8	B
	☉✱♅	11 20	
	♃△♆	2pm 14	
	☽☌♄	6 0	B
	☽P♅	10 59	B
10	☿P♀	1am 24	
SU	☽P♄	4 10	B
	☽△♀	4 21	G
	☽☌♃	8 19	G
	☽△♆	8 31	G
	☽⚼♂	0pm 45	b
	☽P♆	5 25	D
	☽☍☿	6 31	B
	☽☍♇	10 13	B
11	☽P♃	3am 28	G
M	☽△♅	6 0	G

	☽⚼♀	7 4	b
	☽☍☉	9 3	B
	☽⚼♆	9 6	b
	☉∠♆	9 46	
	☽△♂	2pm 15	G
	☽P♀	5 45	G
	☽⚺♄	6 58	g
12	♀△♃	1am 16	
TU	☿☌♇	6 11	
	☽⚼♅	6 19	b
	☽⚺♃	8 40	g
	♀☌♆	9 24	
	☽∠♄	7pm 1	b
13	☽∠♃	8am 36	b
W	☽□♂	4pm 36	B
	☽✱♄	7 4	G
	☽⚼♇	11 4	b
14	☉P☿	1am 42	
TH	☽⚼☿	3 45	b
	☽✱♃	8 39	G
	☽☍♆	9 51	B
	☽P♀	10 44	G
	☽☍♀	1pm 53	B
	☽⚼☉	3 2	b
	☽P♃	4 14	G
	☽△♇	11 33	G
15	☽P♆	1am 54	D
F	☽△☿	7 10	G
	☽☍♅	7 24	B
	☿✱♅	9 24	
	☽P♄	3pm 23	B
	☽△☉	5 35	G
	☽✱♂	7 45	G
	☽□♄	7 57	B
	☽P♅	8 32	B
	♂∇♄	11 54	
16	♀P♃	7am 52	
S	☽□♃	9 49	B
	☿∠♆	2pm 36	
	☽P♇	6 30	D
	☽∠♂	10 8	b
17	☉∇♄	1am 18	
SU	☽□♇	1 53	B
	☽P♂	10 29	B
	☽⚼♆	1pm 17	b
	☽□☿	4 7	B
	☽△♄	10 51	G
18	☽⚼♀	0am 19	b
M	☽□☉	0 41	B
	☽⚺♂	1 13	g
	☽⚼♅	0pm 23	b
	☽△♃	1 13	G
	☽△♆	3 39	G
	☉✱♂	5 8	
19	☽⚼♄	1am 16	b
TU	☽△♀	5 23	G
	☽✱♇	6 42	G
	♂±♃	6 44	
	☉∠♀	1pm 15	
	☽△♅	3 22	G
	☽⚼♃	3 54	b
	♀P♆	5 46	
	♀✱♇	9 7	
20	☿∇♄	1am 15	
W	☽✱☿	4 48	G
	☽☌♂	9 41	B
	☽∠♇	10 8	b
	☽✱☉	11 7	G
	☉⊥♆	0pm 39	

	♂∠♇	8 10	
	☽□♆	10 24	B
21	☽P♂	5am 14	B
TH	☽∠☿	0pm 37	b
	☽⚺♇	2 13	g
	☽∠☉	5 35	b
	☽□♀	6 9	B
	☽P♇	6 37	D
	☽□♅	11 19	B
22	☿⊥♆	10am 55	
F	☽☍♄	0pm 28	B
	☉±♄	2 43	
	☿✱♂	6 31	
	☽P♅	6 49	B
	☽⚺♂	9 7	g
	☽⚺☿	9 21	g
23	☽P♄	0am 49	B
S	☽⚺☉	0 50	g
	☽☍♃	3 46	B
	☽P♀	6 6	G
	☽✱♆	7 42	G
	☽P♆	4pm 44	D
	☿±♄	5 15	
24	☽☌♇	0am 11	D
SU	☽P♃	3 5	G
	☽∠♂	3 49	b
	♀☌♅	5 52	
	☉∇♃	9 31	
	☽✱♅	9 40	G
	☽✱♀	10 3	G
	☽∠♆	1pm 11	b
	☉∠♅	7 41	
	☿∇♃	8 58	
25	♀P♄	2am 1	
M	☿∠♅	4 27	
	☽✱♂	11 5	G
	☽∠♅	3pm 36	b
	☽☌☿	5 15	G
	☽☌●	5 22	D
	☽∠♀	6 58	b
	☽⚺♆	7 7	g
	☉☌☿	7 23	
26	☽⚼♄	4am 40	b
TU	☿⚺♆	7 35	
	☽⚺♇	0pm 7	g
	☉⚺♆	2 42	
	☽⚼♃	8 21	b
	☽⚺♅	9 54	g
27	☽⚺♀	4am 22	g
W	♀P♅	6 26	
	☿∠♀	8 42	
	☽△♄	10 52	G
	☽∠♇	6pm 36	b
	♂∇♃	10 0	
28	☽△♃	2am 34	G
TH	☽□♂	2 50	B
	☽☌♆	8 0	D
	☿±♃	10 5	
	☽⚺☉	11 47	g
	☽⚺☿	3pm 27	g
	☽P♃	5 56	G
29	☽✱♇	1am 15	G
F	☽P♆	4 21	D
	☿⚼♄	4 21	
	☽☌♅	11 9	B
	☉±♃	6pm 50	
	☽P♄	9 3	B
	☽∠☉	9 13	b
	♀□♄	10 35	

DEC.-cont			
	☽□♄	11 40	B
	☽☌♀	11 47	G
30	☽∠☿	2am 48	b
S	☽P♅	3 40	B
	☽P♀	1pm 0	G
	☽□♃	3 7	B
	☽△♂	7 0	G
	♀Q♇	9 8	
	☽⚺♆	9 8	g
	☿⊥♅	11 14	
31	☉⚼♄	0am 29	
SU	☽P♇	4 14	D
	☽✱☉	6 23	G
	☽P♂	6 29	B
	☽✱☿	1pm 47	G
	☽□♇	2 8	B
	☿⚺♇	4 22	
	☽⚺♅	11 53	g

Note: The Distances Apart are in Declination

JANUARY

Day	Aspect	Time	Distance
1	☽☍♄	6am10	2 38
3	☽☌♀	4am52	2 30
3	☽☌♇	8pm54	6 39
6	☽☌☿	5am13	3 35
6	☽☌☉	6pm14	1 37
8	☽☌♆	5am44	0 12
9	☽☌♅	5am04	0 23
9	♀☌♇	9pm14	9 0
10	☽☌♂	8pm02	1 41
14	☽☌♃	5pm47	3 47
15	☽☌♄	6pm23	2 44
16	☉☌☿	1am19	1 58
17	☽☍♇	11pm02	6 41
18	☽☍♀	3pm55	2 4
21	☽●–●☉	4am40	0 18
21	☿☌♆	6am05	2 15
21	☽☍♆	10am18	0 15
21	☽☍☿	10am50	1 59
22	☽☍♅	5am48	0 27
24	☽☍♂	7am47	2 33
24	☉☌♆	6pm08	0 13
27	☽☍♃	11am59	3 52
28	☿☌♅	9am55	1 11
28	☽☍♄	1pm31	2 48
31	☽☌♇	5am17	6 44

FEBRUARY

Day	Aspect	Time	Distance
2	☽☌♀	3pm04	1 21
4	☽☌♆	2pm22	0 17
5	☽●☉	1pm03	1 5
5	☽☌♅	2pm28	0 31
6	☉☌♅	7am14	0 37
6	☽☌☿	8pm52	1 36
8	☽☌♂	7pm46	3 23
11	☽☌♃	5am19	3 55
12	☽☌♄	1am56	2 50
14	☽☍♇	7am47	6 51
17	☽☍♀	0pm51	0 26
17	☽☍♆	10pm21	0 20
18	☽☍♅	7pm05	0 35
19	☽☍☉	4pm27	2 12
20	☽☍☿	8pm59	5 35
22	♀☌♆	8am06	0 29
22	☽☍♂	9am19	3 58
24	☽☍♃	4am59	3 56
25	☽☍♄	0am52	2 50
27	☽☌♇	1pm54	6 59

MARCH

Day	Aspect	Time	Distance
1	☉☌☿	3pm10	3 25
2	☽☌♆	11pm59	0 25
4	♀☌♅	0am39	0 4
4	☽☌♅	1am09	0 39
4	☽●♀	1am12	0 36
5	☽☌☿	1pm19	5 46
6	☽☌☉	5am17	3 14
8	☽☌♂	5pm25	4 26
9	☽☌♃	7pm41	3 55
10	☽☌♄	10am58	2 47
12	☽☍♇	1pm47	7 9
15	☿☌♀	6pm23	2 1
16	☽☍♆	7am36	0 31
17	☽☍♅	6am00	0 45
18	☽☍☿	6am33	2 53
18	☽☍♀	11am24	1 32
20	☽☍☉	4am44	3 57
22	☽☍♂	10am26	4 43
23	☽☍♃	0am45	3 53
23	☽☍♄	2pm47	2 44
25	☽☌♇	10pm16	7 19
30	☽☌♆	9am51	0 38
31	☽☌♅	0pm19	0 53

APRIL

Day	Aspect	Time	Distance
2	☽☌☿	1pm46	1 24
3	☽☌♀	7am44	2 25
4	☽☌☉	6pm12	4 28
6	♂☌♃	6am41	0 59
6	☽☌♃	1pm09	3 50
6	☽☌♂	1pm23	4 50
6	☽☌♄	10pm50	2 40
8	☽☍♇	7pm17	7 29
12	☽☍♆	2pm15	0 46
13	☽☍♅	2pm03	1 1
15	♂☌♄	8pm28	2 10
16	☽☍☿	11pm52	1 54
17	☽☍♀	0pm39	3 4
18	☽☍☉	5pm41	4 41
19	☽☍♃	9pm09	3 47
20	☽☍♄	5am20	2 37
20	☽☍♂	10am36	4 46
22	☽☌♇	5am40	7 36
26	☽☌♆	6pm52	0 55
27	☽☌♅	10pm39	1 10
28	☿☌♀	1pm27	0 17

MAY

Day	Aspect	Time	Distance
3	☽☌♀	9am37	3 33
3	☽☌☿	4pm57	3 50
4	☽☌☉	4am12	4 37
4	☽☌♃	9am05	3 43
4	☽☌♄	1pm27	2 34
5	☽☌♂	8am08	4 31
6	☽☍♇	2am16	7 41
8	☉☌♃	4am08	0 50
8	☿☌♃	6pm53	0 47
9	☉☌☿	3am50	0 1
9	☽☍♆	8pm10	1 2
9	☿☌♄	8pm11	2 3
10	☉☌♄	7pm45	1 56
10	☽☍♅	8pm31	1 17
17	♀☌♃	10am30	0 1
17	☽☍♃	4pm54	3 39
17	☽☍♀	5pm28	3 40
17	☽☍♄	7pm14	2 31
18	☽☍☉	7am34	4 13
18	♀☌♄	0pm56	1 9
19	☽☍☿	9am14	5 12
19	☽☍♂	9am37	4 8
19	☽☌♇	11am40	7 42
19	☿☌♂	0pm26	1 5
19	☿☍♇	11pm41	12 55
20	♂☍♇	8pm25	11 47
24	☽☌♆	2am12	1 8
25	☽☌♅	6am59	1 24
28	♃☌♄	4pm04	1 7

JUNE

Day	Aspect	Time	Distance
1	☽☌♄	5am30	2 29
1	☽☌♃	6am08	3 35
1	☉☍♇	6pm17	11 13
2	☽☌♀	8am01	3 24
2	☽☍♇	11am03	7 40
2	☽☌☉	0pm14	3 30
3	☽☌♂	2am03	3 35
3	♀☍♇	8pm30	11 1
4	☽☌☿	3am36	3 34
6	☽☍♆	3am12	1 11
7	☽☍♅	3am13	1 27
11	☉☌♀	10am31	0 6
14	☽☍♄	7am58	2 27
14	☽☍♃	11am31	3 30
15	☽☌♇	4pm31	7 36
16	☽☍☉	10pm27	2 31
17	☽☍♀	1am50	2 42
17	☽☍♂	7am31	2 55
18	☽☍☿	9pm28	0 6
20	☽☌♆	7am51	1 13
21	☽☌♅	0pm58	1 30
21	♀☌♂	7pm27	0 18
28	☽☌♄	9pm06	2 24
29	☽☌♃	2am34	3 24
29	☽☍♇	8pm33	7 30

JULY

Day	Aspect	Time	Distance
1	☉☌♂	3pm50	0 52
1	☽☌♂	7pm16	2 11
1	☽●☉	7pm20	1 19
2	☽☌♀	4am56	1 37
2	☽☌☿	6am23	3 18
2	☿☌♀	5pm39	4 57
3	☽☍♆	11am55	1 12
4	☽☍♅	11am11	1 29
6	☉☌☿	11am35	4 38
7	☿☌♂	2pm08	5 39
11	☽☍♄	7pm36	2 20
12	☽☍♃	4am52	3 17
12	☽☌♇	9pm09	7 24
15	☽☍☿	9am59	3 16
16	☽☍♂	4am27	1 24
16	☽●–●☉	1pm55	0 2
17	☽☍♀	11am48	0 18
17	☽☌♆	0pm30	1 10
17	♀☍♆	6pm30	1 27
18	☽☌♅	5pm17	1 27
26	☽☌♄	10am20	2 15
26	☽☌♃	8pm35	3 8
27	☽☍♇	5am18	7 18
27	☉☍♆	10pm49	0 12
29	♀☍♅	2am00	0 40
29	☽●☿	5pm19	0 49
30	☽●♂	11am47	0 37
30	☽☍♆	9pm30	1 8
31	☽●☉	2am25	1 12
31	☽☍♅	8pm06	1 24

AUGUST

Day	Aspect	Time	Distance
1	☽●♀	2am14	1 0
8	☽☍♄	6am17	2 8
8	♂☍♆	2pm04	1 15
8	☽☍♃	8pm41	2 58
9	☽☌♇	2am44	7 14
9	☿☍♆	8pm33	1 4
10	☿☌♂	0pm37	0 5
11	☉☍♅	5am20	0 42
13	☽☌♆	5pm16	1 6
14	☽☍♂	0am35	0 9
14	☽☍☿	11am53	0 16
14	☽☌♅	9pm17	1 20
15	☽☍☉	5am13	2 20
16	☿☍♅	6pm43	0 51
16	☽☍♀	7pm58	2 17
22	☉☌☿	1am05	1 39
22	☽☌♄	7pm57	1 59
23	☽☌♃	10am33	2 46
23	☽☍♇	0pm27	7 11
27	☽☍♆	6am25	1 6
28	☽●♂	3am28	0 52
28	☽☍♅	4am44	1 19
29	♂☍♅	7am22	0 24
29	☽☌☉	10am19	3 14
29	☽☌☿	11pm33	2 23
31	☽☌♀	1am21	3 17

SEPTEMBER

Day	Aspect	Time	Distance
4	♃☍♇	10am53	9 48
4	☽☍♄	3pm56	1 52
5	☽☌♇	10am09	7 11
5	☽☍♃	10am17	2 36
9	☽☌♆	11pm05	1 7
11	☽☌♅	2am17	1 19
11	☽☍♂	8pm09	1 31
13	☽☍☉	7pm37	3 58
15	☽☍☿	9am57	4 56
15	☽☍♀	11pm54	4 10
19	☽☌♄	2am01	1 42
19	☽☍♇	6pm30	7 13
19	☽☌♃	7pm40	2 25
23	☽☍♆	1pm34	1 12
24	☽☍♅	11am54	1 21
25	☽☌♂	6pm13	2 5
27	☽☌☉	7pm53	4 25
29	☽☌☿	6pm06	6 42
30	☽☌♀	3am35	4 40

OCTOBER

Day	Aspect	Time	Distance
2	☽☍♄	0am03	1 35
2	☽☌♇	7pm22	7 15
2	☽☍♃	8pm28	2 17
7	☽☌♆	6am17	1 17
8	☽☌♅	8am55	1 26
10	☽☍♂	3pm18	2 35
13	♃☍♇	8am24	9 29
13	☽☍☉	8am53	4 38
15	☽☍☿	4am36	7 29
15	☽☍♀	11pm26	4 47
16	☽☌♄	6am17	1 29
17	☽☌♃	0am42	2 11
17	☽☍♇	1am13	7 18
19	♀☍♄	2am46	3 16
20	☽☍♆	7pm10	1 25
21	☽☍♅	5pm31	1 33
24	☽☌♂	7am59	2 58
27	☽☌☉	7am58	4 33
27	♀☍♃	11am17	2 21
27	☽☌☿	6pm20	5 48
28	♀☌♇	3pm32	11 48
29	☽☍♄	6am04	1 27
30	☉☌☿	2am09	0 38
30	☽☍♃	2am13	2 10
30	☽☌♇	5am32	7 21
30	☽☌♀	9am33	4 23

DISTANCES APART OF ALL ☌s AND ☍s IN 2000

Note: The Distances Apart are in Declination

NOVEMBER															
				19	☉☍♄	0pm42	2 15	2	☽☌♅	2am00	1 56	15	☽☍♅	7am24	2 2
				21	☽☌♂	9pm00	3 30	4	☉☌♇	2pm03	10 14	20	☽☌♂	9am41	3 37
3	☽☌♆	2pm36	1 33	24	☽☌☿	1pm00	2 39	7	☿☍♃	1am10	0 37	22	☽☍♄	0pm28	1 47
4	☽☌♅	5pm03	1 41	25	☽☍♄	9am52	1 33	7	☽☍♂	3am50	3 37	23	☽☍♃	3am46	2 41
8	☽☍♂	10am00	3 18	25	☽☌☉	11pm11	3 24	9	☽☌♄	6pm00	1 41	24	☽☌♇	0am11	7 27
10	☽☍☿	0pm00	2 36	26	☽☍♃	3am50	2 21	10	☽☌♃	8am19	2 31	24	♀☌♅	5am52	1 10
11	☽☍☉	9pm15	4 8	26	☽☌♇	3pm27	7 25	10	☽☍☿	6pm31	3 8	25	☽☌☿	5pm15	2 39
12	☽☌♄	11am12	1 29	28	☉☍♃	2am12	0 54	10	☽☍♇	10pm13	7 25	25	☽●☉	5pm22	1 2
13	☽☌♃	4am03	2 14	29	☽☌♀	5pm49	1 59	11	☽☍☉	9am03	2 18	25	☉☌☿	7pm23	1 37
13	☽☍♇	10am22	7 23	30	☽☌♆	11pm22	1 47	12	☿☌♇	6am11	10 34	28	☽☌♆	8am00	1 54
14	☽☍♀	7pm47	3 24	DECEMBER				12	♀☌♆	9am24	2 23	29	☽☌♅	11am09	2 6
17	☽☍♆	1am11	1 40					14	☽☍♆	9am51	1 51	29	☽☌♀	11pm47	1 37
17	☽☍♅	11pm12	1 49	1	☿☍♄	2pm07	1 21	14	☽☍♀	1pm53	0 17				

TIME WHEN THE SUN, MOON AND PLANETS ENTER THE ZODIACAL SIGNS IN 2000

JANUARY			FEBRUARY			MARCH			APRIL			MAY			JUNE		
2	☽♐	9pm32	1	☽♑	5pm10	2	☽♒	1pm14	1	☽♓	8am12	1	☽♈	0am55	1	☽♊	4pm34
4	♂♓	3am01	4	☽♒	5am31	4	☽♓	11pm30	3	☽♈	3pm22	1	♀♉	2am49	3	☽♋	4pm30
5	☽♑	10am24	5	☿♓	8am09	7	☽♈	6am54	5	☽♉	7pm29	3	☽♉	4am54	5	☽♌	4pm45
7	☽♒	10pm53	6	☽♓	4pm02	9	☽♉	0pm01	6	♀♈	6pm37	3	♂♊	7pm18	7	☽♍	6pm57
10	☽♓	9am59	9	☽♈	0am17	11	☽♊	3pm46	7	☽♊	9pm58	5	☽♊	6am23	9	☽♎	11pm59
12	☽♈	6pm48	11	☽♉	6am21	13	♀♓	11am36	10	☽♋	0am16	7	☽♋	7am14	12	☽♏	7am55
15	☽♉	0am38	12	♂♈	1am04	13	☽♋	6pm51	12	☽♌	3am16	9	☽♌	9am01	14	☽♐	6pm18
17	☽♊	3am25	13	☽♊	10am23	15	☽♌	9pm43	13	☿♈	0am17	11	☽♍	0pm41	16	♂♋	0pm30
18	☿♒	10pm20	14	♃♉	9pm39	18	☽♍	0am48	14	☽♍	7am19	13	☽♎	6pm27	17	☽♑	6am26
19	☽♋	4am01	15	☽♋	0pm45	20	☽♎	4am57	16	☽♎	0pm36	14	☿♊	7am10	18	♀♋	10pm15
20	☉♒	6pm23	17	☽♌	2pm11	20	☉♈	7am35	18	☽♏	7pm35	16	☽♏	2am16	19	☽♒	7pm26
21	☽♌	3am58	18	♀♒	4am43	22	☽♏	11am17	19	☉♉	6pm39	18	☽♐	0pm09	21	☉♋	1am48
23	☽♍	5am07	19	☉♓	8am33	23	♂♉	1am25	21	☽♐	4am58	20	☉♊	5pm49	22	☽♓	7am52
24	♀♑	7pm52	19	☽♍	3pm53	24	☽♐	8pm43	23	☽♑	4pm47	21	☽♑	0am01	24	☽♈	5pm55
25	☽♎	9am09	21	☽♎	7pm21	27	☽♑	8am51	26	☽♒	5am42	23	☽♒	1pm00	27	☽♉	0am19
27	☽♏	5pm01	24	☽♏	1am58	29	☽♒	9pm34	28	☽♓	5pm06	25	♀♊	0pm15	29	☽♊	2am59
30	☽♐	4am17	26	☽♐	0pm10				30	☿♉	3am53	26	☽♓	1am07	30	♃♊	7am34
			29	☽♑	0am45							28	☽♈	10am08			
												30	☿♋	4am27			
												30	☽♉	3pm02			

JULY			AUGUST			SEPTEMBER			OCTOBER			NOVEMBER			DECEMBER		
1	☽♋	3am09	1	♂♌	1am21	2	☽♏	5am55	1	☽♐	10pm50	3	☽♒	6am41	3	☽♓	3am23
3	☽♌	2am38	1	☽♍	1pm27	4	☽♐	2pm08	4	☽♑	9am42	4	♂♎	2am00	3	☿♐	8pm26
5	☽♍	3am19	3	☽♎	3pm31	7	☽♑	1am47	6	☽♒	10pm33	5	☽♓	7pm13	5	☽♈	2pm17
7	☽♎	6am47	5	☽♏	9pm04	7	☿♎	10pm22	9	☽♓	10am36	7	☿♎	7am28	7	☽♉	9pm27
9	☽♏	1pm48	6	♀♍	5pm32	9	☽♒	2pm44	11	☽♈	7pm51	8	☽♈	5am02	8	♀♒	8am48
12	☽♐	0am06	7	☿♌	5am42	12	☽♓	2am34	14	☽♉	2am06	8	☿♏	9pm42	10	☽♊	0am50
13	♀♌	8am02	8	☽♐	6am30	14	☽♈	0pm00	16	♄♉	0am46	10	☽♉	11am12	12	☽♋	1am48
14	☽♑	0pm28	10	♄♊	2am25	16	☽♉	7pm05	16	☽♊	6am19	12	☽♊	2pm27	14	☽♌	2am09
17	☽♒	1am27	10	☽♑	6pm44	17	♂♍	0am19	18	☽♋	9am37	13	♀♑	2am14	16	☽♍	3am30
19	☽♓	1pm44	13	☽♒	7am43	19	☽♊	0am22	19	♀♐	6am18	14	☽♋	4pm21	18	☽♎	7am01
22	☽♈	0am09	15	☽♓	7pm41	21	☽♋	4am16	20	☽♌	0pm42	16	☽♌	6pm19	20	☽♏	1pm12
22	☉♌	0pm43	18	☽♈	5am44	22	☉♎	5pm28	22	☽♍	3pm52	18	☽♍	9pm15	21	☉♑	1pm37
24	☽♉	7am44	20	☽♉	1pm31	23	☽♌	7am00	23	☉♏	2am47	21	☽♎	1am35	22	☽♐	9pm57
26	☽♊	0pm01	22	☿♍	10am11	24	♀♏	3pm26	24	☽♎	7pm30	22	☉♐	0am19	23	☿♑	2am03
28	☽♋	1pm30	22	☽♊	6pm55	25	☽♍	9am02	27	☽♏	0am23	23	☽♏	7am33	23	♂♏	2pm37
30	☽♌	1pm23	22	☉♍	7pm49	27	☽♎	11am22	29	☽♐	7am40	25	☽♐	3pm33	25	☽♑	8am54
			24	☽♋	10pm00	28	☿♏	1pm28	31	☽♑	6pm01	28	☽♑	1am57	27	☽♒	9pm25
			26	☽♌	11pm17	29	☽♏	3pm29				30	☽♒	2pm26	30	☽♓	10am27
			28	☽♍	11pm55												
			31	☽♎	1am33												
			31	♀♎	3am35												

LOCAL MEAN TIME OF SUNRISE FOR LATITUDES 60° North to 50° South

FOR ALL SUNDAYS IN 2000. (ALL TIMES ARE A.M.)

Date	NORTHERN LATITUDES								SOUTHERN LATITUDES					
	LONDON	60°	55°	50°	40°	30°	20°	10°	0°	10°	20°	30°	40°	50°
1999	H M	H M	H M	H M	H M	H M	H M	H M	H M	H M	H M	H M	H M	H M
Dec. 26	8 5	9 4	8 25	7 58	7 20	6 54	6 32	6 14	5 57	5 39	5 20	4 58	4 30	3 50
2000														
Jan. 2	8 6	9 2	8 25	7 58	7 22	6 56	6 35	6 17	6 0	5 43	5 24	5 2	4 35	3 55
9	8 4	8 57	8 21	7 57	7 22	6 57	6 37	6 19	6 3	5 46	5 29	5 8	4 41	4 3
16	8 0	8 48	8 16	7 53	7 20	6 57	6 38	6 22	6 6	5 50	5 33	5 13	4 49	4 13
23	7 52	8 35	8 7	7 46	7 16	6 55	6 38	6 22	6 8	5 54	5 38	5 20	4 57	4 25
30	7 43	8 21	7 56	7 38	7 11	6 52	6 37	6 23	6 9	5 56	5 42	5 26	5 5	4 37
Feb. 6	7 32	8 4	7 43	7 27	7 4	6 48	6 34	6 22	6 11	5 59	5 46	5 32	5 14	4 49
13	7 20	7 46	7 29	7 16	6 57	6 43	6 31	6 21	6 11	6 1	5 50	5 38	5 23	5 1
20	7 6	7 27	7 13	7 3	6 48	6 36	6 27	6 19	6 11	6 2	5 53	5 44	5 31	5 14
27	6 51	7 7	6 57	6 50	6 38	6 29	6 22	6 15	6 9	6 3	5 57	5 48	5 39	5 25
Mar. 5	6 36	6 47	6 40	6 35	6 27	6 22	6 17	6 12	6 8	6 4	5 59	5 54	5 47	5 37
12	6 21	6 26	6 23	6 20	6 16	6 14	6 11	6 9	6 7	6 4	6 1	5 59	5 54	5 49
19	6 5	6 5	6 5	6 5	6 5	6 5	6 5	6 5	6 4	6 4	6 4	6 3	6 2	6 0
26	5 49	5 44	5 47	5 50	5 54	5 57	5 59	6 1	6 2	6 4	6 5	6 7	6 9	6 11
Apr. 2	5 34	5 22	5 29	5 35	5 42	5 49	5 53	5 57	6 1	6 4	6 7	6 11	6 16	6 22
9	5 18	5 1	5 12	5 20	5 32	5 40	5 47	5 53	5 58	6 4	6 9	6 15	6 23	6 33
16	5 2	4 40	4 55	5 5	5 21	5 32	5 41	5 49	5 56	6 4	6 11	6 20	6 30	6 44
23	4 47	4 20	4 38	4 51	5 11	5 25	5 36	5 46	5 55	6 4	6 13	6 24	6 37	6 55
30	4 34	4 1	4 22	4 38	5 1	5 18	5 32	5 43	5 54	6 4	6 16	6 28	6 44	7 5
May 7	4 21	3 42	4 8	4 26	4 53	5 12	5 28	5 41	5 53	6 5	6 18	6 33	6 51	7 15
14	4 10	3 25	3 54	4 16	4 46	5 7	5 25	5 39	5 53	6 6	6 20	6 37	6 57	7 25
21	4 1	3 9	3 43	4 6	4 40	5 3	5 22	5 38	5 53	6 8	6 24	6 41	7 3	7 35
28	3 52	2 56	3 33	3 59	4 35	5 0	5 20	5 38	5 54	6 9	6 26	6 45	7 9	7 43
June 4	3 46	2 45	3 26	3 54	4 32	4 59	5 20	5 38	5 54	6 11	6 29	6·49	7 15	7 50
11	3 43	2 39	3 21	3 51	4 30	4 58	5 20	5 39	5 56	6 13	6 32	6 52	7 18	7 55
18	3 42	2 36	3 20	3 50	4 31	4 59	5 21	5 40	5 57	6 15	6 33	6 55	7 21	7 59
25	3 43	2 37	3 21	3 52	4 32	5 0	5 23	5 41	5 59	6 16	6 35	6 56	7 22	8 0
July 2	3 47	2 43	3 26	3 55	4 35	5 3	5 25	5 43	6 1	6 18	6 36	6 56	7 22	7 59
9	3 53	2 53	3 33	4 1	4 39	5 6	5 27	5 45	6 2	6 18	6 36	6 56	7 21	7 56
16	4 1	3 5	3 42	4 8	4 45	5 10	5 29	5 46	6 2	6 18	6 35	6 54	7 17	7 51
23	4 11	3 20	3 54	4 17	4 50	5 13	5 32	5 48	6 3	6 17	6 33	6 51	7 13	7 43
30	4 20	3 36	4 5	4 26	4 56	5 18	5 35	5 49	6 3	6 16	6 31	6 47	7 7	7 34
Aug. 6	4 31	3 52	4 18	4 36	5 3	5 22	5 37	5 50	6 2	6 15	6 27	6 41	6 59	7 23
13	4 42	4 9	4 31	4 46	5 9	5 26	5 39	5 51	6 1	6 12	6 23	6 36	6 50	7 12
20	4 53	4 26	4 44	4 57	5 16	5 30	5 41	5 51	6 0	6 9	6 18	6 29	6 41	6 59
27	5 5	4 43	4 47	5 7	5 23	5 34	5 43	5 51	5 58	6 5	6 12	6 21	6 31	6 45
Sept. 3	5 16	5 0	5 10	5 18	5 29	5 38	5 45	5 51	5 56	6 1	6 7	6 13	6 21	6 30
10	5 27	5 16	5 23	5 28	5 36	5 42	5 46	5 50	5 54	5 57	6 1	6 5	6 9	6 15
17	5 38	5 32	5 36	5 38	5 43	5 46	5 47	5 50	5 52	5 53	5 54	5 56	5 57	6 0
24	5 49	5 49	5 49	5 49	5 49	5 49	5 49	5 49	5 49	5 49	5 48	5 47	5 46	5 44
Oct. 1	6 1	6 5	6 3	6 0	5 56	5 53	5 51	5 49	5 46	5 44	5 42	5 39	5 35	5 29
8	6 12	6 22	6 16	6 11	6 3	5 58	5 52	5 48	5 45	5 40	5 35	5 30	5 23	5 14
15	6 23	6 39	6 30	6 22	6 11	6 2	5 55	5 48	5 42	5 36	5 30	5 22	5 13	4 59
22	6 36	6 57	6 43	6 33	6 18	6 7	5 57	5 49	5 41	5 33	5 25	5 15	5 2	4 45
29	6 49	7 15	6 57	6 45	6 25	6 12	6 0	5 50	5 40	5 31	5 20	5 8	4 53	4 32
Nov. 5	7 1	7 33	7 12	6 56	6 34	6 17	6 3	5 52	5 40	5 29	5 16	5 2	4 44	4 20
12	7 13	7 51	7 26	7 8	6 42	6 22	6 7	5 53	5 40	5 28	5 14	4 58	4 37	4 9
19	7 25	8 8	7 39	7 19	6 50	6 28	6 11	5 56	5 42	5 28	5 12	4 54	4 31	4 0
26	7 36	8 25	7 52	7 30	6 58	6 34	6 15	5 59	5 44	5 28	5 11	4 52	4 27	3 53
Dec. 3	7 46	8 39	8 4	7 39	7 5	6 40	6 20	6 3	5 46	5 30	5 12	4 51	4 25	3 48
10	7 55	8 50	8 14	7 47	7 11	6 45	6 25	6 6	5 49	5 32	5 13	4 52	4 25	3 45
17	8 1	8 59	8 20	7 53	7 15	6 49	6 28	6 10	5 53	5 35	5 16	4 54	4 26	3 46
24	8 4	9 3	8 24	7 57	7 20	6 53	6 32	6 13	5 56	5 38	5 19	4 57	4 29	3 49
31	8 3	9 3	8 25	7 58	7 22	6 55	6 34	6 16	6 0	5 43	5 24	5 2	4 34	3 54

Example:—To find the time of Sunrise in Jamaica (Latitude 18° N.) on Wednesday, June 21st, 2000. On June 18th, L.M.T.=5h. 21m.+$\frac{2}{10}$×19m.=5h. 25m., on June 25th, L.M.T.=5h. 23m.+$\frac{2}{10}$×18m.=5h. 27m., therefore L.M.T., on June 21st=5h. 25m.+$\frac{3}{7}$×2m.=5h. 26m. A.M.

LOCAL MEAN TIME OF SUNSET FOR LATITUDES

60° North to 50° South

FOR ALL SUNDAYS IN 2000. (ALL TIMES ARE P.M.)

Date	NORTHERN LATITUDES									SOUTHERN LATITUDES				
	LONDON	60°	55°	50°	40°	30°	20°	10°	0°	10°	20°	30°	40°	50°
1999	H M	H M	H M	H M	H M	H M	H M	H M	H M	H M	H M	H M	H M	H M
Dec. 26	3 55	2 57	3 36	4 3	4 41	5 7	5 28	5 47	6 4	6 22	6 40	7 2	7 30	8 11
2000														
Jan. 2	4 2	3 5	3 43	4 9	4 46	5 12	5 32	5 50	6 7	6 25	6 43	7 5	7 32	8 12
9	4 10	3 17	3 53	4 17	4 52	5 17	5 37	5 54	6 10	6 27	6 45	7 6	7 32	8 9
16	4 20	3 32	4 4	4 27	4 59	5 23	5 41	5 58	6 13	6 29	6 46	7 5	7 30	8 5
23	4 31	3 49	4 17	4 38	5 7	5 29	5 46	6 1	6 15	6 30	6 45	7 3	7 26	7 58
30	4 44	4 7	4 31	4 50	5 15	5 35	5 50	6 4	6 17	6 30	6 44	7 0	7 20	7 49
Feb. 6	4 57	4 25	4 45	5 1	5 24	5 40	5 54	6 7	6 18	6 29	6 41	6 56	7 13	7 38
13	5 9	4 43	5 0	5 13	5 32	5 46	5 58	6 8	6 18	6 27	6 38	6 50	7 5	7 26
20	5 22	5 2	5 15	5 26	5 40	5 52	6 1	6 9	6 17	6 25	6 34	6 44	6 56	7 13
27	5 35	5 20	5 29	5 37	5 49	5 57	6 4	6 10	6 16	6 22	6 29	6 37	6 46	6 59
Mar. 5	5 47	5 38	5 44	5 49	5 56	6 2	6 7	6 11	6 15	6 19	6 24	6 29	6 36	6 45
12	5 59	5 55	5 58	6 1	6 4	6 7	6 9	6 11	6 13	6 15	6 18	6 21	6 24	6 30
19	6 11	6 12	6 12	6 11	6 11	6 11	6 11	6 11	6 11	6 11	6 12	6 12	6 13	6 14
26	6 23	6 29	6 26	6 23	6 18	6 15	6 13	6 11	6 9	6 7	6 6	6 4	6 2	5 59
Apr. 2	6 35	6 46	6 39	6 34	6 25	6 19	6 14	6 11	6 7	6 3	6 0	5 56	5 50	5 44
9	6 46	7 3	6 53	6 44	6 32	6 23	6 17	6 10	6 5	5 59	5 54	5 47	5 40	5 29
16	6 58	7 21	7 6	6 55	6 39	6 28	6 19	6 11	6 3	5 56	5 48	5 40	5 29	5 15
23	7 10	7 38	7 20	7 6	6 46	6 32	6 21	6 11	6 2	5 53	5 43	5 32	5 19	5 1
30	7 21	7 55	7 33	7 18	6 54	6 36	6 24	6 12	6 0	5 50	5 39	5 26	5 10	4 49
May 7	7 32	8 13	7 47	7 28	7 1	6 41	6 26	6 13	6 0	5 48	5 35	5 20	5 2	4 37
14	7 43	8 29	8 0	7 38	7 7	6 46	6 28	6 14	6 0	5 46	5 32	5 15	4 55	4 27
21	7 54	8 46	8 12	7 48	7 14	6 50	6 32	6 16	6 0	5 45	5 29	5 12	4 50	4 18
28	8 3	9 0	8 22	7 56	7 20	6 54	6 34	6 17	6 1	5 45	5 28	5 9	4 45	4 11
June 4	8 11	9 12	8 33	8 3	7 25	6 58	6 37	6 19	6 2	5 45	5 28	5 7	4 42	4 7
11	8 16	9 22	8 38	8 8	7 29	7 1	6 40	6 21	6 3	5 46	5 28	5 7	4 41	4 4
18	8 20	9 27	8 42	8 12	7 31	7 3	6 41	6 22	6 5	5 47	5 29	5 8	4 41	4 3
25	8 21	9 28	8 43	8 13	7 33	7 5	6 43	6 24	6 6	5 49	5 30	5 9	4 42	4 5
July 2	8 20	9 24	8 41	8 12	7 32	7 5	6 43	6 25	6 8	5 51	5 33	5 12	4 46	4 9
9	8 17	9 16	8 36	8 9	7 31	7 4	6 43	6 26	6 9	5 52	5 35	5 15	4 50	4 15
16	8 11	9 5	8 29	8 3	7 27	7 2	6 43	6 26	6 10	5 54	5 37	5 18	4 55	4 22
23	8 2	8 51	8 19	7 55	7 22	6 59	6 40	6 25	6 10	5 55	5 40	5 22	5 0	4 30
30	7 52	8 35	8 6	7 46	7 16	6 55	6 38	6 23	6 10	5 56	5 42	5 26	5 7	4 39
Aug. 6	7 40	8 17	7 53	7 34	7 8	6 49	6 34	6 22	6 9	5 57	5 44	5 31	5 13	4 48
13	7 28	7 59	7 38	7 22	6 59	6 43	6 30	6 18	6 8	5 58	5 47	5 34	5 19	4 59
20	7 13	7 39	7 22	7 9	6 50	6 36	6 25	6 16	6 7	5 58	5 49	5 38	5 26	5 9
27	6 58	7 18	7 5	6 55	6 39	6 28	6 19	6 12	6 5	5 58	5 50	5 42	5 32	5 19
Sept. 3	6 43	6 58	6 47	6 40	6 29	6 20	6 14	6 8	6 2	5 57	5 52	5 46	5 39	5 29
10	6 27	6 36	6 30	6 25	6 17	6 12	6 7	6 4	6 0	5 57	5 54	5 50	5 45	5 39
17	6 11	6 15	6 12	6 9	6 5	6 3	6 1	5 59	5 58	5 56	5 55	5 54	5 52	5 50
24	5 55	5 54	5 54	5 54	5 54	5 54	5 55	5 55	5 55	5 56	5 57	5 57	5 58	6 0
Oct. 1	5 38	5 33	5 36	5 39	5 43	5 46	5 48	5 51	5 53	5 55	5 58	6 1	6 5	6 11
8	5 23	5 12	5 18	5 24	5 31	5 38	5 42	5 47	5 51	5 55	6 0	6 6	6 12	6 22
15	5 8	4 51	5 1	5 9	5 21	5 29	5 37	5 43	5 49	5 55	6 2	6 10	6 20	6 33
22	4 53	4 31	4 44	4 55	5 11	5 22	5 32	5 40	5 48	5 56	6 5	6 15	6 27	6 45
29	4 39	4 12	4 29	4 42	5 2	5 15	5 27	5 38	5 47	5 57	6 8	6 20	6 35	6 57
Nov. 5	4 27	3 54	4 15	4 31	4 53	5 10	5 24	5 36	5 47	5 59	6 11	6 25	6 44	7 8
12	4 16	3 37	4 2	4 20	4 46	5 6	5 21	5 35	5 48	6 1	6 15	6 31	6 52	7 21
19	4 6	3 22	3 51	4 11	4 41	5 3	5 20	5 35	5 49	6 3	6 19	6 37	7 0	7 32
26	3 58	3 10	3 42	4 5	4 37	5 0	5 19	5 36	5 51	6 7	6 23	6 43	7 8	7 43
Dec. 3	3 53	3 0	3 35	4 0	4 35	5 0	5 20	5 37	5 54	6 10	6 28	6 49	7 15	7 53
10	3 51	2 55	3 32	3 58	4 35	5 1	5 21	5 39	5 57	6 14	6 33	6 54	7 22	8 1
17	3 52	2 53	3 32	3 59	4 37	5 3	5 24	5 43	6 0	6 18	6 36	6 58	7 26	8 7
24	3 55	2 56	3 35	4 2	4 40	5 6	5 27	5 46	6 3	6 21	6 40	7 2	7 30	8 11
31	4 1	3 3	3 41	4 8	4 45	5 11	5 32	5 49	6 6	6 24	6 42	7 4	7 32	8 12

Example:—To find the time of Sunset in Canberra (Latitude 35°.3S.) on Thursday, August 3rd, 2000. On July 30th, L.M.T.=5h. 26m. $-\frac{5.3}{10}\times$19m.=5h. 16m., on August 6th, L.M.T.=5h. 31m. $-\frac{5.3}{10}\times$18m.=5h. 21m., therefore L.M.T. on August 3rd=5h. 16m.$+\frac{4}{7}\times$5m.=5h. 19m. P.M.

TABLES OF HOUSES FOR LONDON, Latitude 51° 32' N.

Sidereal Time.	10 ♈	11 ♉	12 ♊	Ascen ♋	2 ♌	3 ♍
H. M. S.	°	°	°	° '	°	°
0 0 0	0	9	22	26 36	12	3
0 3 40	1	10	23	27 17	13	3
0 7 20	2	11	24	27 56	14	4
0 11 0	3	12	25	28 42	15	5
0 14 41	4	13	25	29 17	15	6
0 18 21	5	14	26	29 55	16	7
0 22 2	6	15	27	0♌34	17	8
0 25 42	7	16	28	1 14	18	8
0 29 23	8	17	29	1 55	18	9
0 33 4	9	18	♋	2 33	19	10
0 36 45	10	19	1	3 14	20	11
0 40 26	11	20	1	3 54	20	12
0 44 8	12	21	2	4 33	21	13
0 47 50	13	22	3	5 12	22	14
0 51 32	14	23	4	5 52	23	15
0 55 14	15	24	5	6 30	23	15
0 58 57	16	25	6	7 9	24	16
1 2 40	17	26	6	7 50	25	17
1 6 23	18	27	7	8 30	26	18
1 10 7	19	28	8	9 9	26	19
1 13 51	20	29	9	9 48	27	19
1 17 35	21	♊	10	10 28	28	20
1 21 20	22	1	10	11 8	28	21
1 25 6	23	2	11	11 48	29	22
1 28 52	24	3	12	12 28	♍	23
1 32 38	25	4	13	13 8	1	24
1 36 25	26	5	14	13 48	1	25
1 40 12	27	6	14	14 28	2	25
1 44 0	28	7	15	15 8	3	26
1 47 48	29	8	16	15 48	4	27
1 51 37	30	9	17	16 28	4	28

Sidereal Time.	10 ♉	11 ♊	12 ♋	Ascen ♌	2 ♍	3 ♍
H. M. S.	°	°	°	° '	°	°
1 51 37	0	9	17	16 28	4	28
1 55 27	1	10	18	17 8	5	29
1 59 17	2	11	19	17 48	6	♎
2 3 8	3	12	19	18 28	7	1
2 6 59	4	13	20	19 9	8	2
2 10 51	5	14	21	19 49	9	2
2 14 44	6	15	22	20 29	9	3
2 18 37	7	16	22	21 10	10	4
2 22 31	8	17	23	21 51	11	5
2 26 25	9	18	24	22 32	11	6
2 30 20	10	19	25	23 14	12	7
2 34 16	11	20	25	23 55	13	8
2 38 13	12	21	26	24 36	14	9
2 42 10	13	22	27	25 17	15	10
2 46 8	14	23	28	25 58	15	11
2 50 7	15	24	29	26 40	16	12
2 54 7	16	25	29	27 22	17	12
2 58 7	17	26	♌	28 4	18	13
3 2 8	18	27	1	28 46	18	14
3 6 9	19	27	2	29 28	19	15
3 10 12	20	28	3	0♍12	20	16
3 14 15	21	29	3	0 54	21	17
3 18 19	22	♋	4	1 36	22	18
3 22 23	23	1	5	2 20	22	19
3 26 29	24	2	6	3 2	23	20
3 30 35	25	3	7	3 45	24	21
3 34 41	26	4	7	4 28	25	22
3 38 49	27	5	8	5 11	26	23
3 42 57	28	6	9	5 54	27	24
3 47 6	29	7	10	6 38	27	25
3 51 15	30	8	11	7 21	28	25

Sidereal Time.	10 ♊	11 ♋	12 ♌	Ascen ♍	2 ♍	3 ♎
H. M. S.	°	°	°	° '	°	°
3 51 15	0	8	11	7 21	28	25
3 55 25	1	9	12	8 5	29	26
3 59 36	2	10	12	8 49	♎	27
4 3 48	3	10	13	9 33	1	28
4 8 0	4	11	14	10 17	2	29
4 12 13	5	12	15	11 2	2	♏
4 16 26	6	13	16	11 46	3	1
4 20 40	7	14	17	12 30	4	2
4 24 55	8	15	17	13 15	5	3
4 29 10	9	16	18	14 0	6	4
4 33 26	10	17	19	14 45	7	5
4 37 42	11	18	20	15 30	8	6
4 41 59	12	19	21	16 15	8	7
4 46 16	13	20	21	17 0	9	8
4 50 34	14	21	22	17 45	10	9
4 54 52	15	22	23	18 30	11	10
4 59 10	16	23	24	19 16	12	11
5 3 29	17	24	25	20 3	13	12
5 7 49	18	25	26	20 49	14	13
5 12 9	19	25	27	21 35	14	14
5 16 29	20	26	28	22 20	15	14
5 20 49	21	27	28	23 6	16	15
5 25 9	22	28	29	23 51	17	16
5 29 30	23	29	♏	24 37	18	17
5 33 51	24	♌	1	25 23	19	18
5 38 12	25	1	2	26 9	20	19
5 42 34	26	2	3	26 55	21	20
5 46 55	27	3	4	27 41	21	21
5 51 17	28	4	4	28 27	22	22
5 55 38	29	5	5	29 13	23	23
6 0 0	30	6	6	30 0	24	24

Sidereal Time.	10 ♋	11 ♌	12 ♍	Ascen ♎	2 ♎	3 ♏
H. M. S.	°	°	°	° '	°	°
6 0 0	0	6	6	0 0	24	24
6 4 22	1	7	7	0 47	25	25
6 8 43	2	8	8	1 33	26	26
6 13 5	3	9	9	2 19	27	27
6 17 26	4	10	10	3 5	27	28
6 21 48	5	11	10	3 51	28	29
6 26 9	6	12	11	4 37	29	♐
6 30 30	7	13	12	5 23	♏	1
6 34 51	8	14	13	6 9	1	2
6 39 11	9	15	14	6 55	2	3
6 43 31	10	16	15	7 40	2	4
6 47 51	11	16	16	8 26	3	4
6 52 11	12	17	16	9 12	4	5
6 56 31	13	18	17	9 58	5	6
7 0 50	14	19	18	10 43	6	7
7 5 8	15	20	19	11 28	7	8
7 9 26	16	21	20	12 14	8	9
7 13 44	17	22	21	12 59	8	10
7 18 1	18	23	22	13 45	9	11
7 22 18	19	24	23	14 30	10	12
7 26 34	20	25	24	15 15	11	13
7 30 50	21	26	25	16 0	12	14
7 35 5	22	27	25	16 45	13	15
7 39 20	23	28	26	17 30	13	16
7 43 34	24	29	27	18 15	14	17
7 47 47	25	♍	28	18 59	15	18
7 52 0	26	1	29	19 43	16	19
7 56 12	27	2	29	20 27	17	20
8 0 24	28	3	♎	21 11	18	20
8 4 35	29	4	1	21 56	18	21
8 8 45	30	5	2	22 40	19	22

Sidereal Time.	10 ♌	11 ♍	12 ♎	Ascen ♎	2 ♏	3 ♐
H. M. S.	°	°	°	° '	°	°
8 8 45	0	5	2	22 40	19	22
8 12 54	1	5	3	23 24	20	23
8 17 3	2	6	3	24 7	21	24
8 21 11	3	7	4	24 50	22	25
8 25 19	4	8	5	25 34	23	26
8 29 26	5	9	6	26 18	23	27
8 33 31	6	10	7	27 1	24	28
8 37 37	7	11	8	27 44	25	29
8 41 41	8	12	8	28 26	26	♑
8 45 45	9	13	9	29 8	27	1
8 49 48	10	14	10	29 50	27	2
8 53 51	11	15	11	0♏32	28	3
8 57 52	12	16	12	1 15	29	4
9 1 53	13	17	12	1 58	♐	4
9 5 53	14	18	13	2 39	1	5
9 9 53	15	18	14	3 21	1	6
9 13 52	16	19	15	4 3	2	7
9 17 50	17	20	16	4 44	3	8
9 21 47	18	21	16	5 26	3	9
9 25 44	19	22	17	6 7	4	10
9 29 40	20	23	18	6 48	5	11
9 33 35	21	24	18	7 29	5	12
9 37 29	22	25	19	8 9	6	13
9 41 23	23	26	20	8 50	7	14
9 45 16	24	27	21	9 31	8	15
9 49 9	25	28	22	10 11	9	16
9 53 1	26	28	23	10 51	9	17
9 56 52	27	29	23	11 32	10	18
10 0 43	28	♎	24	12 12	11	19
10 4 33	29	1	25	12 53	12	20
10 8 23	30	2	26	13 33	13	20

Sidereal Time.	10 ♍	11 ♎	12 ♎	Ascen ♏	2 ♐	3 ♑
H. M. S.	°	°	°	° '	°	°
10 8 23	0	2	26	13 33	13	20
10 12 12	1	3	26	14 13	14	21
10 16 0	2	4	27	14 53	15	22
10 19 48	3	5	28	15 33	15	23
10 23 35	4	5	29	16 13	16	24
10 27 22	5	6	29	16 52	17	25
10 31 8	6	7	♏	17 32	18	26
10 34 54	7	8	1	18 12	19	27
10 38 40	8	9	2	18 52	20	28
10 42 25	9	10	2	19 31	20	29
10 46 9	10	11	3	20 11	21	♒
10 49 53	11	11	4	20 50	22	1
10 53 37	12	12	4	21 30	23	2
10 57 20	13	13	5	22 9	24	3
11 1 3	14	14	6	22 49	24	4
11 4 46	15	15	7	23 28	25	5
11 8 28	16	16	7	24 8	26	6
11 12 10	17	17	8	24 47	27	8
11 15 52	18	17	9	25 27	28	9
11 19 34	19	18	10	26 6	29	10
11 23 15	20	19	10	26 45	♑	11
11 26 56	21	20	11	27 25	0	12
11 30 37	22	21	12	28 5	1	13
11 34 18	23	22	13	28 44	2	14
11 37 58	24	23	13	29 24	3	15
11 41 39	25	23	14	0♐3	4	16
11 45 19	26	24	15	0 43	5	17
11 49 0	27	25	15	1 23	6	18
11 52 40	28	26	16	2 3	6	19
11 56 20	29	27	17	2 43	7	20
12 0 0	30	27	17	3 23	8	21

TABLES OF HOUSES FOR LONDON, Latitude 51º 32' *N.*

Sidereal Time.	10 ♎	11 ♎	12 ♏	Ascen ♐	2 ♑	3 ♒
H. M. S.	°	°	°	° '	°	°
12 0 0	0	27	17	3 23	8	21
12 3 40	1	28	18	4 4	9	23
12 7 20	2	29	19	4 45	10	24
12 11 0	3	♏	20	5 26	11	25
12 14 41	4	1	20	6 7	12	26
12 18 21	5	1	21	6 48	13	27
12 22 2	6	2	22	7 29	14	28
12 25 42	7	3	23	8 10	15	29
12 29 23	8	4	23	8 51	16	♓
12 33 4	9	5	24	9 33	17	2
12 36 45	10	6	25	10 15	18	3
12 40 26	11	6	25	10 57	19	4
12 44 8	12	7	26	11 40	20	5
12 47 50	13	8	27	12 22	21	6
12 51 32	14	9	28	13 4	22	7
12 55 14	15	10	28	13 47	23	9
12 58 57	16	11	29	14 30	24	10
13 2 40	17	11	♐	15 14	25	11
13 6 23	18	12	1	15 59	26	12
13 10 7	19	13	1	16 44	27	13
13 13 51	20	14	2	17 29	28	15
13 17 35	21	15	3	18 14	29	16
13 21 20	22	16	4	19 0	♒	17
13 25 6	23	16	4	19 45	1	18
13 28 52	24	17	5	20 31	2	20
13 32 38	25	18	6	21 18	4	21
13 36 25	26	19	7	22 6	5	22
13 40 12	27	20	7	22 54	6	23
13 44 0	28	21	8	23 42	7	25
13 47 48	29	21	9	24 31	8	26
13 51 37	30	22	10	25 20	10	27

Sidereal Time.	10 ♏	11 ♏	12 ♐	Ascen ♐	2 ♒	3 ♓
H. M. S.	°	°	°	° '	°	°
13 51 37	0	22	10	25 20	10	27
13 55 27	1	23	11	26 10	11	28
13 59 17	2	24	11	27 2	12	♈
14 3 8	3	25	12	27 53	14	1
14 6 59	4	26	13	28 45	15	2
14 10 51	5	26	14	29 36	16	4
14 14 44	6	27	15	0♑29	18	5
14 18 37	7	28	15	1 23	19	6
14 22 31	8	29	16	2 18	20	8
14 26 25	9	♐	17	3 14	22	9
14 30 20	10	1	18	4 11	23	10
14 34 16	11	2	19	5 9	25	11
14 38 13	12	2	20	6 7	26	13
14 42 10	13	3	20	7 6	28	14
14 46 8	14	4	21	8 6	29	15
14 50 7	15	5	22	9 8	♓	17
14 54 7	16	6	23	10 11	2	18
14 58 7	17	7	24	11 15	4	19
15 2 8	18	8	25	12 20	6	21
15 6 9	19	9	26	13 27	8	22
15 10 12	20	9	27	14 35	9	23
15 14 15	21	10	27	15 43	11	24
15 18 19	22	11	28	16 52	13	26
15 22 23	23	12	29	18 3	14	27
15 26 29	24	13	♑	19 16	16	28
15 30 35	25	14	1	20 32	17	29
15 34 41	26	15	2	21 48	19	♉
15 38 49	27	16	3	23 8	21	2
15 42 57	28	17	4	24 29	22	3
15 47 6	29	18	5	25 51	24	5
15 51 15	30	18	6	27 15	26	6

Sidereal Time.	10 ♐	11 ♐	12 ♑	Ascen ♑	2 ♓	3 ♉
H. M. S.	°	°	°	° '	°	°
15 51 15	0	18	6	27 15	26	6
15 55 25	1	19	7	28 42	28	7
15 59 36	2	20	8	0♒11	♈	9
16 3 48	3	21	9	1 42	2	10
16 8 0	4	22	10	3 16	3	11
16 12 13	5	23	11	4 53	5	12
16 16 26	6	24	12	6 32	7	14
16 20 40	7	25	13	8 13	9	15
16 24 55	8	26	14	9 57	11	16
16 29 10	9	27	16	11 44	12	17
16 33 26	10	28	17	13 34	14	18
16 37 42	11	29	18	15 26	16	20
16 41 59	12	♑	19	17 20	18	21
16 46 16	13	1	20	19 18	20	22
16 50 34	14	2	21	21 22	21	23
16 54 52	15	3	22	23 29	23	25
16 59 10	16	4	24	25 36	25	26
17 3 29	17	5	25	27 46	27	27
17 7 49	18	6	26	0♓ 0	28	28
17 12 9	19	7	27	2 19	♉	29
17 16 29	20	8	29	4 40	2	♊
17 20 49	21	9	♒	7 2	3	1
17 25 9	22	10	1	9 26	5	2
17 29 30	23	11	3	11 54	7	3
17 33 51	24	12	4	14 24	8	5
17 38 12	25	13	5	17 0	10	6
17 42 34	26	14	7	19 33	11	7
17 46 55	27	15	8	22 6	13	8
17 51 17	28	16	10	24 40	14	9
17 55 38	29	17	11	27 20	16	10
18 0 0	30	18	13	30 0	17	11

Sidereal Time.	10 ♑	11 ♑	12 ♒	Ascen ♈	2 ♉	3 ♊
H. M. S.	°	°	°	° '	°	°
18 0 0	0	18	13	0 0	17	11
18 4 22	1	20	14	2 39	19	13
18 8 43	2	21	16	5 19	20	14
18 13 5	3	22	17	7 55	22	15
18 17 26	4	23	19	10 29	23	16
18 21 48	5	24	20	13 2	25	17
18 26 9	6	25	22	15 36	26	18
18 30 30	7	26	23	18 6	28	19
18 34 51	8	27	25	20 34	29	20
18 39 11	9	29	27	22 59	♊	21
18 43 31	10	♒	28	25 22	1	22
18 47 51	11	1	♓	27 42	2	23
18 52 11	12	2	2	29 58	4	24
18 56 31	13	3	3	2♉13	5	25
19 0 50	14	4	5	4 24	6	26
19 5 8	15	6	7	6 30	8	27
19 9 26	16	7	9	8 36	9	28
19 13 44	17	8	10	10 40	10	29
19 18 1	18	9	12	12 39	11	♋
19 22 18	19	10	14	14 35	12	1
19 26 34	20	12	16	16 28	13	2
19 30 50	21	13	18	18 17	14	3
19 35 5	22	14	19	20 3	16	4
19 39 20	23	15	21	21 48	17	5
19 43 34	24	16	23	23 29	18	6
19 47 47	25	18	25	25 9	19	7
19 52 0	26	19	27	26 45	20	8
19 56 12	27	20	28	28 18	21	9
20 0 24	28	21	♈	29 49	22	10
20 4 35	29	23	2	1♊19	23	11
20 8 45	30	24	4	2 45	24	12

Sidereal Time.	10 ♒	11 ♒	12 ♈	Ascen ♊	2 ♊	3 ♋
H. M. S.	°	°	°	° '	°	°
20 8 45	0	24	4	2 45	24	12
20 12 54	1	25	6	4 9	25	12
20 17 3	2	27	7	5 32	26	13
20 21 11	3	28	9	6 53	27	14
20 25 19	4	29	11	8 12	28	15
20 29 26	5	♓	13	9 27	29	16
20 33 31	6	2	14	10 43	♋	17
20 37 37	7	3	16	11 58	1	18
20 41 41	8	4	18	13 9	2	19
20 45 45	9	6	19	14 18	3	20
20 49 48	10	7	21	15 25	3	21
20 53 51	11	8	23	16 32	4	21
20 57 52	12	9	24	17 39	5	22
21 1 53	13	11	26	18 44	6	23
21 5 53	14	12	28	19 48	7	24
21 9 53	15	13	29	20 51	8	25
21 13 52	16	15	♉	21 53	9	26
21 17 50	17	16	2	22 53	10	27
21 21 47	18	17	4	23 52	10	28
21 25 44	19	19	5	24 51	11	28
21 29 40	20	20	7	25 48	12	29
21 33 35	21	22	8	26 44	13	♌
21 37 29	22	23	10	27 40	14	1
21 41 23	23	24	11	28 34	15	2
21 45 16	24	25	13	29 29	15	3
21 49 9	25	26	14	0♋22	16	4
21 53 1	26	28	15	1 15	17	4
21 56 52	27	29	16	2 7	18	5
22 0 43	28	♈	18	2 57	19	6
22 4 33	29	2	19	3 48	19	7
22 8 23	30	3	20	4 38	20	8

Sidereal Time.	10 ♓	11 ♈	12 ♉	Ascen ♋	2 ♋	3 ♌
H. M. S.	°	°	°	° '	°	°
22 8 23	0	3	20	4 38	20	8
22 12 12	1	4	21	5 28	21	8
22 16 0	2	6	23	6 17	22	9
22 19 48	3	7	24	7 5	23	10
22 23 35	4	8	25	7 53	23	11
22 27 22	5	9	26	8 42	24	12
22 31 8	6	10	28	9 29	25	13
22 34 54	7	12	29	10 16	26	14
22 38 40	8	13	♊	11 2	26	14
22 42 25	9	14	1	11 47	27	15
22 46 9	10	15	2	12 31	28	16
22 49 53	11	17	3	13 16	29	17
22 53 37	12	18	4	14 1	29	18
22 57 20	13	19	5	14 45	♌	19
23 1 3	14	20	6	15 28	1	19
23 4 46	15	21	7	16 11	2	20
23 8 28	16	23	8	16 54	2	21
23 12 10	17	24	9	17 37	3	22
23 15 52	18	25	10	18 20	4	23
23 19 34	19	26	11	19 3	5	24
23 23 15	20	27	12	19 45	5	24
23 26 56	21	29	13	20 26	6	25
23 30 37	22	♉	14	21 8	7	26
23 34 18	23	1	15	21 50	7	27
23 37 58	24	2	16	22 31	8	28
23 41 39	25	3	17	23 12	9	28
23 45 19	26	4	18	23 53	9	29
23 49 0	27	5	19	24 32	10	♍
23 52 40	28	6	20	25 15	11	1
23 56 20	29	8	21	25 56	12	2
24 0 0	30	9	22	26 36	13	3

TABLES OF HOUSES FOR LIVERPOOL, Latitude 53º 25' N.

Sidereal Time.	10 ♈	11 ♉	12 ♊	Ascen ♋	2 ♌	3 ♍
H. M. S.	°	°	°	° '	°	°
0 0 0	0	9	24	28 12	14	3
0 3 40	1	10	25	28 51	14	4
0 7 20	2	12	25	29 30	15	4
0 11 0	3	13	26	0♌ 9	16	5
0 14 41	4	14	27	0 48	17	6
0 18 21	5	15	28	1 27	17	7
0 22 2	6	16	29	2 6	18	8
0 25 42	7	17	♋	2 44	19	9
0 29 23	8	18	1	3 22	19	10
0 33 4	9	19	1	4 1	20	10
0 36 45	10	20	2	4 39	21	11
0 40 26	11	21	3	5 18	22	12
0 44 8	12	22	4	5 56	22	13
0 47 50	13	23	5	6 34	23	14
0 51 32	14	24	6	7 13	24	14
0 55 14	15	25	6	7 51	24	15
0 58 57	16	26	7	8 30	25	16
1 2 40	17	27	8	9 8	26	17
1 6 23	18	28	9	9 47	26	18
1 10 7	19	29	10	10 25	27	19
1 13 51	20	♊	11	11 4	28	19
1 17 35	21	1	11	11 43	28	20
1 21 20	22	2	12	12 21	29	21
1 25 6	23	3	13	13 0	♍	22
1 28 52	24	4	14	13 39	1	23
1 32 38	25	5	15	14 17	1	24
1 36 25	26	6	15	14 56	2	25
1 40 12	27	7	16	15 35	3	25
1 44 0	28	8	17	16 14	3	26
1 47 48	29	9	18	16 53	4	27
1 51 37	30	10	18	17 32	5	28

Sidereal Time.	10 ♉	11 ♊	12 ♋	Ascen ♌	2 ♍	3 ♍
H. M. S.	°	°	°	° '	°	°
1 51 37	0	10	18	17 32	5	28
1 55 27	1	11	19	18 11	6	29
1 59 17	2	12	20	18 51	6	♎
2 3 8	3	13	21	19 30	7	1
2 6 59	4	14	22	20 9	8	2
2 10 51	5	15	22	20 49	9	2
2 14 44	6	16	23	21 28	9	3
2 18 37	7	17	24	22 8	10	4
2 22 31	8	18	25	22 48	11	5
2 26 25	9	19	25	23 28	12	6
2 30 20	10	20	26	24 8	12	7
2 34 16	11	21	27	24 48	13	8
2 38 13	12	22	28	25 28	14	9
2 42 10	13	23	29	26 8	15	10
2 46 8	14	24	29	26 49	15	10
2 50 7	15	25	♌	27 29	16	11
2 54 7	16	26	1	28 10	17	12
2 58 7	17	27	2	28 51	18	13
3 2 8	18	28	2	29 32	19	14
3 6 9	19	29	3	0♍13	19	15
3 10 12	20	29	4	0 54	20	16
3 14 15	21	♋	5	1 36	21	17
3 18 19	22	1	5	2 17	22	18
3 22 23	23	2	6	2 59	23	19
3 26 29	24	3	7	3 41	23	20
3 30 35	25	4	8	4 23	24	21
3 34 41	26	5	9	5 5	25	22
3 38 49	27	6	10	5 47	26	22
3 42 57	28	7	10	6 29	27	23
3 47 6	29	8	11	7 12	27	24
3 51 15	30	9	12	7 55	28	25

Sidereal Time.	10 ♊	11 ♋	12 ♌	Ascen ♍	2 ♍	3 ♎
H. M. S.	°	°	°	° '	°	°
3 51 15	0	9	12	7 55	28	25
3 55 25	1	10	13	8 37	29	26
3 59 36	2	11	13	9 20	♎	27
4 3 48	3	12	14	10 3	1	28
4 8 0	4	12	15	10 46	2	29
4 12 13	5	13	16	11 30	2	♏
4 16 26	6	14	17	12 13	3	1
4 20 40	7	15	18	12 56	4	2
4 24 55	8	16	18	13 40	5	3
4 29 10	9	17	19	14 24	6	4
4 33 26	10	18	20	15 8	7	5
4 37 42	11	19	21	15 52	7	6
4 41 59	12	20	21	16 36	8	6
4 46 16	13	21	22	17 20	9	7
4 50 34	14	22	23	18 4	10	8
4 54 52	15	23	24	18 48	11	9
4 59 10	16	24	25	19 32	12	10
5 3 29	17	24	26	20 17	12	11
5 7 49	18	25	26	21 1	13	12
5 12 9	19	26	27	21 46	14	13
5 16 29	20	27	28	22 31	15	14
5 20 49	21	28	29	23 16	16	15
5 25 9	22	29	♍	24 0	17	16
5 29 30	23	♌	1	24 45	18	17
5 33 51	24	1	1	25 30	18	18
5 38 12	25	2	2	26 15	19	19
5 42 34	26	3	3	27 0	20	20
5 46 55	27	4	4	27 45	21	21
5 51 17	28	5	5	28 30	22	21
5 55 38	29	6	6	29 15	23	22
6 0 0	30	7	7	30 0	23	23

Sidereal Time.	10 ♋	11 ♌	12 ♍	Ascen ♎	2 ♎	3 ♏
H. M. S.	°	°	°	° '	°	°
6 0 0	0	7	7	0 0	23	23
6 4 22	1	8	7	0 45	24	24
6 8 43	2	9	8	1 30	25	25
6 13 5	3	9	9	2 15	26	26
6 17 26	4	10	10	3 0	27	27
6 21 48	5	11	11	3 45	28	28
6 26 9	6	12	12	4 30	29	29
6 30 30	7	13	12	5 15	29	♐
6 34 51	8	14	13	6 0	♏	1
6 39 11	9	15	14	6 44	1	2
6 43 31	10	16	15	7 29	2	3
6 47 51	11	17	16	8 14	3	4
6 52 11	12	18	17	8 59	4	5
6 56 31	13	19	18	9 43	4	6
7 0 50	14	20	18	10 27	5	6
7 5 8	15	21	19	11 11	6	7
7 9 26	16	22	20	11 56	7	8
7 13 44	17	23	21	12 40	8	9
7 18 1	18	24	22	13 24	8	10
7 22 18	19	24	23	14 8	9	11
7 26 34	20	25	23	14 52	10	12
7 30 50	21	26	24	15 36	11	13
7 35 5	22	27	25	16 20	12	14
7 39 20	23	28	26	17 4	13	15
7 43 34	24	29	27	17 47	13	16
7 47 47	25	♍	28	18 30	14	17
7 52 0	26	1	28	19 13	15	18
7 56 12	27	2	29	19 57	16	18
8 0 24	28	3	♎	20 40	17	19
8 4 35	29	4	1	21 23	17	20
8 8 45	30	5	2	22 5	18	21

Sidereal Time.	10 ♌	11 ♍	12 ♎	Ascen ♎	2 ♏	3 ♐
H. M. S.	°	°	°	° '	°	°
8 8 45	0	5	2	22 5	18	21
8 12 54	1	6	2	22 48	19	22
8 17 3	2	7	3	23 30	20	23
8 21 11	3	8	4	24 13	20	24
8 25 19	4	8	5	24 55	21	25
8 29 26	5	9	6	25 37	22	26
8 33 31	6	10	7	26 19	23	27
8 37 37	7	11	7	27 1	24	28
8 41 41	8	12	8	27 43	25	29
8 45 45	9	13	9	28 24	25	♑
8 49 48	10	14	10	29 6	26	1
8 53 51	11	15	11	29 47	27	1
8 57 52	12	16	11	0♏28	28	2
9 1 53	13	17	12	1 9	28	3
9 5 53	14	18	13	1 50	29	4
9 9 53	15	19	14	2 31	♐	5
9 13 52	16	19	15	3 11	1	6
9 17 50	17	20	15	3 52	1	7
9 21 47	18	21	16	4 32	2	8
9 25 44	19	22	17	5 12	3	9
9 29 40	20	23	18	5 52	4	10
9 33 35	21	24	18	6 32	5	11
9 37 29	22	25	19	7 12	5	12
9 41 23	23	26	20	7 52	6	13
9 45 16	24	27	21	8 32	7	14
9 49 9	25	27	21	9 12	8	15
9 53 1	26	28	22	9 51	8	16
9 56 52	27	29	23	10 30	9	17
10 0 43	28	♎	24	11 9	10	17
10 4 33	29	1	24	11 49	11	18
10 8 23	30	2	25	12 28	11	19

Sidereal Time.	10 ♍	11 ♎	12 ♎	Ascen ♏	2 ♐	3 ♑
H. M. S.	°	°	°	° '	°	°
10 8 23	0	2	25	12 28	11	19
10 12 12	1	3	26	13 6	12	20
10 16 0	2	4	27	13 45	13	21
10 19 48	3	4	27	14 25	14	22
10 23 35	4	5	28	15 4	15	23
10 27 22	5	6	29	15 42	15	24
10 31 8	6	7	29	16 21	16	25
10 34 54	7	8	♏	17 0	17	26
10 38 40	8	9	1	17 39	18	27
10 42 25	9	10	2	18 17	18	28
10 46 9	10	10	2	18 55	19	29
10 49 53	11	11	3	19 34	20	♒
10 53 37	12	12	4	20 13	21	1
10 57 20	13	13	4	20 52	22	2
11 1 3	14	14	5	21 30	22	3
11 4 46	15	15	6	22 8	23	5
11 8 28	16	16	7	22 46	24	6
11 12 10	17	16	7	23 25	25	7
11 15 52	18	17	8	24 4	26	8
11 19 34	19	18	9	24 42	26	9
11 23 15	20	19	9	25 21	27	10
11 26 56	21	20	10	25 59	28	11
11 30 37	22	20	11	26 38	29	12
11 34 18	23	21	12	27 16	♑	13
11 37 58	24	22	12	27 54	1	14
11 41 39	25	23	13	28 33	1	15
11 45 19	26	24	14	29 11	2	16
11 49 0	27	25	14	29 50	3	17
11 52 40	28	26	15	0♐30	4	18
11 56 20	29	26	16	1 9	5	20
12 0 0	30	27	16	1 48	6	21

TABLES OF HOUSES FOR LIVERPOOL, Latitude 53º 25' N.

Sidereal Time.	10 ♎	11 ♎	12 ♏	Ascen ♐	2 ♑	3 ♒
H. M. S.	º	º	º	º '	º	º
12 0 0	0	27	16	1 48	6	21
12 3 40	1	28	17	2 27	7	22
12 7 20	2	29	18	3 6	8	23
12 11 0	3	♏	18	3 46	9	24
12 14 41	4	0	19	4 25	10	25
12 18 21	5	1	20	5 6	10	26
12 22 2	6	2	21	5 46	11	28
12 25 42	7	3	21	6 26	12	29
12 29 23	8	4	22	7 6	13	♓
12 33 4	9	4	23	7 46	14	1
12 36 45	10	5	24	8 27	15	2
12 40 26	11	6	24	9 8	16	3
12 44 8	12	7	25	9 49	17	5
12 47 50	13	8	26	10 30	18	6
12 51 32	14	9	26	11 12	19	7
12 55 14	15	9	27	11 54	20	8
12 58 57	16	10	28	12 36	21	10
13 2 40	17	11	28	13 19	22	11
13 6 23	18	12	29	14 2	23	12
13 10 7	19	13	♐	14 45	25	13
13 13 51	20	13	1	15 28	26	15
13 17 35	21	14	1	16 12	27	16
13 21 20	22	15	2	16 56	28	17
13 25 6	23	16	3	17 41	29	18
13 28 52	24	17	4	18 26	♒	19
13 32 38	25	17	4	19 11	1	21
13 36 25	26	18	5	19 57	3	22
13 40 12	27	19	6	20 44	4	23
13 44 0	28	20	7	21 31	5	24
13 47 48	29	21	7	22 18	7	26
13 51 37	30	21	8	23 6	8	27

Sidereal Time.	10 ♏	11 ♏	12 ♐	Ascen ♐	2 ♒	3 ♓
H. M. S.	º	º	º	º '	º	º
13 51 37	0	21	8	23 6	8	27
13 55 27	1	22	9	23 55	9	28
13 59 17	2	23	10	24 43	10	♈
14 3 8	3	24	10	25 33	12	1
14 6 59	4	25	11	26 23	13	2
14 10 51	5	26	12	27 14	15	4
14 14 44	6	26	13	28 6	16	5
14 18 37	7	27	13	28 59	18	6
14 22 31	8	28	14	29 52	19	8
14 26 25	9	29	15	0♑46	20	9
14 30 20	10	♐	16	1 41	22	10
14 34 16	11	1	17	2 36	23	11
14 38 13	12	2	18	3 33	25	13
14 42 10	13	2	18	4 30	26	14
14 46 8	14	3	19	5 29	28	16
14 50 7	15	4	20	6 29	♓	17
14 54 7	16	5	21	7 30	1	18
14 58 7	17	6	22	8 32	3	20
15 2 8	18	7	23	9 35	5	21
15 6 9	19	8	24	10 39	6	22
15 10 12	20	8	24	11 45	8	23
15 14 15	21	9	25	12 52	10	25
15 18 19	22	10	26	14 1	11	26
15 22 23	23	11	27	15 11	13	27
15 26 29	24	12	28	16 23	15	29
15 30 35	25	13	29	17 37	17	♉
15 34 41	26	14	♑	18 53	19	1
15 38 49	27	15	1	20 10	21	3
15 42 57	28	16	2	21 29	22	4
15 47 6	29	16	3	22 51	24	5
15 51 15	30	17	4	24 15	26	7

Sidereal Time.	10 ♐	11 ♐	12 ♑	Ascen ♑	2 ♓	3 ♉
H. M. S.	º	º	º	º '	º	º
15 51 15	0	17	4	24 15	26	7
15 55 25	1	18	5	25 41	28	8
15 59 36	2	19	6	27 10	♈	9
16 3 48	3	20	7	28 41	2	10
16 8 0	4	21	8	0♒14	4	12
16 12 13	5	22	9	1 50	5	13
16 16 26	6	23	10	3 30	7	14
16 20 40	7	24	11	5 13	9	15
16 24 55	8	25	12	6 58	11	17
16 29 10	9	26	13	8 46	13	18
16 33 26	10	27	14	10 38	15	19
16 37 42	11	28	15	12 32	17	20
16 41 59	12	29	16	14 31	19	22
16 46 16	13	♑	18	16 33	20	23
16 50 34	14	1	19	18 40	22	24
16 54 52	15	2	20	20 50	24	25
16 59 10	16	3	21	23 4	26	26
17 3 29	17	4	22	25 21	28	28
17 7 49	18	5	24	27 42	29	29
17 12 9	19	6	25	0♓8	♉	♊
17 16 29	20	7	26	2 37	3	1
17 20 49	21	8	28	5 10	5	3
17 25 9	22	9	29	7 46	6	4
17 29 30	23	10	♒	10 24	8	5
17 33 51	24	11	2	13 7	10	6
17 38 12	25	12	3	15 52	11	7
17 42 34	26	13	4	18 38	13	8
17 46 55	27	14	6	21 27	15	9
17 51 17	28	15	7	24 17	16	10
17 55 38	29	16	9	27 8	18	12
18 0 0	30	17	11	30 0	19	13

Sidereal Time.	10 ♑	11 ♑	12 ♒	Ascen ♈	2 ♉	3 ♊
H. M. S.	º	º	º	º '	º	º
18 0 0	0	17	11	0 0	19	13
18 4 22	1	18	12	2 52	21	14
18 8 43	2	20	14	5 43	23	15
18 13 5	3	21	15	8 33	24	16
18 17 26	4	22	17	11 22	25	17
18 21 48	5	23	19	14 8	27	18
18 26 9	6	24	20	16 53	28	19
18 30 30	7	25	22	19 36	♊	20
18 34 51	8	26	24	22 14	1	21
18 39 11	9	27	25	24 50	2	22
18 43 31	10	29	27	27 23	4	23
18 47 51	11	♒	28	29 52	5	24
18 52 11	12	1	♓	2♉18	6	25
18 56 31	13	2	2	4 39	8	26
19 0 50	14	4	4	6 56	9	27
19 5 8	15	5	6	9 10	10	28
19 9 26	16	6	8	11 20	11	29
19 13 44	17	7	10	13 27	12	♋
19 18 1	18	8	11	15 29	14	1
19 22 18	19	9	13	17 28	15	2
19 26 34	20	11	15	19 22	16	3
19 30 50	21	12	17	21 14	17	4
19 35 5	22	13	19	23 2	18	5
19 39 20	23	15	21	24 47	19	6
19 43 34	24	16	23	26 30	20	7
19 47 47	25	17	25	28 10	21	8
19 52 0	26	18	26	29 46	22	9
19 56 12	27	20	28	1♊19	23	10
20 0 24	28	21	♈	2 50	24	11
20 4 35	29	22	2	4 19	25	12
20 8 45	30	23	4	5 45	26	13

Sidereal Time.	10 ♒	11 ♒	12 ♈	Ascen ♊	2 ♊	3 ♋
H. M. S.	º	º	º	º '	º	º
20 8 45	0	23	4	5 45	26	13
20 12 54	1	25	6	7 9	27	14
20 17 3	2	26	8	8 31	28	14
20 21 11	3	27	9	9 50	29	15
20 25 19	4	29	11	11 7	♋	16
20 29 26	5	♓	13	12 23	1	17
20 33 31	6	1	15	13 37	2	18
20 37 37	7	3	17	14 49	3	19
20 41 41	8	4	19	15 59	4	20
20 45 45	9	5	20	17 8	5	21
20 49 48	10	7	22	18 15	6	22
20 53 51	11	8	24	19 21	7	22
20 57 52	12	10	25	20 25	7	23
21 1 53	13	11	27	21 28	8	24
21 5 53	14	12	29	22 30	9	25
21 9 53	15	13	♉	23 31	10	26
21 13 52	16	14	2	24 31	11	27
21 17 50	17	16	4	25 30	12	28
21 21 47	18	17	5	26 27	12	28
21 25 44	19	18	7	27 24	13	29
21 29 40	20	20	8	28 19	14	♌
21 33 35	21	21	10	29 14	15	1
21 37 29	22	22	11	0♋8	16	2
21 41 23	23	24	12	1 1	17	3
21 45 16	24	25	14	1 54	17	4
21 49 9	25	26	15	2 46	18	4
21 53 1	26	28	17	3 37	19	5
21 56 52	27	29	18	4 27	20	6
22 0 43	28	♈	20	5 17	20	7
22 4 33	29	2	21	6 5	21	8
22 8 23	30	3	22	6 54	22	8

Sidereal Time.	10 ♓	11 ♈	12 ♉	Ascen ♋	2 ♋	3 ♌
H. M. S.	º	º	º	º '	º	º
22 8 23	0	3	22	6 54	22	8
22 12 12	1	4	23	7 42	23	9
22 16 0	2	5	25	8 29	23	10
22 19 48	3	7	26	9 16	24	11
22 23 35	4	8	27	10 3	25	12
22 27 22	5	9	29	10 49	26	13
22 31 8	6	11	♊	11 34	26	13
22 34 54	7	12	1	12 19	27	14
22 38 40	8	13	2	13 3	28	15
22 42 25	9	14	3	13 48	29	16
22 46 9	10	16	4	14 32	29	17
22 49 53	11	17	5	15 15	♌	17
22 53 37	12	18	7	15 58	1	18
22 57 20	13	19	8	16 41	2	19
23 1 3	14	20	9	17 24	2	20
23 4 46	15	22	10	18 6	3	21
23 8 28	16	23	11	18 48	4	21
23 12 10	17	24	12	19 30	4	22
23 15 52	18	25	13	20 11	5	23
23 19 34	19	27	14	20 52	6	24
23 23 15	20	28	15	21 33	6	25
23 26 56	21	29	16	22 14	7	26
23 30 37	22	♉	17	22 54	8	26
23 34 18	23	1	18	23 34	9	27
23 37 58	24	2	19	24 14	9	28
23 41 39	25	4	20	24 54	10	29
23 45 19	26	5	21	25 35	11	♍
23 49 0	27	6	22	26 14	11	0
23 52 40	28	7	22	26 54	12	1
23 56 20	29	8	23	27 33	13	2
24 0 0	30	9	24	28 12	14	3

TABLES OF HOUSES FOR NEW YORK, *Latitude* 40° 43' N.

Sidereal Time.	10 ♈	11 ♉	12 ♊	Ascen ♋	2 ♌	3 ♍
H. M. S.	°	°	°	° '	°	°
0 0 0	0	6	15	18 53	8	1
0 3 40	1	7	16	19 38	9	2
0 7 20	2	8	17	20 23	10	3
0 11 0	3	9	18	21 12	11	4
0 14 41	4	11	19	21 55	12	5
0 18 21	5	12	20	22 40	12	5
0 22 2	6	13	21	23 24	13	6
0 25 42	7	14	22	24 8	14	7
0 29 23	8	15	23	24 54	15	8
0 33 4	9	16	23	25 37	15	9
0 36 45	10	17	24	26 22	16	10
0 40 26	11	18	25	27 5	17	11
0 44 8	12	19	26	27 50	18	12
0 47 50	13	20	27	28 33	19	13
0 51 32	14	21	28	29 18	19	13
0 55 14	15	22	28	0♌ 3	20	14
0 58 57	16	23	29	0 46	21	15
1 2 40	17	24	♋	1 31	22	16
1 6 23	18	25	1	2 14	22	17
1 10 7	19	26	2	2 58	23	18
1 13 51	20	27	3	3 43	24	19
1 17 35	21	28	3	4 27	25	20
1 21 20	22	29	4	5 12	25	21
1 25 6	23	♊	5	5 56	26	22
1 28 52	24	1	6	6 40	27	22
1 32 38	25	2	7	7 25	28	23
1 36 25	26	2	8	8 9	29	24
1 40 12	27	3	9	8 53	♍	25
1 44 0	28	4	10	9 38	1	26
1 47 48	29	5	10	10 24	1	27
1 51 37	30	6	11	11 8	2	28

Sidereal Time.	10 ♉	11 ♊	12 ♋	Ascen ♌	2 ♍	3 ♍
H. M. S.	°	°	°	° '	°	°
1 51 37	0	6	11	11 8	2	28
1 55 27	1	7	12	11 53	3	29
1 59 17	2	8	13	12 38	4	♎
2 3 8	3	9	14	13 22	5	1
2 6 59	4	10	15	14 8	5	2
2 10 51	5	11	15	14 53	6	3
2 14 44	6	12	16	15 39	7	4
2 18 37	7	13	17	16 24	8	4
2 22 31	8	14	18	17 10	9	5
2 26 25	9	15	19	17 56	10	6
2 30 20	10	16	20	18 41	10	7
2 34 16	11	17	20	19 27	11	8
2 38 13	12	18	21	20 14	12	9
2 42 10	13	19	22	21 0	13	10
2 46 8	14	19	23	21 47	14	11
2 50 7	15	20	24	22 33	15	12
2 54 7	16	21	25	23 20	16	13
2 58 7	17	22	25	24 7	17	14
3 2 8	18	23	26	24 54	17	15
3 6 9	19	24	27	25 42	18	16
3 10 12	20	25	28	26 29	19	17
3 14 15	21	26	29	27 17	20	18
3 18 19	22	27	♌	28 4	21	19
3 22 23	23	28	1	28 52	22	20
3 26 29	24	29	1	29 40	23	21
3 30 35	25	♋	2	0♍29	24	22
3 34 41	26	1	3	1 17	24	23
3 38 49	27	2	4	2 6	25	24
3 42 57	28	3	5	2 55	26	25
3 47 6	29	4	6	3 43	27	26
3 51 15	30	5	7	4 32	28	27

Sidereal Time.	10 ♊	11 ♋	12 ♌	Ascen ♍	2 ♍	3 ♎
H. M. S.	°	°	°	° '	°	°
3 51 15	0	5	7	4 32	28	27
3 55 25	1	6	8	5 22	29	28
3 59 36	2	6	8	6 10	♎	29
4 3 48	3	7	9	7 0	1	♏
4 8 0	4	8	10	7 49	2	1
4 12 13	5	9	11	8 40	3	2
4 16 26	6	10	12	9 30	4	3
4 20 40	7	11	13	10 19	4	4
4 24 55	8	12	14	11 10	5	5
4 29 10	9	13	15	12 0	6	6
4 33 26	10	14	16	12 51	7	7
4 37 42	11	15	16	13 41	8	8
4 41 59	12	16	17	14 32	9	9
4 46 16	13	17	18	15 23	10	10
4 50 34	14	18	19	16 14	11	11
4 54 52	15	19	20	17 5	12	12
4 59 10	16	20	21	17 56	13	13
5 3 29	17	21	22	18 47	14	14
5 7 49	18	22	23	19 39	15	15
5 12 9	19	23	24	20 30	16	16
5 16 29	20	24	25	21 22	17	17
5 20 49	21	25	25	22 13	18	18
5 25 9	22	26	26	23 5	18	19
5 29 30	23	27	27	23 57	19	20
5 33 51	24	28	28	24 49	20	21
5 38 12	25	29	29	25 40	21	22
5 42 34	26	♌	♍	26 32	22	22
5 46 55	27	1	1	27 25	23	23
5 51 17	28	2	2	28 16	24	24
5 55 38	29	3	3	29 8	25	25
6 0 0	30	4	4	30 0	26	26

Sidereal Time.	10 ♋	11 ♌	12 ♍	Ascen ♎	2 ♎	3 ♏
H. M. S.	°	°	°	° '	°	°
6 0 0	0	4	4	0 0	26	26
6 4 22	1	5	5	0 52	27	27
6 8 43	2	6	6	1 44	28	28
6 13 5	3	6	7	2 35	29	29
6 17 26	4	7	8	3 28	♏	♐
6 21 48	5	8	9	4 20	1	1
6 26 9	6	9	10	5 11	2	2
6 30 30	7	10	11	6 3	3	3
6 34 51	8	11	12	6 55	3	4
6 39 11	9	12	13	7 47	4	5
6 43 31	10	13	14	8 38	5	6
6 47 51	11	14	15	9 30	6	7
6 52 11	12	15	15	10 21	7	8
6 56 31	13	16	16	11 13	8	9
7 0 50	14	17	17	12 4	9	10
7 5 8	15	18	18	12 55	10	11
7 9 26	16	19	19	13 46	11	12
7 13 44	17	20	20	14 37	12	13
7 18 1	18	21	21	15 28	13	14
7 22 18	19	22	22	16 19	14	15
7 26 34	20	23	23	17 9	14	16
7 30 50	21	24	23	18 0	15	17
7 35 5	22	25	24	18 50	16	18
7 39 20	23	26	25	19 41	17	19
7 43 34	24	27	26	20 30	18	20
7 47 47	25	28	27	21 20	19	21
7 52 0	26	29	28	22 11	20	22
7 56 12	27	♍	29	23 0	21	23
8 0 24	28	1	♎	23 50	21	24
8 4 35	29	2	1	24 38	22	24
8 8 45	30	3	2	25 28	23	25

Sidereal Time.	10 ♌	11 ♍	12 ♎	Ascen ♎	2 ♏	3 ♐
H. M. S.	°	°	°	° '	°	°
8 8 45	0	3	2	25 28	23	25
8 12 54	1	4	3	26 17	24	26
8 17 3	2	5	4	27 5	25	27
8 21 11	3	6	5	27 54	26	28
8 25 19	4	7	6	28 43	27	29
8 29 26	5	8	7	29 31	28	♑
8 33 31	6	9	7	0♏20	28	1
8 37 37	7	10	8	1 8	29	2
8 41 41	8	11	9	1 56	♐	3
8 45 45	9	12	10	2 43	1	4
8 49 48	10	13	11	3 31	2	5
8 53 51	11	14	12	4 18	3	6
8 57 52	12	15	12	5 6	4	7
9 1 53	13	16	13	5 53	5	8
9 5 53	14	17	14	6 40	5	9
9 9 53	15	18	15	7 27	6	10
9 13 52	16	19	16	8 13	7	10
9 17 50	17	20	17	9 0	8	11
9 21 47	18	21	18	9 46	9	12
9 25 44	19	22	19	10 33	10	13
9 29 40	20	23	19	11 19	10	14
9 33 35	21	24	20	12 4	11	15
9 37 29	22	24	21	12 50	12	16
9 41 23	23	25	22	13 36	13	17
9 45 16	24	26	23	14 21	14	18
9 49 9	25	27	24	15 7	15	19
9 53 1	26	28	24	15 52	15	20
9 56 52	27	29	25	16 38	16	21
10 0 43	28	♎	26	17 22	17	22
10 4 33	29	1	27	18 7	18	23
10 8 23	30	2	28	18 52	19	24

Sidereal Time.	10 ♍	11 ♎	12 ♎	Ascen ♏	2 ♐	3 ♑
H. M. S.	°	°	°	° '	°	°
10 8 23	0	2	28	18 52	19	24
10 12 12	1	3	29	19 36	20	25
10 16 0	2	4	29	20 22	20	26
10 19 48	3	5	♏	21 7	21	27
10 23 35	4	6	1	21 51	22	28
10 27 22	5	7	1	22 35	23	28
10 31 8	6	7	2	23 20	24	29
10 34 54	7	8	3	24 4	25	♒
10 38 40	8	9	4	24 48	25	1
10 42 25	9	10	5	25 33	26	2
10 46 9	10	11	6	26 17	27	3
10 49 53	11	12	7	27 2	28	4
10 53 37	12	13	7	27 46	29	5
10 57 20	13	14	8	28 29	♑	6
11 1 3	14	15	9	29 14	1	7
11 4 46	15	16	10	29 57	1	8
11 8 28	16	17	11	0♐42	2	9
11 12 10	17	17	11	1 27	3	10
11 15 52	18	18	12	2 10	4	11
11 19 34	19	19	13	2 55	5	12
11 23 15	20	20	14	3 38	6	13
11 26 56	21	21	14	4 23	7	14
11 30 37	22	22	15	5 6	7	15
11 34 18	23	23	16	5 52	8	16
11 37 58	24	23	17	6 36	9	17
11 41 39	25	24	18	7 20	10	18
11 45 19	26	25	18	8 5	11	19
11 49 0	27	26	19	8 48	12	20
11 52 40	28	27	20	9 37	13	22
11 56 20	29	28	21	10 22	14	23
12 0 0	30	29	21	11 7	15	24

TABLES OF HOUSES FOR NEW YORK, Latitude 40º 43' *N.*

Sidereal Time.	10 ♎	11 ♎	12 ♏	Ascen ♐	2 ♑	3 ♒
H. M. S.	°	°	°	° '	°	°
12 0 0	0	29	21	11 7	15	24
12 3 40	1	♏	22	11 52	16	25
12 7 20	2	1	23	12 37	17	26
12 11 0	3	1	24	13 19	17	27
12 14 41	4	2	25	14 7	18	28
12 18 21	5	3	25	14 52	19	29
12 22 2	6	4	26	15 38	20	♓
12 25 42	7	5	27	16 23	21	1
12 29 23	8	6	28	17 11	22	2
12 33 4	9	6	28	17 58	23	3
12 36 45	10	7	29	18 45	24	4
12 40 26	11	8	♐	19 32	25	5
12 44 8	12	9	1	20 20	26	7
12 47 50	13	10	2	21 8	27	8
12 51 32	14	11	2	21 57	28	9
12 55 14	15	12	3	22 43	29	10
12 58 57	16	13	4	23 33	♒	11
13 2 40	17	13	5	24 22	1	12
13 6 23	18	14	6	25 11	2	13
13 10 7	19	15	7	26 1	3	15
13 13 51	20	16	7	26 51	5	16
13 17 35	21	17	8	27 40	6	17
13 21 20	22	18	9	28 32	7	18
13 25 6	23	19	10	29 23	8	19
13 28 52	24	19	10	0♑14	9	20
13 32 38	25	20	11	1 7	10	21
13 36 25	26	21	12	2 0	11	23
13 40 12	27	22	13	2 52	12	24
13 44 0	28	23	13	3 46	13	25
13 47 48	29	24	14	4 41	15	26
13 51 37	30	25	15	5 35	16	27

Sidereal Time.	10 ♏	11 ♏	12 ♐	Ascen ♑	2 ♒	3 ♓
H. M. S.	°	°	°	° '	°	°
13 51 37	0	25	15	5 35	16	27
13 55 27	1	25	16	6 30	17	29
13 59 17	2	26	17	7 27	18	♈
14 3 8	3	27	18	8 23	20	1
14 6 59	4	28	18	9 20	21	2
14 10 51	5	29	19	10 18	22	3
14 14 44	6	♐	20	11 16	23	5
14 18 37	7	1	21	12 15	24	6
14 22 31	8	2	22	13 15	26	7
14 26 25	9	2	23	14 16	27	8
14 30 20	10	3	24	15 17	28	9
14 34 16	11	4	24	16 19	♓	11
14 38 13	12	5	25	17 23	1	12
14 42 10	13	6	26	18 27	2	13
14 46 8	14	7	27	19 32	4	14
14 50 7	15	8	28	20 37	5	16
14 54 7	16	9	29	21 44	6	17
14 58 7	17	10	♑	22 51	8	18
15 2 8	18	10	1	23 59	9	19
15 6 9	19	11	2	25 9	11	20
15 10 12	20	12	3	26 19	12	22
15 14 15	21	13	4	27 31	14	23
15 18 19	22	14	5	28 43	15	24
15 22 23	23	15	6	29 57	16	25
15 26 29	24	16	6	1♒14	18	26
15 30 35	25	17	7	2 28	19	28
15 34 41	26	18	8	3 46	21	29
15 38 49	27	19	9	5 5	22	♉
15 42 57	28	20	10	6 25	24	1
15 47 6	29	21	11	7 46	25	3
15 51 15	30	21	13	9 8	27	4

Sidereal Time.	10 ♐	11 ♐	12 ♑	Ascen ♒	2 ♓	3 ♉
H. M. S.	°	°	°	° '	°	°
15 51 15	0	21	13	9 8	27	4
15 55 25	1	22	14	10 31	28	5
15 59 36	2	23	15	11 56	♈	6
16 3 48	3	24	16	13 23	1	7
16 8 0	4	25	17	14 50	3	9
16 12 13	5	26	18	16 9	4	10
16 16 26	6	27	19	17 50	6	11
16 20 40	7	28	20	19 22	7	12
16 24 55	8	29	21	20 56	9	13
16 29 10	9	♑	22	22 30	11	15
16 33 26	10	1	23	24 7	12	16
16 37 42	11	2	24	25 44	14	17
16 41 59	12	3	26	27 23	15	18
16 46 16	13	4	27	29 4	17	19
16 50 34	14	5	28	0♓45	18	20
16 54 52	15	6	29	2 27	20	22
16 59 10	16	7	♒	4 11	21	23
17 3 29	17	8	2	5 56	23	24
17 7 49	18	9	3	7 43	24	25
17 12 9	19	10	4	9 30	26	26
17 16 29	20	11	5	11 18	27	27
17 20 49	21	12	7	13 8	29	28
17 25 9	22	13	8	14 57	♉	♊
17 29 30	23	14	9	16 48	2	1
17 33 51	24	15	10	18 41	3	2
17 38 12	25	16	12	20 33	5	3
17 42 34	26	17	13	22 25	6	4
17 46 55	27	19	14	24 19	7	5
17 51 17	28	20	16	26 12	9	6
17 55 38	29	21	17	28 7	10	7
18 0 0	30	22	18	30 0	12	9

Sidereal Time.	10 ♑	11 ♑	12 ♒	Ascen ♈	2 ♉	3 ♊
H. M. S.	°	°	°	° '	°	°
18 0 0	0	22	18	0 0	12	9
18 4 22	1	23	20	1 53	13	10
18 8 43	2	24	21	3 48	14	11
18 13 5	3	25	23	5 41	16	12
18 17 26	4	26	24	7 35	17	13
18 21 48	5	27	25	9 27	18	14
18 26 9	6	28	27	11 19	20	15
18 30 30	7	29	28	13 12	21	16
18 34 51	8	♒	♓	15 3	22	17
18 39 11	9	2	1	16 52	23	18
18 43 31	10	3	3	18 42	25	19
18 47 51	11	4	4	20 30	26	20
18 52 11	12	5	5	22 17	27	21
18 56 31	13	6	7	24 4	29	22
19 0 50	14	7	9	25 49	♊	23
19 5 8	15	9	10	27 33	1	24
19 9 26	16	10	12	29 15	2	25
19 13 44	17	11	13	0♉56	3	26
19 18 1	18	12	15	2 37	4	27
19 22 18	19	13	16	4 16	6	28
19 26 34	20	14	18	5 53	7	29
19 30 50	21	16	19	7 30	8	♋
19 35 5	22	17	21	9 4	9	1
19 39 20	23	18	22	10 38	10	2
19 43 34	24	19	24	12 10	11	3
19 47 47	25	20	25	13 41	12	4
19 52 0	26	21	27	15 10	13	5
19 56 12	27	23	29	16 37	14	6
20 0 24	28	24	♈	18 4	15	7
20 4 35	29	25	2	19 29	16	8
20 8 45	30	26	3	20 52	17	9

Sidereal Time.	10 ♒	11 ♒	12 ♈	Ascen ♉	2 ♊	3 ♋
H. M. S.	°	°	°	° '	°	°
20 8 45	0	26	3	20 52	17	9
20 12 54	1	27	5	22 14	18	9
20 17 3	2	29	6	23 35	19	10
20 21 11	3	♓	8	24 55	20	11
20 25 19	4	1	9	26 14	21	12
20 29 26	5	2	11	27 32	22	13
20 33 31	6	3	12	28 46	23	14
20 37 37	7	5	14	0♊3	24	15
20 41 41	8	6	15	1 17	25	16
20 45 45	9	7	16	2 29	26	17
20 49 48	10	8	18	3 41	27	18
20 53 51	11	10	19	4 51	28	19
20 57 52	12	11	21	6 1	29	20
21 1 53	13	12	22	7 9	♋	20
21 5 53	14	13	24	8 16	1	21
21 9 53	15	14	25	9 23	2	22
21 13 52	16	16	26	10 30	3	23
21 17 50	17	17	28	11 33	4	24
21 21 47	18	18	29	12 37	5	25
21 25 44	19	19	♉	13 41	6	26
21 29 40	20	21	2	14 43	6	27
21 33 35	21	22	3	15 44	7	28
21 37 29	22	23	4	16 45	8	28
21 41 23	23	24	6	17 45	9	29
21 45 16	24	25	7	18 44	10	♌
21 49 9	25	27	8	19 42	11	1
21 53 1	26	28	9	20 40	12	2
21 56 52	27	29	11	21 37	12	3
22 0 43	28	♈	12	22 33	13	4
22 4 33	29	1	13	23 30	14	5
22 8 23	30	3	14	24 25	15	5

Sidereal Time.	10 ♓	11 ♈	12 ♉	Ascen ♊	2 ♋	3 ♌
H. M. S.	°	°	°	° '	°	°
22 8 23	0	3	14	24 25	15	5
22 12 12	1	4	15	25 19	16	6
22 16 0	2	5	17	26 14	17	7
22 19 48	3	6	18	27 8	17	8
22 23 35	4	7	19	28 0	18	9
22 27 22	5	8	20	28 53	19	10
22 31 8	6	10	21	29 46	20	11
22 34 54	7	11	22	0♋37	21	11
22 38 40	8	12	23	1 28	21	12
22 42 25	9	13	24	2 20	22	13
22 46 9	10	14	25	3 9	23	14
22 49 53	11	15	27	3 59	24	15
22 53 37	12	17	28	4 49	24	16
22 57 20	13	18	29	5 38	25	17
23 1 3	14	19	♊	6 27	26	17
23 4 46	15	20	1	7 17	27	18
23 8 28	16	21	2	8 3	28	19
23 12 10	17	22	3	8 52	28	20
23 15 52	18	23	4	9 40	29	21
23 19 34	19	24	5	10 28	♌	22
23 23 15	20	26	6	11 15	1	23
23 26 56	21	27	7	12 2	2	23
23 30 37	22	28	8	12 49	2	24
23 34 18	23	29	9	13 37	3	25
23 37 58	24	♉	10	14 22	4	26
23 41 39	25	1	11	15 8	5	27
23 45 19	26	2	12	15 53	5	28
23 49 0	27	3	12	16 41	6	29
23 52 40	28	4	13	17 23	7	29
23 56 20	29	5	14	18 8	8	♍
24 0 0	30	6	15	18 53	9	1

PROPORTIONAL LOGARITHMS FOR FINDING THE PLANETS' PLACES

DEGREES OR HOURS

Min	0	1	2	3	4	5	6	7	8	9	10	11	12	13	14	15	Min
0	3.1584	1.3802	1.0792	9031	7781	6812	6021	5351	4771	4260	3802	3388	3010	2663	2341	2041	**0**
1	3.1584	1.3730	1.0756	9007	7763	6798	6009	5341	4762	4252	3795	3382	3004	2657	2336	2036	**1**
2	2.8573	1.3660	1.0720	8983	7745	6784	5997	5330	4753	4244	3788	3375	2998	2652	2330	2032	**2**
3	2.6812	1.3590	1.0685	8959	7728	6769	5985	5320	4744	4236	3780	3368	2992	2646	2325	2027	**3**
4	2.5563	1.3522	1.0649	8935	7710	6755	5973	5310	4735	4228	3773	3362	2986	2640	2320	2022	**4**
5	2.4594	1.3454	1.0614	8912	7692	6741	5961	5300	4726	4220	3766	3355	2980	2635	2315	2017	**5**
6	2.3802	1.3388	1.0580	8888	7674	6726	5949	5289	4717	4212	3759	3349	2974	2629	2310	2012	**6**
7	2.3133	1.3323	1.0546	8865	7657	6712	5937	5279	4708	4204	3752	3342	2968	2624	2305	2008	**7**
8	2.2553	1.3258	1.0511	8842	7639	6698	5925	5269	4699	4196	3745	3336	2962	2618	2300	2003	**8**
9	2.2041	1.3195	1.0478	8819	7622	6684	5913	5259	4690	4188	3737	3329	2956	2613	2295	1998	**9**
10	2.1584	1.3133	1.0444	8796	7604	6670	5902	5249	4682	4180	3730	3323	2950	2607	2289	1993	**10**
11	2.1170	1.3071	1.0411	8773	7587	6656	5890	5239	4673	4172	3723	3316	2944	2602	2284	1988	**11**
12	2.0792	1.3010	1.0378	8751	7570	6642	5878	5229	4664	4164	3716	3310	2938	2596	2279	1984	**12**
13	2.0444	1.2950	1.0345	8728	7552	6628	5866	5219	4655	4156	3709	3303	2933	2591	2274	1979	**13**
14	2.0122	1.2891	1.0313	8706	7535	6614	5855	5209	4646	4148	3702	3297	2927	2585	2269	1974	**14**
15	1.9823	1.2833	1.0280	8683	7518	6600	5843	5199	4638	4141	3695	3291	2921	2580	2264	1969	**15**
16	1.9542	1.2775	1.0248	8661	7501	6587	5832	5189	4629	4133	3688	3284	2915	2574	2259	1965	**16**
17	1.9279	1.2719	1.0216	8639	7484	6573	5820	5179	4620	4125	3681	3278	2909	2569	2254	1960	**17**
18	1.9031	1.2663	1.0185	8617	7467	6559	5809	5169	4611	4117	3674	3271	2903	2564	2249	1955	**18**
19	1.8796	1.2607	1.0153	8595	7451	6546	5797	5159	4603	4109	3667	3265	2897	2558	2244	1950	**19**
20	1.8573	1.2553	1.0122	8573	7434	6532	5786	5149	4594	4102	3660	3258	2891	2553	2239	1946	**20**
21	1.8631	1.2499	1.0091	8552	7417	6519	5774	5139	4585	4094	3653	3252	2885	2547	2234	1941	**21**
22	1.8159	1.2445	1.0061	8530	7401	6505	5763	5129	4577	4086	3646	3246	2880	2542	2229	1936	**22**
23	1.7966	1.2393	1.0030	8509	7384	6492	5752	5120	4568	4079	3639	3239	2874	2536	2223	1932	**23**
24	1.7781	1.2341	1.0000	8487	7368	6478	5740	5110	4559	4071	3632	3233	2868	2531	2218	1927	**24**
25	1.7604	1.2289	0.9970	8466	7351	6465	5729	5100	4551	4063	3625	3227	2862	2526	2213	1922	**25**
26	1.7434	1.2239	0.9940	8445	7335	6451	5718	5090	4542	4055	3618	3220	2856	2520	2208	1917	**26**
27	1.7270	1.2188	0.9910	8424	7318	6438	5706	5081	4534	4048	3611	3214	2850	2515	2203	1913	**27**
28	1.7112	1.2139	0.9881	8403	7302	6425	5695	5071	4525	4040	3604	3208	2845	2509	2198	1908	**28**
29	1.6960	1.2090	0.9852	8382	7286	6412	5684	5061	4516	4032	3597	3201	2839	2504	2193	1903	**29**
30	1.6812	1.2041	0.9823	8361	7270	6398	5673	5051	4508	4025	3590	3195	2833	2499	2188	1899	**30**
31	1.6670	1.1993	0.9794	8341	7254	6385	5662	5042	4499	4017	3583	3189	2827	2493	2183	1894	**31**
32	1.6532	1.1946	0.9765	8320	7238	6372	5651	5032	4491	4010	3576	3183	2821	2488	2178	1889	**32**
33	1.6398	1.1899	0.9737	8300	7222	6359	5640	5023	4482	4002	3570	3176	2816	2483	2173	1885	**33**
34	1.6269	1.1852	0.9708	8279	7206	6346	5629	5013	4474	3994	3563	3170	2810	2477	2168	1880	**34**
35	1.6143	1.1806	0.9680	8259	7190	6333	5618	5003	4466	3987	3556	3164	2804	2472	2164	1875	**35**
36	1.6021	1.1761	0.9652	8239	7174	6320	5607	4994	4457	3979	3549	3157	2798	2467	2159	1871	**36**
37	1.5902	1.1716	0.9625	8219	7159	6307	5596	4984	4449	3972	3542	3151	2793	2461	2154	1866	**37**
38	1.5786	1.1671	0.9597	8199	7143	6294	5585	4975	4440	3964	3535	3145	2787	2456	2149	1862	**38**
39	1.5673	1.1627	0.9570	8179	7128	6282	5574	4965	4432	3957	3529	3139	2781	2451	2144	1857	**39**
40	1.5563	1.1584	0.9542	8159	7112	6269	5563	4956	4424	3949	3522	3133	2775	2445	2139	1852	**40**
41	1.5456	1.1540	0.9515	8140	7097	6256	5552	4947	4415	3942	3515	3126	2770	2440	2134	1848	**41**
42	1.5351	1.1498	0.9488	8120	7081	6243	5541	4937	4407	3934	3508	3120	2764	2435	2129	1843	**42**
43	1.5249	1.1455	0.9462	8101	7066	6231	5531	4928	4399	3927	3501	3114	2758	2430	2124	1838	**43**
44	1.5149	1.1413	0.9435	8081	7050	6218	5520	4918	4390	3919	3495	3108	2753	2424	2119	1834	**44**
45	1.5051	1.1372	0.9409	8062	7035	6205	5509	4909	4382	3912	3488	3102	2747	2419	2114	1829	**45**
46	1.4956	1.1331	0.9383	8043	7020	6193	5498	4900	4374	3905	3481	3096	2741	2414	2109	1825	**46**
47	1.4863	1.1290	0.9356	8023	7005	6180	5488	4890	4365	3897	3475	3089	2736	2409	2104	1820	**47**
48	1.4771	1.1249	0.9330	8004	6990	6168	5477	4881	4357	3890	3468	3083	2730	2403	2099	1816	**48**
49	1.4682	1.1209	0.9305	7985	6975	6155	5466	4872	4349	3882	3461	3077	2724	2398	2095	1811	**49**
50	1.4594	1.1170	0.9279	7966	6960	6143	5456	4863	4341	3875	3454	3071	2719	2393	2090	1806	**50**
51	1.4508	1.1130	0.9254	7947	6945	6131	5445	4853	4333	3868	3448	3065	2713	2388	2085	1802	**51**
52	1.4424	1.1091	0.9228	7929	6930	6118	5435	4844	4324	3860	3441	3059	2707	2382	2080	1797	**52**
53	1.4341	1.1053	0.9203	7910	6915	6106	5424	4835	4316	3853	3434	3053	2702	2377	2075	1793	**53**
54	1.4260	1.1015	0.9178	7891	6900	6094	5414	4826	4308	3846	3428	3047	2696	2372	2070	1788	**54**
55	1.4180	1.0977	0.9153	7873	6885	6081	5403	4817	4300	3838	3421	3041	2691	2367	2065	1784	**55**
56	1.4102	1.0939	0.9128	7854	6871	6069	5393	4808	4292	3831	3415	3034	2685	2362	2061	1779	**56**
57	1.4025	1.0902	0.9104	7836	6856	6057	5382	4798	4284	3824	3408	3028	2679	2356	2056	1774	**57**
58	1.3949	1.0865	0.9079	7818	6841	6045	5372	4789	4276	3817	3401	3022	2674	2351	2051	1770	**58**
59	1.3875	1.0828	0.9055	7800	6827	6033	5361	4780	4268	3809	3395	3016	2668	2346	2046	1765	**59**
	0	1	2	3	4	5	6	7	8	9	10	11	12	13	14	15	

RULE: – Add proportional log. of planet's daily motion to log. of time from noon, and the sum will be the log. of the motion required. Add this to planet's place at noon, if time be p.m., but subtract if a.m., and the sum will be planet's true place. If Retrograde, subtract for p.m., but add for a.m.

What is the Long. of ☽ February 13, 2000 at 2.15 p.m.?

☽'s daily motion—14° 12′

Prop. Log. of 14° 12′ .... .2279

Prop. Log. of 2h. 15m. 1.0280

☽'s motion in 2h. 15m. = 1° 20′ or Log. 1.2559

☽'s Long. = 0° ♊ 57′ + 1° 20′ = 2° ♊ 17′

The Daily Motions of the Sun, Moon, Mercury, Venus and Mars will be found on pages 26 to 28.